shakespeare's

henry IV

parts one and two

shakespeare's

henry IV

parts one and two

harold **bloom**

riverhead books
new york

THE BERKLEY PUBLISHING GROUP
Published by the Penguin Group
Penguin Group (USA) Inc.
375 Hudson Street, New York, New York 10014, U.S.A.
Penguin Group (Canada), 10 Alcorn Avenue, Toronto, Ontario, Canada M4V 3B2
(a division of Pearson Penguin Canada Inc.)
Penguin Books Ltd., 80 Strand, London WC2R 0RL, England
Penguin Group Ireland, 25 St. Stephen's Green, Dublin 2, Ireland (a division of
Penguin Books, Ltd.)
Penguin Group (Australia), 250 Camberwell Road, Camberwell, Victoria 3124, Australia
(a division of Pearson Australia Group Pty., Ltd.)
Penguin Books India Pvt. Ltd., 11 Community Centre, Panchsheel Park, New Delhi–
110 017, India
Penguin Group (NZ), Cnr. Airborne and Rosedale Roads, Albany, Auckland, New Zealand
(a division of Pearson New Zealand, Ltd.)
Penguin Books (South Africa) (Pty.) Ltd., 24 Sturdee Avenue, Rosebank, Johannesburg
2196, South Africa

Penguin Books Ltd., Registered Offices: 80 Strand, London, WC2R 0RL, England

PRINTING HISTORY
Riverhead trade paperback edition: October 2004

Library of Congress Cataloging-in-Publication Data

Bloom, Harold.
    Shakespeare's Henry IV / Harold Bloom.—1st Riverhead trade pbk. ed.
        p. cm.
    The essay "Henry IV" was previously published as part of Shakespeare: invention
    of the human by Harold Bloom—T.p. verso.
    Includes the full text of the play, with editorial revisions by Harold Bloom.
    ISBN 1-59448-010-9 (pbk.)
        1. Shakespeare, William, 1564–1616. King Henry IV. 2. Henry IV, King of England,
    1367–1413—In literature. 3. Henry IV, King of England, 1367–1413—Drama. 4. Great
    Britain—History—Henry IV, 1399–1413—Drama. I. Shakespeare, William, 1564–1616.
    King Henry IV. II. Title.

PR2809.B55 2004
822.3'3—dc22   2004050846

PRINTED IN THE UNITED STATES OF AMERICA

10   9   8   7   6   5   4   3   2   1

contents

The text of the two parts of *Henry IV,* including the synopses, is that of the old Cambridge Edition (1893), as edited by William Aldis Wright. I am grateful to Brett Foster for indispensable advice upon the editorial revisions I have made in the text.

—Harold Bloom

harold bloom on

henry IV

parts one and two

You cannot reduce Shakespeare to any single power, of all his myriad gifts, and assert that he matters most because of that one glory. Yet all his endowments issue from his extraordinary intelligence, which for comprehensiveness is unmatched, and not just among the greatest writers. The true Bardolatry stems from this recognition: Here at last we encounter an intelligence without limits. As we read Shakespeare, we are always engaged in catching up, and our joy is that the process is never-ending: he is still out ahead of us. I marvel at critics, of whatever persuasions, old and new, who substitute their *knowingness* (really their resentment) for Shakespeare's woe and wonder, which are among the prime manifestations of his cognitive power.

I have cited Hegel's fine observation that Shakespeare made his best characters "free artists of themselves." The freest of the free are Hamlet and Falstaff, because they are the most intelligent of Shakespeare's persons (or roles, if you prefer that word). Critics rarely condescend to Hamlet, though some, like Alistair Fowler, morally disapprove of him. With Falstaff, alas, it is different; many critics not only condemn him morally, they also lord it over him, as if Sir John knows less than they do. If one loves Falstaff (as I do, and as we all should, even as a role), they are likely to term one a "sentimentalist." I remember a graduate student in one of my Shakespeare seminars, a few years back, who informed me rather vehemently that Falstaff was not worthy of admiration, whereas the transformation of Prince Hal into King Henry V was exemplary. Her point was that Hal represented rule and that Falstaff was a lord of misrule, and I could not persuade her that Falstaff transcended her categories, as he transcends virtually all our catalogings of human sin and error. That Shakespeare had an intensely personal relation to his Hamlet is clear enough, and he lavished all his powers upon the prince. Falstaff did not trouble Shakespeare for as many years as Hamlet did, and perhaps Falstaff did not at all perplex his creator. I would guess, though, that Falstaff surprised Shakespeare and ran away from the role originally intended for him, which may have been no larger than, say, Ancient Pistol's is in *Henry V*. The two parts of *Henry IV* do not belong to Hal, but to Falstaff, and even Hotspur, in the first part, is dimmed by Falstaff's splendor. I despair of ever again seeing a Falstaff to match Ralph Richardson's, half a century ago, because Richardson did not condescend to Falstaff or underestimate him. The Falstaff he played was neither coward nor jester, but infinite wit delighting in its own inventiveness, and transcending its own darkening pathos. Courage in Falstaff finds expression as a refusal to acknowledge rejection, even though Sir John is aware, as *Henry IV, Part One,* opens, that Hal's ambivalence has resolved itself into a murderous negativity. Hal's displaced paternal love is Falstaff's vulnerability, his one weakness, and the origin of his destruction. Time annihilates other Shakespearean protagonists, but not Falstaff, who dies for love. Critics have insisted that this love is grotesque, but they are grotesque. The greatest of all fictive wits dies the death of a rejected father-substitute, and also of a dishonored mentor.

Most of Shakespeare's mature plays implicitly demand that we provide them with a particular foreground, which we can arrive at by a kind of inference, as scholars from Maurice Morgann to A.D. Nuttall have indicated. The foreground of *Henry IV, Part One,* is only partly supplied by *Richard II,* the drama in which Bolingbroke usurps the crown and becomes King Henry IV. There, in Act V, Scene iii, the new King and Percy, soon to be known as Hotspur, have a prophetic conversation about Prince Hal:

> *Bol.* Can no man tell me of my unthrifty son?
>> 'Tis full three months since I did see him last.
>> If any plague hang over us, 'tis he.
>> I would to God, my lords, he might be found.
>> Inquire at London, 'mongst the taverns there,
>> For there, they say, he daily doth frequent
>> With unrestrained loose companions,
>> Even such, they say, as stand in narrow lanes
>> And beat our watch and rob our passengers,
>> Which he, young wanton, and effeminate boy,
>> Takes on the point of honor to support
>> So dissolute a crew.
> *Percy.* My lord, some two days since I saw the prince,
>> And told him of those triumphs held at Oxford.
> *Bol.* And what said the gallant?
> *Percy.* His answer was, he would unto the stews.
>> And from the common'st creature pluck a glove,
>> And wear it as a favour; and with that
>> He would unhorse the lustiest challenger.
> *Bol.* As dissolute as desperate! But yet
>> Through both I see some sparks of better hope,
>> Which elder years may happily bring forth.
>>> [*Richard II,* V.iii. 1–22]

The leader of this dissolute crew is Falstaff, whose pre-Shakespearean fortunes do not involve *him*—that is to say, the immortal Falstaff (as Bradley and Goddard rightly called him). Immortal Falstaff is Shakespeare's invention, the proverbial fat man who struggled triumphantly to get out of the thin Will Shakespeare. Many critics have pointed to the wordplay that is parallel: Fall/staff; Shake/spear. Others have found in the poet of the Sonnets a Falstaff figure suffering in relation to a Prince Hal–like noble youth. The personal link, though, seems to me strongest when one notes that Falstaff *is* Shakespeare's wit at its very limits, even as Hamlet *is* the farthest reach of Shakespeare's cognitive acuity. Whether we can surmise Shakespeare's human investment in Falstaff to the degree that we surmise it in Hamlet is a puzzle to me. A celebrated New Historicist critic of Shakespeare, responding to a talk I gave on value in the personalities of Hamlet and Falstaff, told the audience that my handling of those characters or roles was "a politics of identity." I don't know what politics have (or had) to do with this, but it is difficult not to speculate upon Shakespeare's identification both with his son Hamlet and with his other self, Falstaff. You don't write Hamlet and Falstaff into existence without something like Cervantes's own reactions to Don Quixote and Sancho Panza. Narrative fiction is not dramatic fiction, and so we cannot have Shakespeare's Cervantes-like expressions of pride and of mock dismay in what he had wrought. William Empson, first, and then C. L. Barber and Richard P. Wheeler, sought Shakespeare's oblique commentary on Falstaff in the Sonnets, with mixed but valuable enough results. I prefer to find Shakespeare's Falstaffian spirit in the plays, if I can, because the Sonnets, at their strongest, seem to me more equivocal than anything else by Shakespeare. Perhaps they can lead us into the plays, but Hamlet and Falstaff illuminate the Sonnets more often than the Sonnets give us new light upon those two giant forms.

In the chronicles of English history, a Sir John Falstolfe figures as a cowardly commander in the French wars, and as such enters *Henry VI, Part One* (Act I, Scene i, 130–40), where his flight leads to the brave Talbot's being wounded and captured. The character who became the Immortal Falstaff (no coward, as Morgann and Bradley insisted, against Prince Hal) was originally called Sir John Oldcastle. But in 1587 or so, the apprentice playwright Shakespeare may have helped botch *The Famous Victories of Henry IV,* a rousing, patriotic rant of a play, perhaps mostly written by the comic actor Dick Tarlton. In this drama, Prince Hal eventually reforms, and banishes his wicked companion, Sir John Oldcastle. But the historical Oldcastle died a Protestant martyr, and his descendants were not pleased to see him as a wicked glutton and walking vice. Shakespeare was compelled to change the name, and so came up with Falstaff instead. Shakespeare, a touch censured, allows Hal to call Falstaff "my old lad of the castle" but then adds to the Epilogue of *Henry IV, Part Two,* a blunt disclaimer: "for Oldcastle died a martyr, and this is not the man." How odd it would sound if Verdi's opera were called *Oldcastle*! Contingency governs the dramatist's choices, at many levels, and Oldcastle's annoyed progeny helped give us what now seems the one possible name for comic genius: Falstaff.

Sir John Oldcastle, in *The Famous Victories,* is only a minor roisterer. Shakespeare found Falstaff in Shakespeare, though the language and personalities of Berowne and of Faulconbridge the Bastard, of Mercutio and of Bottom, do not prepare us adequately for Falstaff, who speaks what is still the best and most vital prose in the English language. Sir John's mastery of language transcends even Hamlet's, since Falstaff has absolute faith both in language and in himself. Falstaff never loses faith either in himself or in language, and so seems to emanate from a more primordial Shakespeare than Hamlet does. Falstaff becomes Shakespeare's greatest and subtlest victory over Barabas and the other Marlovian overreachers, because the fat knight surpasses Marlowe's Machiavels as a rhetorician, yet never uses his magnificent language to persuade anyone of anything. Though Falstaff constantly has to defend himself against Hal's endless and well-nigh murderous aggressivity, even with Hal he seeks neither to persuade nor merely to defend. Wit is Falstaff's god, and since we must assume that God has a sense of humor, we can observe that Falstaff's vitalizing discourse, his beautiful laughing speech (as Yeats said of Blake), is truly Sir John's mode of devotion. Making others wittier is Falstaff's enterprise; not only witty in himself, he is the cause of Hal's wit as well. Sir John is a comic Socrates. What Shakespeare knew of Socrates, he would have learned from Montaigne, whose Plato and whose Socrates were skeptics. Falstaff is more than skeptical, but he is too much of a teacher (his true vocation, more than highwayman) to follow skepticism out to its nihilistic borders, as Hamlet does. Skeptical wit is not witty skepticism, and Sir John is not a master of negation, like Hamlet (or Iago). As the Socrates of Eastcheap, Falstaff need not concern himself with teaching virtue, because the struggle between the usurper Henry IV and the rebels has no possible relation to ethics or to morality. Falstaff jests of the rebels that "they offend only the virtuous," who clearly are not to be found in the England of Henry IV (or of Henry V).

What, then, are the teachings of the philosopher of Eastcheap? Eating, drinking, fornication, and the other obvious indulgences are not the heart of Falstaffianism, though they certainly take up much of the knight's time. This does not matter, because Falstaff, as Hal first tells us, has nothing to do with the time of the day.

That which we are, that only can we teach; Falstaff, who is free, instructs us in freedom—not a freedom *in* society, but *from* society. The sage of Eastcheap inhabits Shakespearean histories but treats them like comedies. Scholars have named the tetralogy of *Richard II, Henry IV, Part One, Henry IV, Part Two,* and *Henry V* as the Henriad, but I regard the two middle plays as the Falstaffiad (to which I would not add *The Merry Wives of Windsor,* whose "Falstaff" is an operatic impostor). The Falstaffiad is tragicomedy; the Henriad is patriotic (with some shadings!) history. I wish that Shakespeare had not told us of the death of Falstaff in *Henry V* but instead had carried Sir John off to the forest of Arden, to exchange wit with Rosalind in *As You Like It*. Though he incarnates freedom, Falstaff's liberty is not absolute, like Rosalind's. As audience, we are given no perspective more privileged than Rosalind's own, whereas we can see Prince Hal's Machiavel-like qualities more clearly than Falstaff can bear to do, and we sense Falstaff's rejection, from Hal's opening speech on, in *Henry IV, Part One*. Edging the Falstaffiad's comic joy is its enclosure by the Henriad, and from one legitimate perspective, what is Hal except Falstaff's evil genius?

E. E. Stoll shrewdly compared Shakespeare's comic art of *isolation* in regard to Shylock and Falstaff. Shylock is never alone on stage; we are allowed only societal perspectives upon him. Falstaff, in the second part of his tragicomedy, is in Hal's company only twice, first to be seen by the prince in a tawdry scene of erotic pathos with Doll Tearsheet, and then to be brutally insulted and rejected by the newly crowned king. We would like Falstaff to enjoy absolute freedom, and something in Shakespeare would like that also, but Shakespearean mimesis is too artful for such a fantasy. Falstaff, as the comic Socrates, represents freedom only as an educational dialectic of conversion. If you come to Falstaff full of your own indignation and fury, whether directed at him or not, Falstaff will transform your dark affect into wit and laughter. If, like Hal, you come to Falstaff with ambivalence, now weighted to the negative side, Falstaff will evade you where he cannot convert you.

I don't believe that this makes Falstaff a pragmatist of economic exchange, as Lars Engle believes, when he says that Falstaff "is a figure not so much of freedom from value systems as of joyous participation in their inevitably contingent and manipulable operation." You can exploit a value system, as Falstaff profits from the civil war, while seeing through and beyond it. The immortal Falstaff, never a hypocrite and rarely ambivalent, decidedly not a counterfeit like Hal, is essentially a satirist turned against all power, which means turned against all historicisms—explanations of history—rather than against history. A veteran warrior, now set against the chivalric code of honor, Falstaff knows that history is an ironic flux of reversals. Prince Hal refuses to learn this lesson from Falstaff, because as a mass of ambivalences toward everyone, including Falstaff, he cannot afford it.

Falstaff's energies are personal: his relative freedom is a dynamic one, which can be transferred to a pupil but at the cost of a dangerous distortion. Despite his current "materialist" critics, Falstaff declines to harvest his affections, but he certainly teaches Hal to harvest everyone: Hotspur, the King his father, and Falstaff himself. Hal is Falstaff's masterpiece: a student of genius who adopts his teacher's stance of freedom in order to exploit a universal ambivalence and turn it into a selective wit. Hal is totally ambivalent toward everyone and everything—his wit is selective, while Falstaff's is universal. Hotspur and King Henry IV are in Hal's way, but they do not menace him inwardly. Falstaff, once Hal is crowned, becomes a figure to be dreaded, to be banished ten miles from the royal person. In the cruel speech of rejection,

Henry V is at some trouble to ensure that Falstaff be given no opportunity for dialogue: "Reply not to me with a fool-born jest" (V.v.55). As "the tutor and the feeder of my riots" (V.v.62), poor Falstaff is allowed no final evasions, and is essentially in receipt of a death sentence. Just as Shylock was ordered immediately to become a Christian, so Falstaff is enjoined to become "more wise and modest" (Prince John to the Lord Chief Justice), to undergo a severe diet, and presumably to get as close to God as Henry V now is. Squadrons of scholars, old-style and new, offer apologies for Henry V, while assuring us that Shakespeare realistically does not share our outrage: Order is in order, Henry V is an ideal monarch, the first authentic English king, the very model for Shakespeare's own political ideal.

On the not unlikely grounds that Shakespeare himself was more Falstaffian than Henrican, I join the now derided "humanist" critics—including Dr. Johnson, Hazlitt, Swinburne, Bradley, and Goddard—in dismissing this idea of order as irrelevant nonsense. To reject Falstaff is to reject Shakespeare. And to speak merely historically, the freedom Falstaff represents is in the first case freedom from Christopher Marlowe, which means that Falstaff is the signature of Shakespeare's originality, of his breakthrough into an art more nearly his own. Engle, speaking for most of his historicizing contemporaries, tells us "that Shakespeare's work is subdued to what it works in," but I wonder why the dyer's hand of tradition subdued Shakespeare less than it did, say, Ben Jonson, let alone the several score minor post-Marlovian dramatists. Falstaff, not a Marlovian, is quite Chaucerian: he is the son of the vitalistic Wife of Bath. Marlowe, after an initial inspiring effect, doubtless oppressed Shakespeare; Chaucer did not, because Shakespeare's own genius for comedy came to him far more spontaneously than did an aptitude for tragedy.

2

Chronologically, *Henry IV, Part One,* comes directly after *The Merchant of Venice,* yet the history and the comedy possess in common only a profound ambivalence, which may be Shakespeare's own, both toward himself and toward the young man and dark woman of the Sonnets. Hal's ambivalence in regard to Falstaff, as every critic has seen, displaces the ambivalence provoked in him by his father, King Henry IV, from whom his son already is in full flight at the close of *Richard II.* Shylock and Falstaff are antithetical to each other: the Jew's bitter eloquence, life-denying and puritanical, is wholly other from the Falstaffian affirmation of a dynamic vitalism. And yet Shylock and Falstaff share an exuberance, negative in Shylock, extravagantly positive in Falstaff. Both are anti-Marlovian emblems; their force is crucial to Shakespeare's invention of the human, of a window onto reality.

Falstaff is anything but an elegiac figure; he would be fully present to consciousness, if only we could summon up a consciousness in ourselves to receive his. It is the comprehensiveness of Falstaff's consciousness that puts him beyond us, not in Hamlet's way of transcendence but in Falstaff's way of immanence. Only a few characters in the world's literature can match the real presence of Falstaff, who in that regard is Hamlet's greatest rival in Shakespeare. Falstaff's presence is more than the presence of mind that Hazlitt praised in him. The illusion of being a real person—if you want to call it "illusion"—attends Falstaff as it does Hamlet. Yet somehow Shakespeare conveys to us that these two charismatics are *in* their plays, but not *of* them; Hamlet is a person, and Claudius and Ophelia are fictions—or Falstaff is a person, while Hal and Hotspur are fictions.

The Shakespearean charismatic has little in common with the sociological charismatic of Max Weber, but anticipates rather more Oscar Wilde's sense that comprehensiveness in consciousness is the sublime of value, when the representation of personality is at the center of one's concern. Shakespeare has other gorgeous triumphs—Rosalind, Iago, Cleopatra among them—but in circumference of consciousness, as I keep insisting, there are no rivals for Falstaff and Hamlet. The Edmund of *King Lear* perhaps is as intelligent as Falstaff and Hamlet, yet he is all but void of affect until he sustains his death wound, and so he must be judged as a negative charismatic in comparison with Sir John and the Prince of Denmark. Weber's sense of charisma, though derived from religion, has clear affinities with Carlyle's and Emerson's exaltation of heroic genius. Institution and routine, in Weber's vision, quickly absorb the effect of the charismatic individual on his followers. But Caesarism and Calvinism are not *aesthetic* movements; Falstaff and Hamlet scarcely can be routinized or institutionalized. Falstaff disdains any task or mission, and Hamlet cannot tolerate being the protagonist of a revenge tragedy. In both figures, charisma goes back beyond the model of Jesus to his ancestor King David, who uniquely held the blessing of Yahweh. Falstaff, though derided by virtuous scholars and rejected by the newly virtuous King Henry V, nevertheless retains the blessing, in its truest sense: more life.

Personality, even upon its deathbed, retains its unique value. I have known a number of intelligent philosophers and a vast multitude of poets, novelists, storytellers, playwrights. No one should expect them to talk as well as they write, yet even the best of them, on their best day, cannot equal those men made out of words, Falstaff and Hamlet. One wonders: Just how does the representation of cognition, in Shakespeare, differ from cognition, itself? Pragmatically, can we tell the difference? One wonders again: Just how does the representation of charisma, in Shakespeare, differ from charisma itself? Charisma, by definition, is not a social energy; it originates outside society. Shakespeare's uniqueness, his greatest originality, can be described either as a charismatic cognition, which comes from an individual before it enters group thinking, or as a cognitive charisma, which cannot be routinized. The decisive theatrical experience of my life came half a century ago, in 1946, when I was sixteen, and watched Ralph Richardson play Falstaff. Even the bravura of Laurence Olivier, playing Hotspur in Part One, and Shallow in Part Two, could not divert me from the Richardsonian Falstaff. When he was off stage, then an absence in reality was felt by all the audience, and we waited, in helpless impatience, for Shakespeare to set Sir John before us again. W. H. Auden, commenting upon this phenomenon, rather oddly explained that Falstaff was "a comic symbol for the supernatural order of charity." Though I admire Auden's essays on Shakespeare, I am baffled by Auden's Christian Falstaff. The superb Sir John is neither Christ nor Satan, nor an imitation of either.

And yet a representation of secular immanence upon a stage, the most persuasive representation that we have, is going to tempt even the wisest critics into extravagant interpretations. I do not think that Shakespeare set out to show Falstaff as supremely immanent, or Hamlet as eminently transcendent. Ben Jonson composed ideograms and called them characters; at their best, as in Volpone and Sir Epicure Mammon, they are rammed with life, and yet they are not portrayals of persons. Though most current Shakespeare scholars in the Anglophonic academies refuse to confront Shakespeare's peopling of a world, that remains his appeal to almost all who attend performances of the plays, or who continue to read them. And while it is true that Shakespeare's persons are only images or complex metaphors, our pleasure in Shakespeare primarily comes from the persuasive illusion that these shadows are cast by entities as substantial as ourselves. Shakespeare's powers of persuading us of this magnificent illusion all stem from his astonishing ability to represent change, an ability unmatched in the world's literature. Our own personalities may well reduce to a flux of sensations, but that concourse of impressions requires presentation in detailed vividness if any one of us is to be distinguished from any other. A Ben Jonson version of Falstaff would indeed be only a "trunk of humours," as Hal angrily terms Sir John when the prince acts the part of his father in the skit of Act II, Scene iv, *Henry IV, Part One*. Not even Volpone, greatest of Jonson's characters, undergoes significant change, but Falstaff, like Hamlet, is always transforming himself, always thinking, speaking, and overhearing himself in a quicksilver metamorphosis, always willing the change and suffering the change that is Shakespeare's tribute to the reality of our lives.

Algernon Charles Swinburne, now mostly forgotten as both poet and critic, yet frequently superb as both, adroitly compared Falstaff to his true companions, the Sancho Panza of Cervantes and the Panurge of Rabelais. He awarded the palm to Falstaff, not just for his massive intellect but for his range of feeling and indeed even for his "possible moral elevation." Swinburne meant a morality of the heart, and of the imagination, rather than the social morality that is the permanent curse of Shakespearean scholarship and criticism, afflicting historicists old and new, and Puritans sacred and secular. Here Swinburne anticipated A. C. Bradley, who rightly remarked that all adverse moral judgments upon Falstaff are antithetical to the nature of Shakespearean comedy. One can add Chaucer's Wife of Bath to form a foursome of great vitalists, all bearing the Blessing—which means "more life"—and all impressing us as superb comedians. Shakespeare's abandonment of judgment to his audience allows Falstaff to be even more unsponsored and free than Sancho, Panurge, and the Wife. The will to live, immense in all four, has a particular poignance in Sir John, a professional soldier long since turned against the nonsense of military "glory" and "honor." We have no reason to believe that Shakespeare set any supposed societal good over an individual good, and considerable reason—based on the plays and the Sonnets—to believe something close to the opposite. After a lifetime surrounded by other professors, I question their experiential qualifications to apprehend, let alone judge, the Immortal Falstaff. The late Anthony Burgess, who gave us a splendid, rather Joycean version of Falstaff in his wastrel poet, Enderby, also gave us critical wisdom on Falstaff:

> The Falstaffian spirit is a great sustainer of civilization. It disappears when the state is too powerful and when people worry too much about their souls. . . . There is little of Falstaff's substance in the world now, and, as the power of the state expands, what is left will be liquidated.

The power of the state will be personified by King Henry V, whose attitude toward Falstaff differs scarcely a jot from that of academic puritans and professorial power freaks. Falstaff's irreverence is life-enhancing but state-destroying; it strains pragmatic sense to believe that Shakespeare shared the Henrican attitude toward Falstaff. To say that Shakespeare is also Hotspur, or Hal, or King Henry IV, is of little interest: he then also would be Romeo, Juliet, Mercutio, and the Nurse, and many hundreds of others. Falstaff, like and unlike Hamlet, has another kind of relation to his playwright. The instant popularity of Sir John with Shakespeare's audience prompted first *The Merry Wives of Windsor*, and next *Henry IV, Part Two*. Falstaff's death scene, brilliantly recounted by the Hostess in *Henry V*, testifies both to Shakespeare's inability to let the great wit's story go unfinished, and to the dramatist's shrewd awareness that the heroic posturings at Agincourt could not withstand Falstaffian commentary, a counterchorus that would have sunk the play, however gloriously.

When Falstaff captured Queen Elizabeth and everyone else in Shakespeare's public, whatever had been the playwright's relation to his exorbitant comic character had to change. I hear a certain anxiety in *The Merry Wives of Windsor,* where Falstaff is travestied, and a struggle in *Henry IV, Part Two,* where Shakespeare seems, at moments, vexed as to whether to extend Falstaff's splendor or to darken it. Scholars can write what they will, but a diminished Falstaff is their creation, not Shakespeare's. Falstaff's festival of language cannot be reduced or melted down. Mind in the largest sense, more even than wit, is Falstaff's greatest power; who can settle which is the more intelligent consciousness, Hamlet's or Falstaff's? For all its comprehensiveness, Shakespearean drama is ultimately a theater of mind, and what matters most about Falstaff is his vitalization of the intellect, in direct contrast to Hamlet's conversion of the mind to the vision of annihilation.

I have suffered through recent performances of the *Henry IV* plays that debased Falstaff into a cowardly braggart, a sly instigator to vice, a fawner for the Prince's favor, a besotted old scoundrel, and much more of that sort of desecration of Shakespeare's actual text. The proper response is to give a brief cento of Sir John's own utterances:

> O, thou host damnable iteration, and art indeed able to corrupt a saint: thou hast done much harm upon me, Hal, God forgive thee for it: before I knew thee, Hal, I knew nothing, and now am I, if a man should speak truly, little better than one of the wicked.

> But to say I know more harm in him than in myself were to say more than I know. That he is old, the more the pity,

his white hairs do witness it, but that he is, saving your reverence, a whoremaster, that I utterly deny. If sack and sugar be a fault, God help the wicked! If to be old and merry be a sin, then many an old host that I know is damned: if to be fat be to be hated, then Pharaoh's lean kine are to be loved. No, my good lord; banish Peto, banish Bardolph, banish Poins—but for sweet Jack Falstaff, kind Jack Falstaff, true Jack Falstaff, valiant Jack Falstaff, and therefore more valiant, being as he is old Jack Falstaff, banish not him thy Harry's company, banish not him thy Harry's company, banish plump Jack, and banish all the world.

Well, if Percy be alive, I'll pierce him. If he do come in my way, so: if he do not, if I come in his willingly, let him make a carbonado of me. I like not such grinning honour as Sir Walter hath. Give me life, which if I can save, so: if not, honour comes unlooked for, and there's an end.

Embowelled? If thou embowel me today, I'll give you leave to powder me and eat me too tomorrow. 'Sblood, 'twas time to counterfeit, or that hot termagant Scot had paid me, scot and lot too. Counterfeit? I lie, I am no counterfeit: to die is to be a counterfeit, for he is but the counterfeit of a man, who hath not the life of a man: but to counterfeit dying, when a man thereby liveth, is to be no counterfeit, but the true and perfect image of life indeed.

Call these four extracts Sir John Falstaff on popular piety, personal wickedness, military honor, and the blessing of life itself. I hear a great wit, but also an authentic sage, destroying illusions. I do not hear mere *knowingness,* which is the professional disease of resentful academic clerks, who see Falstaff, like themselves, as questing for room at the top. Sir John is anything but a lovable old darling; he personally is bad news, rather in the mode of certain great poets who were not exactly wholesome and productive citizens: Villon, Marlowe, Rimbaud among them. You wouldn't want to dine with any of them, or pick pockets with Villon, spy with Marlowe, work at gun running with Rimbaud, or go highway robbing with Falstaff. But like those reprobate poets, Sir John has genius, more of Shakespeare's own genius than any other character save Hamlet. As for exercising moral disapproval upon Falstaff—why, who is there in the Henriad whom we could prefer to Fat Jack? Henry IV, hypocrite and usurper, is not an option, nor is Hal/Henry V, hypocrite and brutal soldier, slaughterer of prisoners and of his old companion Bardolph. Are we to prefer Hotspur's "die all, die merrily" to Falstaff's "Give me life"? Is Falstaff morally inferior to the treacherous Prince John? There is, of course, the Lord Chief Justice, if you have a strong taste for law enforcement as such. Shakespeare, and his contemporary audience, got Falstaff right; it is much of the scholarly tradition that goes on getting Falstaff wrong. The Wife of Bath, Falstaff's literary mother, divides critics pretty much the way that Falstaff does. One wouldn't want to marry the Wife of Bath, or carouse with Falstaff, but if you crave vitalism and vitality, then you turn to the Wife of Bath, Panurge (in Rabelais), Sancho Panza (in Cervantes), but most of all to Sir John Falstaff, the true and perfect image of life itself.

Graham Bradshaw argues for a much more limited Falstaff, on the curious grounds that Falstaff speaks only in prose, like Thersites in *Troilus and Cressida*. But Shakespeare is not composing opera, and I do not think we as yet know whether there were, for him, crucial intentions that accompany a choice between prose or verse. Here is Bradshaw's contention:

Like Iago, Falstaff prides himself on truth-telling but speaks
a language in which it is only possible to tell some kinds of

truth. His language speaks him, and its limited registers are placed within the incomparably large range of registers within the play as a whole (or two wholes: that issue need not distract us here). Our corresponding sense that various human potentialities and aspirations are entirely beyond Falstaff's range has important consequences. It should ensure that our delighted response to Falstaff's wonderful catechism on Honour commits us no further than Gloster's response to Edgar's 'Ripeness is all': 'And *that's* true *too,*' says Gloster.

The comparison to Iago is surprising in the astute Bradshaw, who is momentarily too invested in his prose/poetry hypothesis to remember that Falstaff betrays and harms no one, and does not write with the lives of the other characters, as Iago always does. The contrasts between the humane wit of Fat Jack and the murderous ironies of Iago are almost too palpable to be mentioned. But Bradshaw's true sin is elsewhere, in his quest to find a middle path between Falstaffian celebrants and statist moralists. Who is Bradshaw (or any other among us) to judge that "various human potentialities and aspirations are entirely beyond Falstaff's range," *because he speaks prose,* and the best prose at that in any modern language? What are those aspirations and potentialities?

They turn out to be what Hal/Henry V, King Henry IV, Prince John, and Hotspur and company are all about: power, usurpation, rule, grand extortion, treachery, violence, hypocrisy, fake piety, the murder of prisoners and of those who surrender under truce. For Bradshaw, all these come under the category of Honor, to which Falstaff–Shakespeare responds: "I like not such grinning honour as [the dead!] Sir Walter hath. Give me life, which if I can save; so: if not, honour comes unlooked for, and there's an end." Do we hear wider ranges of human aspirations and potentialities in this, or in Hal's threat to Hotspur:

And all the budding honours on thy crest
I'll crop to make a garland for my head.

That is royal verse (and royal rant), but can anyone of sensibility prefer it to Falstaff's "Give me life"? Hal wins: He kills Hotspur, becomes Henry V, rejects Falstaff, conquers France, and dies
young (in history, not on Shakespeare's stage), whereas Falstaff
breaks, dies sadly (but to the astonishing music of Mistress
Quickly's prose), resurrects perpetually in his own immortal
prose, and haunts us ever since, as one of Shelley's "forms more
real than living man." Shakespeare goes neither with the great
wits nor with the big battalions, but we hardly can forget that he
himself was the greatest of wits, a shrewd and peaceful scribbler,
who perhaps sat quietly in the tavern and listened to Ben Jonson's truthful boasts that the author of *Volpone* had killed his man
in single combat between, and in the sight of, two warring armies.
Sir John, a battered old soldier, wanders about Shrewsbury battlefield with a bottle of sack in his holster, intending neither to
kill nor to be killed, though he boldly takes his chances with his
ragged recruits ("I have *led* my ragamuffins where they are peppered"). Shakespeare himself is neither an upholder of order nor
a lord of disorder. I do not know why Shylock sometimes speaks
verse and sometimes prose, but I don't *want* Sir John Falstaff to
speak verse. The Falstaffian prose is suppler and ampler than
Prince Hal's verse, and far more of the vast range of human po-
tentiality is contained in it than in Hal's formulations.

3

Samuel Butler, Victorian novelist and independent thinker, observed in a notebook jotting that "the great characters live as
truly as the memory of dead men. For the life after death, it is

not necessary that a man or woman have lived." Falstaff—like Hamlet, Don Quixote, and Mr. Pickwick—is still alive because Shakespeare knew something like the Gnostic secret of resurrection, which is that Jesus first arose and *then* he died. Shakespeare shows Falstaff rising from the dead, and only later has Mrs. Quickly narrate the death of Sir John. The critic John Bayley wisely remarks that "character is what other people have, 'consciousness' is ourselves," but his observation pertains more to life than to literature, since the miracle of Hamlet and of Falstaff is that they manifest a consciousness that is and is not "ourselves." The understanding of Falstaff must begin not necessarily with affection for him, but with an acute apprehension of the nature and extent of his consciousness. Immanent Falstaff and transcendent Hamlet are the two largest representations of consciousness in Shakespeare, and indeed in all of literature. Consciousness must be consciousness of something; in Hamlet of all things in heaven or earth. Moralists and historicists (two names for the same persons) see Falstaff's consciousness as being rather more confined: food, drink, sex, power, money. We cannot know whether Shakespeare was more Falstaff or Hamlet, though the formidable E.A.J. Honigmann shakes me by arguing for Hamlet. Yet while dramatic irony sometimes victimizes Hamlet, and we are allowed to see him as he cannot see himself, Falstaff, like Rosalind, gazes in all directions, and beholds himself with a serio-comic self-acceptance that Hamlet is not allowed. Honigmann warns us that the Falstaff–Hal relationship does not yield to psychological analysis. Not completely perhaps, but well enough. Its paradigm for Shakespeare, by general consent, is his relationship to the young nobleman of the Sonnets, whether Southampton or Pembroke. To say that Shakespeare *is* Falstaff plainly is absurd; it was not a part he could play, even on the stage. You can brood upon Shakespeare-as-Antonio in *The Merchant of Venice,* should you want to; he probably acted the role, well aware of all its implications. Yet both Falstaff's vivacity and his darkening reaction to Hal's ambivalences have some connections to the Sonnets. And it cannot be affirmed too often that Falstaff's most salient qualities are his astonishing intellect and his exuberant vitality, the second probably not so outward a personal endowment of the man William Shakespeare.

Shakespeare has Hal kill Hotspur at the close of *Henry IV, Part One,* but Douglas fails to slay Falstaff. Consider how we would react if the "hot termagant Scot" indeed had carved up Sir John. We wince, and not just because we wish to preserve Part Two. The Epilogue to Part Two promises that Falstaff will appear in what became *Henry V,* a pledge Shakespeare thought better than to keep, though is there anything better in that play than Mrs. Quickly's sketch of Falstaff's death scene? What would happen to Sir John if he had appeared in *Henry V*? Would he be hanged, like poor Bardolph, or beaten up like the wretched Pistol? Whatever the aesthetic virtues of *Henry V* may or may not be, it does not play itself out in the Theater of Mind, as do both parts of *Henry IV.* If you are greatly concerned with the history and theory of Renaissance kingship, then *Henry V* has a strong cognitive interest. But common readers and playgoers tend not to be spurred to deep thought by the Battle of Agincourt, its foregrounds and aftermath. King Henry V broods on the burdens of monarchy, and on the obligations of subjects, but most among us do not. Falstaff, to most scholars, is the emblem of self-indulgence, but to most playgoers and readers Sir John is the representative of imaginative freedom, of a liberty set against time, death, and the state, which is a condition that we crave for ourselves. Add a fourth freedom to timelessness, the blessing of more life, and the evasion of the state, and call it freedom from censoriousness, from the superego, from guilt. I hesitate to select any single power out of Shakespeare's infinite variety of powers as being foremost, but sometimes I would vote that eminence to confidence in his audience. You define who you are by your re-action to Falstaff, or to his younger sister, Cleopatra, even as Chaucer had you define yourself by your judgment of (or refusal to judge) the Wife of Bath. Those who do not care for Falstaff are in love with time, death, the state, and the censor. They have their reward. I prefer to love Falstaff, the image of freedom's wit, and the language of wit's freedom. There is a middle way, of be-ing dispassionate about Falstaff, but it vanishes if you attend a good performance of the *Henry IV* plays. W. H. Auden caught this with great vividness:

> At a performance, my immediate reaction is to wonder what Falstaff is doing in this play at all. . . . As the play proceeds, our surprise is replaced by another kind of puzzle, for the better we come to know Falstaff, the clearer it becomes that the world of historical reality which a Chronicle Play claims to imitate is not a world which he can inhabit.

One can agree with this, and still dissent when Auden insists that the only world appropriate for Falstaff is Verdi's opera. Au-den also, rather oddly, calls Falstaff a troll, in the Ibsenite sense of *Peer Gynt,* but that is an error. Trolls are daemonic, yet are more animal than human, and Falstaff dies a martyr to human love, to his unrequited affection for his displaced son, Prince Hal. Again, if you dislike Falstaff, you can dismiss this love as grotesque or as self-serving, but then you may as well dismiss the *Henry IV* plays. I hardly am determined to vindicate Falstaff, but to Shakespeare, clearly, the poet's own love for the young nobleman in the Sonnets was anything but grotesque or self-serving, and it does seem to be the paradigm for the Falstaff–Hal relationship. The personality of Shakespeare remains an enigma; some contemporaries thought him warm and open, though a touch ruthless in his financial dealings. Some, however, found him withdrawn, even a little cold. Perhaps he went from one kind of person to another, in his quarter century of a career. Shakespeare certainly never acted Falstaff upon a stage, any more than he acted Hamlet. Perhaps he played King Henry IV, or one of the older rebels. But his full exuberance of language, his festival self, is as present in Falstaff's prose as in Hamlet's verse. If you love language, then you love Falstaff, and Shakespeare palpably loved language. Falstaff's resourcefulness gathers together the florabundance of *Love's Labour's Lost* with the more aggressive verbal energies of Faulconbridge the Bastard and the negative exuberance of Shylock. After Falstaff's prose, Shakespeare was ready for Hamlet's prose, which rivals the Prince of Denmark's verse.

There are fewer than a double handful (at most) of Shakespearean characters who are truly endless to meditation: Falstaff, Rosalind, Hamlet, Iago, Lear, Edgar, Edmund, Macbeth, Cleopatra. A considerable portrait gallery of the others is not quite that profound and problematical: the Bastard Faulconbridge, Richard II, Juliet, Bottom, Portia, Shylock, Prince Hal/Henry V, Brutus, Malvolio, Helena, Parolles, Isabella, Othello, Desdemona, Lear's Fool, Lady Macbeth, Antony, Coriolanus, Timon, Imogen, Leontes, Prospero, Caliban. These are two dozen great roles, but you cannot say of any of them what Milton's Satan says of himself, that "in every deep a lower deep opens." The great villains—Iago, Edmund, Macbeth—invent Western nihilism, and each is an abyss in himself. Lear and his godson Edgar are studies so profound in human torment and endurance that they carry biblical resonances in a pre-Christian, pagan play. But Falstaff, Rosalind, Hamlet, and Cleopatra are something apart in world literature: through them Shakespeare essentially invented human personality as we continue to know and value it. Falstaff has priority in this invention; not to appreciate his personal largeness, which surpasses even his sublime girth, would be to miss the greatest of Shakespearean originalities: the invention of the human.

How far back should we take our apprehension of Falstaff? Inference, as first practiced by Maurice Morgann in the eighteenth century, and refined by A. D. Nuttall in our era, is the mode offered us by Shakespeare himself. One of the neglected aspects of *Henry IV, Part Two,* is its subtle reach back to Falstaff's earlier years. It cannot be said that Shakespeare provides all the information we might hope for concerning the life and death of Sir John Falstaff, but we certainly are given more than enough to help us appreciate Falstaff's enormous personality. Shakespeare is no more a field anthropologist than his Prince Hal is: the Falstaffiad is intricately interwoven with the Henriad, each as the stuff of saga. What Shakespeare challenges us to imagine is left almost clueless by him: How did Hal and Falstaff enter upon their original friendship?

I am aware that partisans of supposed common sense will find my question mostly an irritant. But I am in no danger of believing that Sir John was a flesh-and-blood creature, merely as real as you and I. Falstaff would hardly matter if he did not greatly exceed all of us in vitality, exuberance, and wit. That is why Nuttall, mildly disputing Maurice Morgann, is so precise in his dissent:

> The objection to Morgann's speculations is not that Falstaff has no previous life but that Shakespeare does not give us enough clues to render Morgann's more detailed inferences probable.

The proper issue, then, is to judge just how many and how extensive the clues are, while accepting (as Nuttall wisely does), Morgann's notion of latent meaning, the Shakespearean play's undersong:

If the characters of Shakespeare are thus *whole,* and as it were original, whilst those of almost all other writers are mere imitation, it may be fit to consider them rather as Historic than Dramatic beings; and when occasion requires, to account for their conduct from the *whole* of character, from general principles, from latent motives, and from policies not avowed.

Morgann is calling for an *experiential* criticism of Shakespeare, which alas is light-years away from nearly all current interpretation of Shakespeare. Leo Salingar, who joins Nuttall as one of Morgann's few recent defenders, nevertheless pursues Shakespeare's hints to discover a darker Falstaff than Morgann, Hazlitt, and A. C. Bradley gave us. Though Salingar suggests that critical agreement on Falstaff (and on Hal's rejection of him) is not possible, I want to sketch as comprehensive a view of the Falstaff–Hal relationship as Shakespeare allows us to infer, from the origins of so unlikely a friendship, on to the expulsion of Sir John from the righteously offended royal presence. That returns me to my question: how might we give a Shakespearean description of Prince Hal's initial choice of Falstaff as wayward mentor, as the alternative to Hal's mere repetition of his own usurping father?

When Hal's disaffection from Henry IV is first noted by Shakespeare, in Act V, Scene iii, of *Richard II,* Falstaff is unmentioned. Presumably, he is one of Hal's "unrestrained loose companions," highwaymen and tavern denizens. Since King Richard II has not yet been murdered, Hal's flight from his father can have reference only to evading the guilt of usurpation, and not the still greater guilt of regicide. Still, what Hal flees from must be his father's drive to power, an impulse the prince more than shares, so that Hal represses his own ambitions—or is he merely postponing them, a rather more conscious process? Shakespeare gives us more than enough evidence to suggest that part of Hal is a colder hypocrite than even his father Bolingbroke is and was. Yet another part of him is (or becomes) Falstaffian, in the deepest sense of the Falstaffian: a genius for language and its rhetorical control of others through psychological insight.

Falstaff is an outrageous version of Socrates, but then Socrates outraged his contemporaries to the point of provoking them to execute him. There is a link between Shakespeare's Falstaff and Montaigne's Socrates, a connection that may be a direct influence, since Shakespeare probably had access to John Florio's translation of Montaigne while it was still in manuscript. Scholars have recognized that Mistress Quickly's account of Falstaff's death, in *Henry V,* clearly alludes to Plato's story of the death of Socrates, in the *Phaedo.* Montaigne's Socrates resembles aspects of Falstaff in more than his death, and it may be that Prince Hal has a touch of Alcibiades in him, though hardly of Shakespeare's later Alcibiades as he appears in *Timon of Athens.* One can object that Falstaff teaches wit rather than wisdom, as Socrates did, but then Falstaff's wit is raffishly wise, and Socrates is so frequently witty.

Despite Hal's obsessive accusations of cowardice, I will vindicate Maurice Morgann's defense of Falstaff's courage, a pragmatic courage that scorns the pretenses of chivalric "honor," of the Hotspur variety. Falstaff's sensible courage resembles that of Socrates, who knew how to retreat intrepidly. Like Socrates, Falstaff will fight only so long as he sees reason, as Poins acknowledges to Hal.

The most authentic parallel between Falstaff and Montaigne's Socrates is in their shared contrast of outer deformity and inner genius. Socrates, Montaigne's hero throughout many of the *Essays,* is particularly lauded in the two final essays, "Of Physiognomy" and "Of Experience." We are reasonably certain that Shakespeare read "Of Physiognomy," because Hamlet almost certainly echoes it, while "Of Experience" is Montaigne's masterpiece and is profoundly Shakespearean in spirit. The ugliness of Socrates is the vessel that contains wisdom and knowledge, even as the grotesque Falstaff exceeds every Shakespearean character except Hamlet as an intellect.

Montaigne's Socrates is both skeptical and affirmative, questioning everything, while remaining positive in his values. Falstaff is both a superb ironist, like Hamlet, and a great vitalist, as that master of negations, Hamlet, might have been, except for the Ghost's intervention. In "Of Experience," Montaigne says he has a vocabulary, all his own, and so do Socrates and Falstaff, overwhelmingly. All three—Montaigne, Socrates, Falstaff—are great educators, little as scholars credit Falstaff in this regard. What the three teach is the great lesson of experience, the perfection and virtual divinity of knowing how to enjoy our being rightfully.

One can surmise, then, that Hal first came to Falstaff as Alcibiades and so many other young men (Plato included) first came to Socrates: the disreputable sage was the authentic teacher of wisdom. But of Hal's earlier phase, or phases, in Falstaff's company, we know almost nothing. When we first see the two on stage together, Hal is on the attack, ambivalence toward Falstaff dominating every utterance he directs at him. Sir John parries nimbly, yet he must begin to recognize, as the audience does, that the prince's ambivalence has turned murderous. But such a turn argues implicitly for a prior relationship of great closeness and importance between the prince and the fat knight. Only Falstaff has maintained the positive affection of the earlier relationship, and yet why does Hal continue to seek Falstaff out? Evidently, the prince needs both to convict Falstaff of cowardice and to show himself that rhetorically he can not only hold his own against his teacher of wit but overgo Falstaff as well, bettering his instruction.

William Empson wrote brilliantly about a Falstaff not wholly different from the one I follow Morgann, Hazlitt, Bradley, and Goddard in reading. Empson's Falstaff is "a scandalous gentleman," descended among the lower orders:

> Falstaff is the first major joke by the English against their class system; he is a picture of how badly you can behave, and still get away with it, if you are a gentleman—a mere common rogue would not have been nearly so funny.

That seems to me a little reductive, yes behind it is Empson's sensible conviction that Falstaff's relation to Hal may well be influenced by Shakespeare's playing the role of Socrates to the Earl of Southampton's (or another nobleman's) Alcibiades, at least in the story intimated by the Sonnets. Shakespeare, we know, badly wished to restore his family's status as gentlemen, and was fiercely satirized by Ben Jonson for securing a coat of arms, with its motto, "Not without right," which became "Not without mustard" in Jonson's *Every Man Out of His Humor* (1599). But to center upon Falstaff as an exemplification of Shakespeare's class consciousness, while clearly not wrong, is ultimately inadequate. Empson's Falstaff is something of a patriotic Machiavel, and thus a fit teacher for the future Henry V. Going interestingly further, Empson sees Falstaff as a potential mob leader—charismatic, unscrupulous, and able to sway people lower in the social order than himself. Does that not wholly decenter the magnificent Falstaff?

Critics regularly have called Sir John one of the lords of language, which beggars him: he is the veritable monarch of language, unmatched whether elsewhere in Shakespeare or in all of Western literature. His superbly supple and copious prose is astonishingly attractive: Samuel Johnson and Oscar Wilde's Lady

Bracknell (in *The Importance of Being Earnest*) alike are legatees of Falstaff's amazing resourcefulness of speech. What can a great teacher possess except high intellect and the language appropriate to it? Fluellen in *Henry V* happily compares his hero-king to Alexander the Great, pointing out that the former Prince Hal "turned away the fat knight with the great-belly doublet—he was full of jests, and gipes, and knaveries, and mocks" even as Alexander murdered his best friend, Cleitus. One feels that Fluellen did not get that right; Falstaff is no Cleitus, but as much Prince Hal's tutor as Aristotle was Alexander's. The implicit comparison to Aristotle is outrageous, yet it is Shakespeare's, not mine. What is the difference between Henry IV and Henry V? Falstaff, because the fat knight so "full of jests, and gipes, and knaveries, and mocks" taught the son how to transcend the usurping and joyless father without rejecting him. That is not exactly what Falstaff attempted to teach Hal, one can sensibly insist, but Hal (much as I dislike him) is almost as much a student of genius as Falstaff is a teacher of genius. Henry V is an authentic charismatic, who has learned the uses of charisma from his disreputable but endlessly gifted teacher. It is one of Shakespeare's harshest dramatic ironies that Falstaff prepares his own destruction not only by teaching too well but by loving much too well. Henry V is no man's teacher and loves no one; he is a great leader and exploiter of power, and destroying Falstaff causes him not an iota of regret.

The rejection of Falstaff possibly is a deep echo of Shakespeare's own sense of betrayal by the young nobleman of the Sonnets, except that Shakespeare manifests extraordinary ambivalence toward himself in the Sonnets, while Falstaff's almost innocent self-love is part of the secret of the fat knight's genius. Like his admirer Oscar Wilde, Sir John was always right, except in blinding himself to Hal's hypocrisy, just as the sublime Oscar was wrong only about Lord Alfred Douglas, poetaster and narcissist. Just before the battle of Shrewsbury, Falstaff, most probably the oldest and certainly the fattest soldier about to risk death, sensibly and rather movingly says, "I would 'twere bed-time, Hal, and all well." The prince grimly retorts, "Why, thou owest God a death," and exits, with the pun of "death" and "debt" (in Elizabethan pronunciation) still reverberating. I can still hear Ralph Richardson as Falstaff responding to the warlike Hal's nasty pun:

'Tis not due yet: I would be loath to pay him before his day—what need I be so forward with him that calls not on me? Well, 'tis no matter, honour pricks me on. Yea, but how if honour prick me off when I come on, how then? Can honour set to a leg? No. Or an arm? No. Or take away the grief of a wound? No. Honour hath no skill in surgery then? No. What is honour? A word. What is in that word honour? What is that honour? Air. A trim reckoning! Who hath it? He that died a-Wednesday. Doth he feel it? No. Doth he hear it? No. 'Tis insensible, then? Yea, to the dead. But will it not live with the living? No. Why? Detraction will not suffer it. Therefore I'll none of it. Honour is a mere scutcheon—and so ends my catechism.

[V.i.127–41]

Can there be an audience that will not learn from this, in a society still given to military fantasies? Are there any societies not so given, past or present? Falstaff, like his reluctantly charmed admirer, Dr. Samuel Johnson, urges us to clear our minds of cant, and Falstaff is even freer of societal delusions than was the Grand Cham, Johnson. Shakespeare, we can surmise from his life as well as from his work, had a horror of violence, including the organized violence of warfare. *Henry V* hardly exalts battle; its ironies are subtle but palpable. "Honor" is the sphere of Hotspur, and of the Hal who slays Hotspur and thus usurps the throne of this "Air. A trim reckoning!" Going to the battle, Hotspur cries out, "Doomsday is near; die all, die merrily," while Falstaff, on the battlefield, says, "Give me life."

Shakespeare gave Sir John such abundant life that even Shakespeare had a very hard (and reluctant) time in ending Falstaff, who never owed Shakespeare a death. The debt (as Shakespeare knew) was to Falstaff, both for finally emancipating him from Marlowe, and for making him the most successful of Elizabethan dramatists, thus dwarfing Marlowe, Kyd, and all other rivals, Ben Jonson included. Ralph Richardson, exactly half a century ago, implicitly understood that Falstaff had absolute presence of mind, and could triumph over every challenger, until the terrible rejection by Hal. At sixty-seven, I again remember vividly my re-actions as a boy of sixteen, educated by Richardson's Falstaff to a first understanding of Shakespeare. What Richardson played was the essence of playing, in every sense of playing, and his Falstaff (whether he knew it or not) was the Falstaff of A. C. Bradley, now absurdly deprecated but still the best English critic of Shakespeare since William Hazlitt:

The bliss of freedom gained in humour is the essence of Falstaff. His humour is not directed only or chiefly against obvious absurdities; he is the enemy of everything that would interfere with his ease, and therefore of anything serious, and especially of everything respectable and moral. For these things impose limits and obligations, and make us the subjects of old father antic the law, and the categorical imperative, and our station and its duties, and conscience, and reputation, and other people's opinions, and all sorts of nuisances. I say he is therefore their enemy; but I do him wrong; to say that he is their enemy implies that he regards them as serious and recognises their power, when in truth he refuses to recognise them at all. They are to him absurd; and to reduce a thing ad absurdum is to reduce it to nothing and to walk about free and rejoicing. This is what Falstaff does with all the would-be serious things of life, sometimes only by his words, sometimes by his actions too. He will make truth appear absurd by solemn statements, which he utters with perfect gravity and which he expects nobody to believe; and honour, by demonstrating that it cannot set a leg, and that neither the living nor the dead can possess it; and law, by evading all the attacks of its highest representative and almost forcing him to laugh at his own defeat; and patriotism, by filling his pockets with the bribes offered by competent soldiers who want to escape service, while he takes in their stead the halt and maimed and gaol-birds; and duty, by showing how he labours in his vocation—of thieving; and courage, alike by mocking at his own capture of Colevile and gravely claiming to have killed Hotspur; and war, by offering the Prince his bottle of sack when he is asked for a sword; and religion, by amusing himself with remorse at odd times when he has nothing else to do; and the fear of death, by maintaining perfectly untouched, in the face of imminent peril and even while he feels the fear of death, the very same power of dissolving it in persiflage that he shows when he sits at ease in his inn. These are the wonderful achievements which he performs, not with the sourness of a cynic, but with the gaiety of a boy. And therefore, we praise him, we laud him, for he offends none but the virtuous, and denies that life is real or life is earnest, and delivers us from the oppression of such nightmares, and lifts us into the atmosphere of perfect freedom.

I remember first reading this grand paragraph by Bradley a few months after seeing Richardson as Falstaff, and my shock of pleasure at recognizing how well the interpretations of this critic and this actor confirmed each other. Bradley's Falstaff is not sentimentalized; the critic knows full well that he would literally not be safe in Falstaff's company. But he knows also that Falstaff teaches us *not to moralize.* Hal's belated espousal of courage and honor is one kind of moralizing, and the Lord Chief Justice's is another; Falstaff wants childlike (not childish) play, which exists in another order than that of morality. As Bradley says, Falstaff simply refuses to recognize the social institutions of reality; he is neither immoral nor amoral but of another realm, the order of play. Hal entered that order as Falstaff's disciple, and sojourned there rather longer than he may have intended. Despite his presumably long-gathering ambivalence toward Falstaff, Hal struggles all through *Henry IV, Part One,* against the fascination exercised by the great wit. It seems just to observe that Falstaff charms the tough and resistant prince for many of the same reasons that Falstaff, properly played, dominates any audience.

4

Antithetical forces seem to drive Shakespeare's characterization of Falstaff in Part Two, if only to prepare us for Hal's climactic rejection. Still triumphant over the Lord Chief Justice and Prince John, the law and the state, Falstaff remains nimble at bidding the world of "honour" pass. Hal is the spokesperson for so-called honor's indictment of Falstaff, and he performs the rule with an exuberance learned from the teacher, though all the accusations fall flat. The sublime Falstaff simply is not a coward, a court jester or fool, a confidence man, a bawd, another politician, an opportunistic courtier, an alcoholic seducer of the young. Falstaff, as I remarked earlier, is the Elizabethan Socrates, and in the wit combat with Hal, the prince is a mere sophist, bound to lose. Falstaff, like Socrates, is wisdom, wit, self-knowledge, mastery of reality. Socrates too seemed disreputable to the powermongers of Athens, who finally condemned him to death. Hal, who plays with the possibility of hanging Falstaff, doubtless would have executed his mentor at Agincourt if the antics performed at Shrewsbury had been repeated there. Instead, Bardolph swings as the master's surrogate, and Sir John, heartbroken into acceptance of his old age, dies offstage to Mistress Quickly's loving, cockney elegy.

I wish that Shakespeare had put Socrates on stage in *Timon of Athens,* in company with Alcibiades, so as to give us an after-image of the Hal-Falstaff relationship. Perhaps Shakespeare felt that his Falstaff made Montaigne's Socrates redundant. Falstaff or Socrates? That may sound outrageous, since the two great challengers of moral values practiced very different styles: Socrates' dialectic, and Falstaff's perpetual reinvention of language. Socrates teases you into truth; Falstaff the parodist inundates you with wordplay. Those who detest Falstaff, in and out of his plays, insist that the fat knight drowns himself in his tidal wave of language. "The question is which is to be master?" Humpty Dumpty says to Alice, after that imitation Falstaff has boasted: "When I use a word it means just what I choose it to mean." Falstaff finishes at the head of Humpty Dumpty's class. Sir John is the master, as Hamlet and Rosalind are also masters. The witty knight is hardly the prisoner of his phonemes. Shakespeare gives Falstaff one of his own greatest gifts: the florabundant language of Shakespeare's own youth, not a style of old age.

For Hal, more than ironically, Falstaff is "the latter spring . . . all-hallow summer," ageless in his exuberance. Descending as a highwayman against travelers, Falstaff chants, "Ah, whoreson caterpillars, bacon-fed knaves, they hate us youth!" "What, ye knaves!" he adds, "young men must live." Outrageously parodistic,

Falstaff mocks his own years, and persuasively continues a military career (when he has to) that he both scorns and indulges, primarily as *materia poetica* for further mockery, by others as by himself. "We must all to the wars," Hal tells his Eastcheap roisterers, and plans fresh exploits for Falstaff: "I'll procure this fat rogue a charge of foot, and I know his death will be a march of twelve score." Informed by the prince, Falstaff will not cease jesting: "Well God be thanked for these rebels, they offend none but the virtuous: I laud them, I praise them." "Rebellion lay in his way, and he found it" is the Falstaffian formula for civil war. Since Hal's kingdom (and his life) is at stake, the prince's growl of: "Peace, chewet, peace," is hardly excessive. Falstaff has outlived his function for a prince who means to conquer "honour," England, and France, in that order.

Yet Falstaff is the poem of Shakespeare's climate, not an idea of disorder but the essence of Shakespeare's dramatic art: the principle of play. If Falstaff's nature is subdued at all, it is to the element of play, without which he will die. This is the most intimate link between playwright and comedic genius: Falstaff's high theatricalism is prophetic of Hamlet, of Duke Vincentio in *Measure for Measure,* most darkly of Iago, most gloriously of Cleopatra, Falstaff's truest child. Falstaff, always himself, surpasses the selfsame in the improvised but elaborate plays-within-the-play that present shadows of the forthcoming confrontation between King Henry IV and the prince. First, Falstaff portrays the king, while Hal plays himself. Parodying John Lyly's *Euphues,* of twenty years before, Falstaff leaves little of either father or son, while enjoying a vision of the greatness of Falstaff:

> *Fal.* Harry, I do not only marvel where thou spendest thy
> time, but also how thou art accompanied. For though
> the camomile, the more it is trodden on the faster it
> grows, yet youth, the more it is wasted the sooner it

wears. That thou art my son I have partly thy mother's
word, partly my own opinion, but chiefly a villainous
trick of thine eye, and a foolish hanging of thy nether
lip, that doth warrant me. If then thou be son to me,
here lies the point—why, being son to me, art thou so
pointed at? Shall the blessed sun of heaven prove a
micher, and eat blackberries? A question not to be
asked. Shall the son of England prove a thief, and take
purses? A question to be asked. There is a thing, Harry,
which thou hast often heard of, and it is known to
many in our land by the name of pitch. This pitch (as
ancient writers do report) doth defile, so doth the company thou keepest: for, Harry, now I do not speak to
thee in drink, but in tears; not in pleasure, but in passion; not in words only, but in woes also. And yet there
is a virtuous man whom I have often noted in thy
company, but I know not his name.

Prince. What manner of man, and it like your Majesty?

Fal. A goodly portly man, i' faith, and a corpulent; of a
cheerful look, a pleasing eye, and a most noble carriage;
and, as I think, his age some fifty, or, by'r lady, inclining
to threescore; and now I remember me, his name is Falstaff. If that man should be lewdly given, he deceiveth
me; for, Harry, I see virtue in his looks. If then the tree
may be known by the fruit, as the fruit by the tree, then
peremptorily I speak it, there is virtue in that Falstaff;
him keep with, the rest banish.

[II.iv.393–425]

Falstaff, who has been absorbing much abuse from Hal, triumphantly betters the scoffing, though in a far finer tone than
the prince's murderous aggressivity. Royal father and holidaying

son are rendered charmingly foolish, while Falstaff's Falstaff is beheld in the light of Swinburne's "possible moral elevation." All this is play in its sweetest and purest sense, an exercise that heals and restores. Very different is Hal's thunderous version, after he commands that he is to play his own father, while Falstaff stands in for the prince:

Prince. Now, Harry, whence come you?

Fal. My noble lord, from Eastcheap.

Prince. The complaints I hear of thee are grievous.

Fal. 'Sblood, my lord, they are false: nay, I'll tickle ye for a young prince, i'faith.

Prince. Swearest thou, ungracious boy? Henceforth ne'er look on me. Thou art violently carried away from grace, there is a devil haunts thee in the likeness of an old fat man, a tun of man is thy companion. Why dost thou converse with that trunk of humours, that bolting-hutch of beastliness, that swoll'n parcel of drop-sies, that huge bombard of sack, that stuffed cloak-bag of guts, that roasted Manningtree ox with the pudding in his belly, that reverend vice, that grey iniquity, that fa-ther ruffian, that vanity in years? Wherein is he good, but to taste sack and drink it? wherein neat and cleanly, but to carve a capon and eat it? wherein cunning, but in craft? wherein crafty, but in villainy? wherein villain-ous, but in all things? wherein worthy, but in nothing?

Fal. I would your Grace would take me with you: whom means your Grace?

Prince. That villainous abominable misleader of youth, Falstaff, that old white-bearded Satan.

Fal. My lord, the man I know.

Prince. I know thou dost.

Fal. But to say I know more harm in him that in myself
were to say more than I know. That he is old, the more
the pity, his white hairs do witness it, but that he is, saving your reverence, a whoremaster, that I utterly deny.
If sack and sugar be a fault, God help the wicked! If to
be old and merry be a sin, then many an old host that I
know is damned: if to be fat be to be hated, then
Pharaoh's lean kine are to be loved. No, my good lord;
banish Peto, banish Bardolph, banish Poins—but for
sweet Jack Falstaff, kind Jack Falstaff, true Jack Falstaff,
valiant Jack Falstaff, and therefore more valiant, being as
he is old Jack Falstaff, banish not him thy Harry's company, banish plump Jack, and banish all the world.
Prince. I do, I will.

[II.iv.434–75]

This is the glowing center of *Henry IV, Part One,* intense with
Falstaff's poignant wit and Hal's cold fury. Ambivalence ex-
plodes into positive hatred in Hal's final summation: "That villainous abominable misleader of youth, Falstaff, that old
white-bearded Satan." The Prince is not acting, and speaks from
his whole mind and heart. How are we to account for this un-
justified malevolence, this exorcism that transcends rejection?
Whom do we credit, Hal's "old white-bearded Satan" or "sweet
Jack Falstaff, kind Jack Falstaff, true Jack Falstaff, valiant Jack Falstaff, and therefore more valiant, being as he is old Jack Falstaff"? Hal is so extreme that surely we have no choice. Always
Falstaff's student, he has one insult worthy of the old professor:
"that roasted Manningtree ox with the pudding in his belly,"
but that is hardly in a class with "if to be fat be to be hated, then
Pharaoh's lean kine are to be loved." No scholarly detractor of
Falstaff, old- or new-style, is so disgusted by Sir John as Hal re-
veals himself to be. I have mentioned Honigmann's assertion

that Shakespeare does not allow us to unravel the psychological perplexities of the Falstaff–Hal relationship, but while a puzzling matter, it is not beyond all conjecture. Hal has fallen out of love. Iris Murdoch remarks that this is one of the great human experiences, in which you see the world with newly awakened eyes. "But being awak'd I do despise my dream," the newly crowned Henry V virtuously assures us. Alas, he has been awake as long as we have known him, since the start of *Henry IV, Part One,* where he manifests three ambitions of equal magnitude: wait for Henry IV to die (as quickly as possible), kill Hotspur and appropriate his "honour," have Falstaff hanged. He very nearly does place Falstaff in the hangman's hands, but forbears, reasoning that it is more appropriate to kill the aged reprobate by a forced march, or even (honorably) in battle. Some residue of former affection for Falstaff could be argued, though I myself doubt it. Sir John has outlived his educational function, but he is annoyingly indestructible, as the marvelous Battle of Shrewsbury, so much livelier than the Falstaffless Agincourt, will demonstrate.

Shakespeare's charming disrespect for slaughter is frequently an undersong throughout the plays, but it is never quite as pungent as in Falstaff's audacious contempt at Shrewsbury:

> *Prince.* What, stands thou idle here? Lend me thy sword:
> Many a nobleman lies stark and stiff
> Under the hoofs of vaunting enemies,
> Whose deaths are yet unrevenged. I prithee lend me
> thy sword.
> *Fal.* O Hal, I prithee give me leave to breathe awhile—
> Turk Gregory never did such deeds in arms as I have
> done this day; I have paid Percy, I have made him sure.
> *Prince.* He is indeed, and living to kill thee:
> I prithee lend me thy sword.

Fal. Nay, before God, Hal, if Percy be alive, thou gets not
   my sword, but take my pistol if thou wilt.
Prince. Give it me: what, is it in the case?
Fal. Ay, Hal, 'tis hot, 'tis hot; there's that will sack a city.
   The Prince draws it out, and finds it to be a bottle of sack.
Prince. What, is it a time to jest and dally now?
          He throws the bottle at him. Exit.
Fal. Well, if Percy be alive, I'll pierce him. If he do come
   in my way, so: if he do not, if I come in his willingly, let
   him make a carbonado of me. I like not such grinning
   honour as Sir Walter hath. Give me life; which if I can
   save, so: honour comes unlooked for, and there's an end.
                    [Exit.]

                              [V.iii.40–61]

In one sense, Falstaff here pays Hal back for many imputations
of supposed cowardice, yet this is so fine a Falstaffian moment that
it transcends their waning relationship. Having "led" his hundred
and fifty men into their all-but-total destruction, the huge target
Falstaff remains not only unscathed but replete with sublime
mockery of the absurd slaughter. His grand contempt for Hot-
spurian "honour" allows him to take the risk of substituting a
bottle of sack for the pistol his rank merits. After a half century, I
retain the vivid image of Ralph Richardson gleefully and nimbly
dodging the thrown bottle, with an expressive gesture indicating
that indeed this was much the best time to jest and dally! Is there,
in all Shakespeare, anything more useful than "I like not such
grinning honour as Sir Walter hath. Give me life"? For Falstaff,
Shrewsbury becomes an insane spectator sport, as when Sir John
ironically cheers the prince on in the duel with Hotspur.
Shakespeare's gusto is at its height when the ferocious Douglas
charges on stage and forces Falstaff to fight. The wily Falstaff

falls down as if dead, just as Hal gives Hotspur a death wound. Even as we wonder what the dying Hotspur "could prophesy" (the vanity of "honour"?), Shakespeare affords Hal his great moment when the prince believes that he beholds the corpse of Falstaff:

> What, old acquaintance, could not all this flesh
> Keep in a little life? Poor Jack, farewell!
> I could have better spared a better man:
> O, I should have a heavy miss of thee
> If I were much in love with vanity:
> Death hath not struck so fat a deer today,
> Though many dearer, in this bloody fray.
> Embowell'd will I see thee by and by,
> Till then in blood by noble Percy lie.
>
> *[Exit.]*
>
> [V.iv.101–9]

These intricate lines are not so much ambivalent as they are revelatory of Henry V, whose kingship is formed at Shrewsbury. "Poor Jack, farewell!" is almost as much authentic grief as the warlike Harry can summon for the apostle of "vanity," who was so frivolous as to gambol about and jest upon a royal battleground. As an epitaph for Falstaff, this does not even achieve the dignity of being absurd, and is properly answered by the resurrection of "the true and perfect image of life," immortal spirit worth a thousand Hals. Here is the truest glory of Shakespeare's invention of the human:

> Embowelled? If thou embowel me today, I'll give you
> leave to powder me and eat me too tomorrow. 'Sblood,
> 'twas time to counterfeit, or that hot termagant Scot had

paid me, scot and lot too. Counterfeit? I lie, I am no counterfeit: to die is to be a counterfeit, for he is but the counterfeit of a man, who hath not the life of a man: but to
counterfeit dying, when a man thereby liveth, is to be no
counterfeit, but the true and perfect image of life indeed.
The better part of valor is discretion, in the which better
part I have saved my life. 'Zounds, I am afraid of this gunpowder Percy, though he be dead; how if he should counterfeit too and rise? By my faith, I am afraid he would
prove the better counterfeit; therefore I'll make him sure,
yea, and I'll swear I killed him. Why may not he rise as
well as I? Nothing confutes me but eyes, and nobody sees
me: therefore, sirrah [*stabbing him*], with a new wound in
your thigh, come you along with me.

[V.iv.110–28]

To have seen Richardson bounding up was to have beheld the
most joyous representation of secular resurrection ever staged:
Falstaff's Wake would be an apt title for *Henry IV, Part One*. Ma-
ligned, threatened with hanging, hated (by the prince) where he
had been loved, the great pariah rises in the flesh, having counterfeited death. As true and perfect image, he has seemed to the
Christian critic Auden a type of Christ, but it is more than
enough that he abides as Falstaff, mocker of hypocritical "honour," parodist of noble butchery, defier of time, law, order, and
the state. He is still irrepressible, and is accurate, as Harold Goddard observed, in asserting that *he* killed the spirit of Hotspur: It
is not the swordplay of Hal that upstages Hotspur; place Hotspur
in any play not inhabited by Falstaff, and Hotspur would fascinate
us, but he fades in the cognitive bonfire of Falstaff's exuberance
and is exposed as only another counterfeit. Shakespearean secu-
larists should manifest their Bardoaltry by celebrating the Resurrection of Sir John Falstaff. It should be made, unofficially but

pervasively, an international holiday, a Carnival of wit, with multiple performances of *Henry IV, Part One*. Let it be a day for loathing political ambition, religious hypocrisy, and false friendship, and let it be marked by wearing bottles of sack in our holsters.

5

Falstaffians, derided by joyless scholars as "sentimentalists," actually are "pataphysicians," knowing that Falstaff's is the true science of imaginary solutions. Alfred Jarry, author of *Ubu Roi*, conceived of the Passion as an Uphill Bicycle Race. *Henry IV, Part Two*, is *The Passion of Sir John Falstaff*, who exuberantly surges on to his humiliation and destruction by the brutal hypocrite, the newly crowned Henry V. If you interpret the play otherwise, doubtless you will have your reward, since you stand with the Lord Chief Justice as he berates and admonishes Falstaff, who gives back much better than he receives, and yet at last will be conveyed to the Fleet, where the Chief Justice, hearing the case, is bound to have the last word. Shakespeare spares us the sadness of the hearing; perhaps we might venture that Shakespeare also spared himself, since nothing appropriate remains for Falstaff to experience, except for his beautiful death scene as reported by Mistress Quickly and his other survivors in *Henry V*.

Falstaff, still in his glory when first we see him in *Henry IV, Part Two*, memorably disputes his age with the Chief Justice:

> *Fal.* You that are old consider not the capacities of us that
> are young; you do measure the heat of our livers with
> the bitterness of your galls; and we that are in the
> vaward of our youth, I must confess, are wags too.

> *Ch. Just.* Do you set down your name in the scroll of
> youth, that are written down old with all the characters
> of age? Have you not a moist eye, a dry hand, a yellow
> cheek, a white beard, a decreasing leg, an increasing
> belly? Is not your voice broken, your wind short, your
> chin double, your wit single, and every part about you
> blasted with antiquity? And will you yet call yourself
> young? Fie, fie, fie, Sir John!
>
> *Fal.* My lord, I was born about three of the clock in the
> afternoon, with a white head, and something a round
> belly. For my voice, I have lost it with hallooing, and
> singing of anthems. To approve my youth further, I will
> not: the truth is, I am only old in judgment and under-
> standing; and he that will caper with me for a thousand
> marks, let him lend me the money, and have at him!
>
> > [I.ii.172–93]

One can start with a good morning's moral disapproval of
Falstaff (very rueful if one is a fat man) and still contend that
only a sensibility of stone will not be charmed by "My lord, I
was born about three of the clock in the afternoon, with a white
head, and something a round belly." Yet Shakespeare will show
time darkening Falstaff, in the pathos of his aged lust for Doll
Tearsheet:

> *Fal.* Thou dost give me flattering busses.
> *Doll.* By my troth, I kiss thee with a most constant heart.
> *Fal.* I am old; I am old.
> *Doll.* I love thee better than I love e'er a scurvy young boy
> of them all.
> *Fal.* What stuff wilt have a kirtle of? I shall receive money
> a-Thursday, shalt have a cap tomorrow. A merry song!

Come, it grows late, we'll to bed. Thou't forget me
when I am gone.

[II.iv.266–74]

The play at perpetual youth yields to "I am old, I am old," in
this giant paradox of an exhausted vitalist, about to be dragged
back to the civil wars by a dozen sweating captains. Beneath
Hal's savage banter and Falstaff's outrageous parries, there abides
the prodigy of an ancient warrior still formidable enough to be
of considerable if highly reluctant service. Coming upon the
rebel Coleville, Falstaff observes his general praxis of playful
pragmatism: "Do ye yield, sir, or shall I sweat for you?" Coleville
surrenders, but it is clear that Falstaff would have sweated to defeat or kill Coleville had it been necessary. And yet Falstaff cheer-
fully mocks his own exploit of capturing Coleville: "But thou
like a kind fellow gavest thyself away gratis, and I thank thee for
thee." This is in the same spirit as Falstaff's insistence that he, not
Hal, gave the death wound, not literally but in spirit. Hotspur,
absurdly courageous and doom-eager, is one of Falstaff's antithe-
ses; the other is John of Lancaster, Hal's warlike younger brother,
who like Hal and the Chief Justice threatens Sir John with hanging. Lancaster, "sober-blooded boy," provokes Falstaff to his great
rhapsody on the virtues of drinking sherry, but otherwise causes
us to reflect that it was an ill hour when the sublime Sir John first
became involved with the royal family. As the shadows of Hal's
forthcoming rejection darken *Henry IV, Part Two,* Shakespeare
distracts us (and himself) by the scenes shared by Falstaff with
the two country justices, Shallow and Silence (Act III, Scene ii,
and Act V, Scenes i and iii). Kenneth Tynan rightly remarked that
"Shakespeare never surpassed these scenes in the vein of pure
naturalism": the fatuousness of Shallow plays off deliciously
against the Falstaffian wit, particularly when the appropriately

named Shallow attempts to revive common memories dating back fifty-five years:

> *Shallow.* Ha, cousin Silence, that thou hadst seen that that
>   this knight and I have seen! Ha, Sir John, said I well?
> *Fal.* We have heard the chimes at midnight, Master
>   Shallow.
>
> [III.ii.206–10]

Falstaff's dry response masks his resolution to return and fleece this country gull, which he will perform on the grand scale. Shallow is Hotspur turned inside out, as was beautifully demonstrated by Laurence Olivier, when he played Hotspur in the afternoon and Shallow in the evening, in the Old Vic productions of 1946. The eloquent swordsman mutated into the aged "forked radish," while Richardson maintained his exuberant wit in a long day's defiance of dying, only to suffer Hal's inevitable betrayal and pragmatic death sentence.

6

Sir John Falstaff is the greatest vitalist in Shakespeare, but while he is certainly not the most intense of Shakespeare's nihilists, his strain of nihilism is extraordinarily virulent. Indeed, Falstaff's nihilism seems to me his version of Christianity, and helps account for the darkest element in the grand wit, his realistic obsession with rejection, massively to be realized at the end of *Henry IV, Part Two.*

It is the image of rejection, rather than of damnation, that accounts for Falstaff's frequent allusions to the frightening parable of the purple-clad glutton, Dives, and poor Lazarus the beggar that Jesus tells in Luke 16:19–26:

There was a certeine riche man, which was clothed in
   purple and fine linen, and fared wel and delicately
   everie day.

Also there was a certeine begger named Lazarus, which was
   laied at his gate ful of sores,

And desired to be refreshed with the crommes that fell
   from the riche mans table: yea, and the dogs came and
   licked his sores.

And it was so that the begger dyed, and was caryed by the
   Angels into Abrahams bosome. The riche man also dyed
   and was buryed.

And being in hel in torments, he lift vp his eyes, and sawe
   Abraham a farre of, & Lazarus in his bosome.

Then he cryed, and sais, Father Abraham, gaue mercie on
   me, and send Lazarus that he may dippe y typ of his finger in water, and coole my tongue: for I am tormented
   in this flame.

But Abraham said, Sonne, remember that thou in thy life
   time receiuedft thy pleasures, and likewise Lazarus
   paines: now therefore is he comforted, and thou art tormented.

Besides all this, betwene you and vs there is a great gulfe set,
   so that they which wolde go from hence to you, can not,
   nether can they come from thence to vs.

[Geneva Bible, Luke 16:19–26]

Three times Falstaff alludes to this fierce parable; I will suggest
that there is a fourth, concealed allusion when Falstaff kneels and is
rejected by King Henry V, in his new royal purple, and manifestly
there is a fifth when the Hostess, describing Falstaff's death in the
play he is not permitted to enter, *Henry V,* assures us that Falstaff is
"in Arthur's bosom," with the British Arthur substituting for Father Abraham. To be sure, Henry V allows that Falstaff is to be fed

crumbs from the royal table, but the initial feeding is held in prison, by order of the Lord Chief Justice. If we are to credit his Sonnets, Shakespeare knew what it was to be rejected, though I certainly do not wish to suggest an affinity between the creator of Falstaff and Falstaff himself. I wonder, though, at the affinities between Prince Hal and the Earl of Southampton, neither of them candidates for Abraham's bosom. What is Sir John's implicit interpretation of the parable of the rich man and the beggar?

Falstaff's first allusion to the parable is the richest and most outrageous, beginning as a meditation on Bardolph's fiery nose, which makes him "the Knight of the Burning Lamp." The hurt Bardolph complains, "Why, Sir John, my face does you no harm," to which Falstaff makes a massive reply:

> No, I'll be sworn, I make as good use of it as many a man doth of a death's-head or a *memento mori.* I never see thy face but I think upon hell-fire, and Dives that lived in purple: for there he is in his robes, burning, burning. If thou wert any way given to virtue, I would swear by thy face; my oath should be "By this fire, that's God's angel!" But thou art altogether given over; and wert indeed, but for the light in thy face, the son of utter darkness. When thou ran'st up Gad's Hill in the night to catch my horse, if I did not think thou hadst been an *ignis fatuus,* or a ball of wildfire, there's no purchase in money. O, thou art a perpetual triumph, an everlasting bonfire-light! Thou hast saved me a thousand marks in links and torches, walking with thee in the night betwixt tavern and tavern: but the sack that thou hast drunk me would have bought me lights as good cheap at the dearest chandler's in Europe. I have maintained that salamander of yours with fire any time this two and thirty years, God reward me for it!

[III.iii.28–47]

"For there he is in his robes, burning, burning": of course we are to note that Falstaff himself is another glutton, but I do not believe we are to take seriously Falstaff's fear of hellfire, any more than we are to identify Bardolph with the Burning Bush. Sir John is at work subverting Scripture, even as he subverts everything else that would constrain him: time, the state, virtue, the chivalric concept of "honour," and all ideas of order whatsoever. The brilliant fantasia upon Bardolph's nose does not allow us much residual awe in relation to Jesus's rather uncharacteristic parable. What chance has the rhetorical threat of hellfire against the dazzling metamorphoses of Bardolph's nose, which goes from a *memento mori* to the Burning Bush to a will-o'-the-wisp to fireworks to a torchlight procession to a bonfire to a fiery salamander, seven amiable variants that far outshine the burning in Jesus's parable. Falstaff, the greatest of Shakespeare's prose poets, leaps from metaphor to metaphor so as to remind us implicitly that the parable's "burning, burning" is metaphor also, albeit a metaphor that Sir John cannot cease to empty out. He returns to it as he marches his wretched recruits on to the hellfire of the battle of Shrewsbury: "slaves as ragged as Lazarus in the painted cloth, where the glutton's dogs lick'd his sores."

Why does the allusion recur in this context? Hal, staring at Falstaff's troop, observes, "I did never see such pitiful rascals," prompting Falstaff's grand rejoinder: "Tut, tut, good enough to toss, food for powder, food for powder; they'll fill a pit as well as better; tush, man, mortal men, mortal men." Would it be more honorable if you tossed on a pike better-fed, better-clothed impressed men? How could one state it more tellingly: Falstaff's recruits have all the necessary qualities: food for powder, corpses to fill a pit, mortal men, who are there to be killed, only to be killed, like their betters, whose "grinning honour" Prince Hal will worship. Falstaff has drafted the poorest, like the beggar

Lazarus, in contrast to the purple glutton he previously named as Dives, a name not to be found in the Geneva Bible or later in the King James. It is not likely that either Shakespeare or Falstaff had read Luke in the Vulgate, where the "certain rich man" is a *dives,* Late Latin for "rich man," but Dives by Shakespeare's day was already a name out of Chaucer and the common tongue. Sir John, after collecting the bribes of the affluent to release them from the service, has put together a fine crew of Lazaruses, who will be stabbed and blown up to serve the Henrys, father and son. Yet, true to his charismatic personality, Falstaff, marching with a bottle of sack in his pistol holster, observes, "I have led my ragamuffins where they are peppered; there's not three of my hundred and fifty alive, and they are for the town's end, to beg during life." All we can ask of Falstaff he has done; a mortal man, he *led* his Lazaruses to their peppering, taking his chances with them where the fire was hottest. Sir John's cognitive contempt for the entire enterprise is his true offense against time and the state; Prince Hal is never less hypocritical than when he bellows at Falstaff, "What, is it a time to jest and dally now?" while throwing at Sir John the bottle of sack the Prince has just drawn from the holster, in attempting to borrow a pistol.

Falstaff's last explicit allusion to Dives omits any mention of Lazarus, since it is turned against a tailor who has denied him credit: "Let him be damned like the glutton! Pray God his tongue be hotter!" Since Falstaff perpetually is in want of money, neither he nor we associate the fat knight with Dives. It is a fearful irony that Sir John must end like Lazarus, rejected by the newly crowned king in order to win admission to "Arthur's bosom," but clearly Shakespeare was not much in agreement with nearly all his modern critics, who mostly unite in defending the rejection of Falstaff, that spirit of misrule. They mistake this great representation of a personality not less than wholly, and I return again to Jesus's parable, for a final time. Falstaff's implicit inter-

pretation of the text is nihilistic: one must either be damned with
Dives, or else be saved with Lazarus, an antithesis that loses one
either the world to come or this world. Emerson once said,
"Other world? There is no other world; here or nowhere is the
whole fact." Falstaff is more than pragmatic enough to agree
with Emerson, and I find nothing in Shakespeare to indicate that
he himself hoped to join Falstaff in Arthur's bosom, or Lazarus in
Abraham's. Falstaff is the prose poet of "the whole fact," and I
venture that for Sir John the "whole fact" is what we call "personality," as opposed to "character."

It is very difficult for me, even painful, to have done with Falstaff,
for no other literary character—not even Don Quixote or Sancho Panza, not even Hamlet—seems to me so infinite in provoking thought and in arousing emotion. Falstaff is a miracle in the
creation of personality, and his enigmas rival those of Hamlet.
Each is first and foremost an absolutely individual *voice,* no other
personages in Western literature rival them in mastery of language. Falstaff's prose and Hamlet's verse give us a cognitive music that overwhelms us even as it expands our minds to the ends
of thought. They are beyond our last thought, and they have an
immediacy that by the pragmatic test constitutes a real presence,
one that all current theorists and ideologues insist literature cannot even intimate, let alone sustain. But Falstaff persists, after four
centuries, and he will prevail centuries after our fashionable know-
ers and resenters have become alms for oblivion. Dr. Johnson, best
and most moral of critics, loved Falstaff almost despite himself,
partly because Sir John had cleared his mind of cant, but primarily because the fat knight's cheerfulness was contagious enough
to banish, however momentarily, Johnson's vile melancholy.
Schlegel, despite his high German seriousness, acutely noted Falstaff's freedom from malice; the critic should have gone further
and emphasized that Sir John is also free of all censoriousness,

free of what Freud came to call the *überich,* the superego. We all of us beat up upon ourselves; the sane and sacred Falstaff does not, and urges us to emulate him. Falstaff has nothing of Hamlet's savagery, or of Prince Hal's.

What Falstaff bears is the Blessing, in the original Yahwistic sense: more life. All the self-contradictions of his complex nature resolve themselves in his exuberance of being, his passion for being alive. Many of us become machines for fulfilling responsibilities; Falstaff is the largest and best reproach we can find. I am aware that I commit the Original Sin that all historicists—of all generations—decry, joined by all formalists as well: I exalt Falstaff above his plays, the two parts of *Henry IV* and Mistress Quickly's deathbed account in *Henry V.* This sin, like Bardolatry, to me seems salvation. No matter how often I reread Shakespeare, or teach him, or endure what currently passes for stagings, like everyone else I am left with memories, of language and of images, or of an image. I write these pages and Richardson's Falstaff rises before me, a vision of perfection in realizing a central Shakespearean role. But like Hamlet, Falstaff is more than a role. Hamlet and Falstaff have become our culture.

What can we do with dramatic and literary characters who are geniuses in their own right? We know in one sense far too little about Shakespeare himself, but in quite another sense we somehow apprehend that he invested himself very deeply in Hamlet and in Falstaff. They are—both of them—enigmatic and self-revelatory, and we never can mark precisely where what is hidden suddenly beacons to us. Hamlet, as I have remarked, sometimes seems a "real" person surrounded by actors; he has depths not suggested by anyone around him. Conversely, Falstaff can seem a great actor, a Ralph Richardson, surrounded by merely "real" people, since even Hotspur and Hal are trivialized when Falstaff stands on stage with them. They duel, and are a distraction, because we want to hear what Falstaff will say next. When Douglas dashes on and has at Falstaff, we wish the hot termagant Scot to get on with it and then leave us, so that we can enjoy the style of Falstaff's resurrection.

Shakespeare's largest tribute to Falstaff is that, belying his own promise to the audience, he dared not allow Sir John to appear on stage in *Henry V*. The playwright understood the magnitude of his creature. Scholars tend not to, which is why we have the nonsense of what they, and not Shakespeare, continue to call the Henriad. We do not need Henry V, and he does not need us. Falstaff needs an audience, and never fails to find it. We need Falstaff because we have so few images of authentic vitalism, and even fewer persuasive images of human freedom.

william shakespeare
henry IV
part one

synopsis

Henry IV quickly drops his plan to lead an expedition to the Holy Land as an act of penance for the death of Richard II when complete information reaches him of the uprisings and battles in Wales and Scotland. He hears with elation of the conquest of the Scotch army under the command of the Earl of Douglas by Henry Percy, nicknamed Hotspur, son of the Earl of Northumberland, but is greatly annoyed when Hotspur sends word that he will not give up the Scottish prisoners he has captured until Henry ransoms Lady Percy's brother, Edmund Mortimer, who was captured by the Welsh warrior, Owen Glendower, while leading an English expedition against him.

Summoned by the King, the three Percys come to London, the cold, impassive Northumberland, his brother, the suspicious insubordinate Worcester, and his son, the sincere, impulsive Hotspur, each of whom was instrumental in placing Henry on the throne. The King again demands the Scottish prisoners, refuses to ransom Mortimer, whom the late King Richard had named as his rightful heir, calls him a traitor because he has recently married

Glendower's daughter, scoffs at Hotspur's staunch defence of his brother-in-law's nobility and valor as a fighter, and peremptorily orders no further mention of his name.

Fuming with angry resentment, Hotspur, his father and uncle return home and plan a rebellion against Henry by combining their forces with those of the Welsh rebel, Glendower; his new son-in-law, Mortimer, claimant to the throne; the Archbishop of York, whose brother, a loyal adherent of King Richard's, was executed by the present King; and Malcolm of Scotland, whose aid they purpose to secure by the release of the Scottish prisoners.

When the King hears of the revolt, he is forcibly reminded of the Bishop of Carlisle's prophecy that kindred should be set against kindred as the result of King Richard's deposition, and he bitterly contrasts the devotion and energy of young Hotspur with the carefree recklessness of his own son, the fun-loving Prince of Wales, whom he has not seen for three months. Just at this time, the madcap Prince is planning a wild escapade with his boon companion, the corpulent Sir John Falstaff, and a few of his disreputable associates. After Falstaff and the others have attacked and robbed some travellers at Gadshill near London, they are put to a comical flight by the Prince and Ned Poins in disguises of buckram. Later, in the Boar's-Head Tavern in Eastcheap, Prince Hal's favorite resort, the irrepressible Falstaff tells of a hand-to-hand fight with eleven men in buckram and is not at all embarrassed when the Prince discloses the real facts.

In the midst of their riotous fun, a messenger from the King arrives with news of the northern rebellion and summoning his son to the palace, whereupon Falstaff seats himself on a chair with impressive dignity, his dagger in his hand for a scepter, and a cushion on his head for a crown, and practices Prince Hal in his answers to his father's questions on his recent doings and companions. Once the Prince of Wales has aroused himself to a full sense of his responsibilities, he pledges the King that he will be worthy of his title and is given command of part of the royal forces, with Falstaff in charge of a company of foot soldiers.

Meanwhile, in the north of Wales, the rebels confer on the plan of campaign against Henry's army and confidently divide the map of England and Wales into three parts for Mortimer, Glendower, and Hotspur. Later, in their camp at Shrewsbury, these plans are disarranged by the desertion of Northumberland himself, who pleads illness, and by Glendower, who sends word that his forces cannot be drawn upon for fourteen days, but in spite of their diminished numbers Hotspur and Douglas are determined to meet the superior royal army advancing to meet them under the command of the Earl of Westmoreland, the Prince of Wales, and his brother, Prince John of Lancaster.

In the parley before battle, the King assures the enemy generals, the Earl of Worcester and Sir Richard Vernon, that he will grant full pardon to the rebels if they will disperse, but Worcester's suspicions of Henry's motives are so deeply rooted that instead of conveying the terms of surrender to Hotspur, or telling him of the Prince of Wales' offer to decide the issue in a personal combat, he delivers a challenge to immediate battle. Douglas, ranging over the field, fights anyone attired like the King and at length encounters Henry himself who is saved at a critical moment by the Prince Hal whose skillful fighting forces Douglas to flight.

The Prince soon afterwards meets the valiant Hotspur whom he fights and kills. Worcester and Vernon are captured and ordered by Henry to execution. As the rebel forces are scattered in utter defeat, Douglas is seized but released through the generosity of the Prince of Wales, Prince John of Lancaster and Westmoreland are dispatched to meet the forces of Northumberland and the Archbishop of York, while the King and the Prince depart for Wales to fight Glendower and Mortimer, Earl of March.

historical data

Holinshed and, to a lesser extent, Halle provide the outline of events covered in this play, which deals with the period of English history from the battle of Holmedon Hill in 1402 to the battle of Shrewsbury in 1403. As usual, Shakespeare elaborated the merest suggestions of fact into dramatic situations, but in general he followed history in this play fairly closely. For the sake of dramatic contrast Prince Hal and Hotspur are made the same age, and the character development is almost altogether Shakespeare's own contribution.

For the comedy elements in the play an older drama, performed as early as 1588, was freely drawn upon. This was called *The Famous Victories of Henry the Fifth* and presented in crude form various episodes at the Tavern in Eastcheap, the robbery at Gadshill, Hal's relationships with his boon companions and the Chief Justice, and a number of other details of which Shakespeare made excellent use.

Falstaff, although based upon Sir John Oldcastle in *The Famous Victories,* is very largely Shakespeare's own creation. The new name may have been suggested by the historical Sir John Fastolfe, who appears in Part One of *Henry VI.*

Contemporary events of 1596 are referred to and the play was entered in the Stationers' Register in 1598, so that 1597 is reasonably well established as the date of its writing.

dramatis personæ

King Henry *the Fourth*.
Henry, *Prince of Wales,* ⎫
John *of Lancaster,* ⎬ *sons to the King.*
  ⎭
Earl of Westmoreland.
Sir Walter Blunt.
Thomas Percy, *Earl of Worcester*.
Henry Percy, *Earl of Northumberland*.
Henry Percy, *surnamed* Hotspur, *his son*.
Edmund Mortimer, *Earl of March*.
Richard Scroop, *Archbishop of York*.
Archibald, *Earl of Douglas*.
Owen Glendower.
Sir Richard Vernon.
Sir John Falstaff.
Sir Michael, *a friend to the Archbishop of York*.
Poins.
Gadshill.
Peto.
Bardolph.

Lady Percy, *wife to Hotspur, and sister to Mortimer*.
Lady Mortimer, *daughter to Glendower, and wife to Mortimer*.
Mistress Quickly, *hostess of a tavern in Eastcheap*.

Lords, Officers, Sheriff, Vintner, Chamberlain, Drawers, *two* Carriers,
  Travellers, *and* Attendants.

Scene: England and Wales.

act 1

scene 1. [*London. The palace*]

Enter King Henry, Lord John of Lancaster, *the* Earl of
Westmoreland, Sir Walter Blunt, *and others*

King. So Shaken as we are, so wan with care,
  Find we a time for frighted peace to pant,
  And breathe short-winded accents of new broils
  To be commenced in stronds afar remote.
  No more the thirsty entrance of this soil
  Shall daub her lips with her own children's blood;
  No more shall trenching war channel her fields,
  Nor bruise her flowerets with the armed hoofs
  Of hostile paces: those opposed eyes,
  Which, like the meteors of a troubled heaven,
  All of one nature, of one substance bred,
  Did lately meet in the intestine shock
  And furious close of civil butchery,
  Shall now, in mutual well-beseeming ranks,
  March all one way, and be no more opposed
  Against acquaintance, kindred and allies:
  The edge of war, like an ill-sheathed knife,

No more shall cut his master. Therefore, friends,
As far as to the sepulchre of Christ,
Whose soldier now, under whose blessed cross
We are impressed and engaged to fight,
Forthwith a power of English shall we levy;
Whose arms were moulded in their mothers' womb
To chase these pagans in those holy fields
Over whose acres walk'd those blessed feet,
Which fourteen hundred years ago were nail'd
For our advantage on the bitter cross.
But this our purpose now is twelve month old,
And bootless 'tis to tell you we will go:
Therefore we meet not now. Then let me hear
Of you, my gentle cousin Westmoreland,
What yesternight our council did decree
In forwarding this dear expedience.

Westmoreland. My liege, this haste was hot in question,
And many limits of the charge set down
But yesternight: when all athwart there came
A post from Wales loaden with heavy news;
Whose worst was, that the noble Mortimer,
Leading the men of Herefordshire to fight
Against the irregular and wild Glendower,
Was by the rude hands of that Welshman taken,
A thousand of his people butchered;
Upon whose dead corpse there was such misuse,
Such beastly shameless transformation,
By those Welshwomen done, as may not be
Without much shame retold or spoken of.

King. It seems then that the tidings of this broil
Brake off our business for the Holy Land.

Westmoreland. This match'd with other did, my gracious lord;
 For more uneven and unwelcome news
 Came from the north and thus it did import:
 On Holy-rood day, the gallant Hotspur there,
 Young Harry Percy, and brave Archibald,
 That ever-valiant and approved Scot,
 At Holmedon met,
 Where they did spend a sad and bloody hour;
 As by discharge of their artillery,
 And shape of likelihood, the news was told;
 For he that brought them, in the very heat
 And pride of their contention did take horse,
 Uncertain of the issue any way.

King. Here is a dear, a true industrious friend,
 Sir Walter Blunt, new lighted from his horse,
 Stain'd with the variation of each soil
 Betwixt that Holmedon and this seat of ours;
 And he hath brought us smooth and welcome news.
 The Earl of Douglas is discomfited:
 Ten thousand bold Scots, two and twenty knights,
 Balk'd in their own blood did Sir Walter see
 On Holmedon's plains. Of prisoners, Hotspur took
 Mordake the Earl of Fife, and eldest son
 To beaten Douglas; and the Earl of Athol,
 Of Murray, Angus, and Menteith:
 And is not this an honourable spoil?
 A gallant prize? ha, cousin, is it not?

Westmoreland. In faith,
 It is a conquest for a prince to boast of.

King. Yea, there thou mak'st me sad and mak'st me sin
 In envy that my Lord Northumberland

Should be the father to so blest a son,
A son who is the theme of honour's tongue;
Amongst a grove, the very straightest plant;
Who is sweet Fortune's minion and her pride:
Whilst I, by looking on the praise of him,
See riot and dishonour stain the brow
Of my young Harry. O that it could be proved
That some night-tripping fairy had exchanged
In cradle-clothes our children where they lay,
And call'd mine Percy, his Plantagenet!
Then would I have his Harry, and he mine.
But let him from my thoughts. What think you, coz,
Of this young Percy's pride? the prisoners,
Which he in this adventure hath surprised,
To his own use he keeps; and sends me word
I shall have none but Mordake Earl of Fife.

Westmoreland. This is his uncle's teaching: this is Worcester,
Malevolent to you in all aspects;
Which makes him prune himself, and bristle up
The crest of youth against your dignity.

King. But I have sent for him to answer this;
And for this cause awhile we must neglect
Our holy purpose to Jerusalem.
Cousin, on Wednesday next our council we
Will hold at Windsor; so inform the lords:
But come yourself with speed to us again;
For more is to be said and to be done
Than out of anger can be uttered.

Westmoreland. I will, my liege.

Exeunt.

scene 2. [*London. An apartment of the* Prince's]

Enter the Prince of Wales *and* Falstaff

Falstaff. Now, Hal, what time of day is it, lad?

Prince. Thou art so fat-witted, with drinking of old sack and
unbuttoning thee after supper and sleeping upon benches after noon, that thou hast forgotten to demand that truly which
thou wouldst truly know. What a devil hast thou to do with
the time of the day? Unless hours were cups of sack, and
minutes capons, and clocks the tongues of bawds, and dials
the signs of leaping-houses, and the blessed sun himself a fair
hot wench in flame-coloured taffeta, I see no reason why thou
shouldst be so superfluous to demand the time of the day.

Falstaff. Indeed, you come near me now, Hal; for we that take
purses go by the moon and the seven stars, and not by
Phœbus, he, 'that wandering knight so fair.' And, I prithee,
sweet wag, when thou art king, as, God save thy grace—
majesty I should say, for grace thou wilt have none—

Prince. What, none?

Falstaff. No, by my troth, not so much as will serve to be pro-
logue to an egg and butter.

Prince. Well, how then? come, roundly, roundly.

Falstaff. Marry, then, sweet wag, when thou art king, let not us
that are squires of the night's body be called thieves of the
day's beauty: let us be Diana's foresters, gentlemen of the
shade, minions of the moon; and let men say we be men of
good government, being governed, as the sea is, by our noble
and chaste mistress the moon, under whose countenance we
steal.

Prince. Thou sayest well, and it holds well too; for the fortune of us that are the moon's men doth ebb and flow like the sea, being governed, as the sea is, by the moon. As, for proof, now: a purse of gold most resolutely snatched on Monday night and most dissolutely spent on Tuesday morning; got with swearing 'Lay by' and spent with crying 'Bring in;' now in as low an ebb as the foot of the ladder, and by and by in as high a flow as the ridge of the gallows.

Falstaff. By the Lord, thou sayest true, lad. And is not my hostess of the tavern a most sweet wench?

Prince. As the honey of Hybla, my old lad of the castle. And is not a buff jerkin a most sweet robe of durance?

Falstaff. How now, how now, mad wag! what, in thy quips and thy quiddities? what a plague have I to do with a buff jerkin?

Prince. Why, what a pox have I to do with my hostess of the tavern?

Falstaff. Well, thou hast called her to a reckoning many a time and oft.

Prince. Did I ever call for thee to pay thy part?

Falstaff. No; I'll give thee thy due, thou hast paid all there.

Prince. Yea, and elsewhere, so far as my coin would stretch; and where it would not, I have used my credit.

Falstaff. Yea, and so used it that, were it not here apparent that thou art heir apparent—But, I prithee, sweet wag, shall there be gallows standing in England when thou art king? and resolution thus fubbed as it is with the rusty curb of old father Antic the law? Do not thou, when thou art king, hang a thief.

Prince. No; thou shalt.

Falstaff. Shall I? O rare! By the Lord, I'll be a brave judge.

Prince. Thou judgest false already: I mean, thou shalt have the hanging of the thieves and so become a rare hangman.

Falstaff. Well, Hal, well; and in some sort it jumps with my humour as well as waiting in the court, I can tell you.

Prince. For obtaining of suits?

Falstaff. Yea, for obtaining of suits, whereof the hangman hath no lean wardrobe. 'Sblood, I am as melancholy as a gib cat or a lugged bear.

Prince. Or an old lion, or a lover's lute.

Falstaff. Yea, or the drone of a Lincolnshire bagpipe.

Prince. What sayest thou to a hare, or the melancholy of Moorditch?

Falstaff. Thou hast the most unsavoury similes, and art indeed the most comparative, rascalliest sweet young prince. But Hal, I prithee, trouble me no more with vanity. I would to God thou and I knew where a commodity of good names were to be bought. An old lord of the council rated me the other day in the street about you, sir, but I marked him not; and yet he talked very wisely, but I regarded him not; and yet he talked wisely, and in the street too.

Prince. Thou didst well; for wisdom cries out in the streets, and no man regards it.

Falstaff. O, thou hast damnable iteration, and art indeed able to corrupt a saint. Thou hast done much harm upon me, Hal; God forgive thee for it! Before I knew thee, Hal, I knew nothing; and now am I, if a man should speak truly, little better than one of the wicked. I must give over this life, and I will give it over: by the Lord, an I do not, I am a villain: I'll be damned for never a king's son in Christendom.

Prince. Where shall we take a purse to-morrow, Jack?

Falstaff. 'Zounds, where thou wilt, lad; I'll make one; an I do not, call me villain and baffle me.

Prince. I see a good amendment of life in thee; from praying to purse-taking.

Falstaff. Why, Hal, 'tis my vocation, Hal; 'tis no sin for a man to labour in his vocation.

Enter Poins. Poins! Now shall we know if Gadshill have set a match.
O, if men were to be saved by merit, what hole in hell were hot enough for him? This is the most omnipotent villain that ever cried 'Stand' to a true man.

Prince. Good morrow, Ned.

Poins. Good morrow, sweet Hal. What says Monsieur Remorse? what says Sir John Sack and Sugar? Jack! how agrees the devil and thee about thy soul, that thou soldest him on Good Friday last for a cup of Madeira and a cold capon's leg?

Prince. Sir John stands to his word, the devil shall have his bargain; for he was never yet a breaker of proverbs: he will give the devil his due.

Poins. Then art thou damned for keeping thy word with the devil.

Prince. Else he had been damned for cozening the devil.

Poins. But, my lads, my lads, to-morrow morning, by four o'clock, early at Gadshill! there are pilgrims going to Canterbury with rich offerings, and traders riding to London with fat purses: I have vizards for you all; you have horses for yourselves: Gadshill lies to-night in Rochester: I have bespoke supper to-morrow night in Eastcheap: we may do it as secure as sleep. If you will go, I will stuff your purses full of crowns; if you will not, tarry at home and be hanged.

Falstaff. Hear ye, Yedward; if I tarry at home and go not, I'll hang you for going.

Poins. You will, chops?

Falstaff. Hal, wilt thou make one?

Prince. Who, I rob? I a thief? not I, by my faith.

Falstaff. There's neither honesty, manhood, nor good fellowship in thee, nor thou camest not of the blood royal, if thou darest not stand for ten shillings.

Prince. Well then, once in my days I'll be a madcap.

Falstaff. Why, that's well said.

Prince. Well, come what will, I'll tarry at home.

Falstaff. By the Lord, I'll be a traitor then, when thou art king.

Prince. I care not.

Poins. Sir John, I prithee, leave the prince and me alone: I will lay him down such reasons for this adventure that he shall go.

Falstaff. Well, God give thee the spirit of persuasion and him the ears of profiting, that what thou speakest may move and what he hears may be believed, that the true prince may, for recreation sake, prove a false thief; for the poor abuses of the time want countenance. Farewell: you shall find me in Eastcheap.

Prince. Farewell, thou latter spring! farewell, All-hallown summer!
Exit Falstaff.

Poins. Now, my good sweet honey lord, ride with us to-morrow: I have a jest to execute that I cannot manage alone. Falstaff, Bardolph, Peto and Gadshill shall rob those men that we have already waylaid; yourself and I will not be there; and when they have the booty, if you and I do not rob them, cut this head off from my shoulders.

Prince. How shall we part with them in setting forth?

Poins. Why, we will set forth before or after them, and appoint them a place of meeting, wherein it is at our pleasure to fail, and then will they adventure upon the exploit themselves; which they shall have no sooner achieved, but we'll set upon them.

Prince. Yea, but 'tis like that they will know us by our horses, by our habits, and by every other appointment, to be ourselves.

Poins. Tut! our horses they shall not see; I'll tie them in the wood; our vizards we will change after we leave them: and, sirrah, I have cases of buckram for the nonce, to immask our noted outward garments.

Prince. Yea, but I doubt they will be too hard for us.

Poins. Well, for two of them, I know them to be as true-bred cowards as ever turned back; and for the third, if he fight longer than he sees reason, I'll forswear arms. The virtue of this jest will be the incomprehensible lies that this same fat rogue will tell us when we meet at supper: how thirty, at least, he fought with; what wards, what blows, what extremities he endured; and in the reproof of this lives the jest.

Prince. Well, I'll go with thee: provide us all things necessary and meet me to-morrow night in Eastcheap; there I'll sup. Farewell.

Poins. Farewell, my lord.

Exit.

Prince. I know you all, and will a while uphold
The unyoked humour of your idleness:
Yet herein will I imitate the sun,
Who doth permit the base contagious clouds
To smother up his beauty from the world,
That, when he please again to be himself,
Being wanted, he may be more wonder'd at,

By breaking through the foul and ugly mists
Of vapours that did seem to strangle him.
If all the year were playing holidays,
To sport would be as tedious as to work;
But when they seldom come, they wish'd for come,
And nothing pleaseth but rare accidents.
So, when this loose behaviour I throw off
And pay the debt I never promised,
By how much better than my word I am,
By so much shall I falsify men's hopes;
And like bright metal on a sullen ground,
My reformation, glittering o'er my fault,
Shall show more goodly and attract more eyes
Than that which hath no foil to set it off.
I'll so offend, to make offence a skill;
Redeeming time when men think least I will.

Exit.

scene 3. [*Windsor. A room in the palace*]

Enter the King, Northumberland, Worcester,
Hotspur, Sir Walter Blunt, *with others*

King. My blood hath been too cold and temperate,
    Unapt to stir at these indignities,
    And you have found me; for accordingly
    You tread upon my patience: but be sure
    I will from henceforth rather be myself,
    Mighty and to be fear'd, than my condition;
    Which hath been smooth as oil, soft as young down,
    And therefore lost that title of respect
    Which the proud soul ne'er pays but to the proud.

Worcester. Our house, my sovereign liege, little deserves
   The scourge of greatness to be used on it;
   And that same greatness too which our own hands
   Have holp to make so portly.

Northumberland. My lord,—

King. Worcester, get thee gone; for I do see
   Danger and disobedience in thine eye:
   O, sir, your presence is too bold and peremptory,
   And majesty might never yet endure
   The moody frontier of a servant brow.
   You have good leave to leave us: when we need
   Your use and counsel, we shall send for you.

                                   Exit Worcester.

   You were about to speak.

                                   To Northumberland.

Northumberland. Yea, my good lord.
   Those prisoners in your highness' name demanded,
   Which Harry Percy here at Holmedon took,
   Were, as he says, not with such strength denied
   As is deliver'd to your majesty:
   Either envy, therefore, or misprision
   Is guilty of this fault and not my son.

Hotspur. My liege, I did deny no prisoners.
   But I remember, when the fight was done,
   When I was dry with rage and extreme toil,
   Breathless and faint, leaning upon my sword,
   Came there a certain lord, neat, and trimly dress'd,
   Fresh as a bridegroom; and his chin new reap'd
   Show'd like a stubble-land at harvest-home;
   He was perfumed like a milliner;
   And 'twixt his finger and his thumb he held

A pouncet-box, which ever and anon
He gave his nose and took 't away again;
Who therewith angry, when it next came there,
Took it in snuff; and still he smiled and talk'd,
And as the soldiers bore dead bodies by,
He call'd them untaught knaves, unmannerly,
To bring a slovenly unhandsome corse
Betwixt the wind and his nobility.
With many holiday and lady terms
He question'd me; amongst the rest, demanded
My prisoners in your majesty's behalf.
I then, all smarting with my wounds being cold;
To be so pester'd with a popinjay,
Out of my grief and my impatience
Answer'd neglectingly I know not what,
He should, or he should not; for he made me mad
To see him shine so brisk, and smell so sweet,
And talk so like a waiting-gentlewoman
Of guns and drums and wounds,—God save the mark!—
And telling me the sovereign'st thing on earth
Was parmaceti for an inward bruise;
And that it was great pity, so it was,
This villanous salt-petre should be digg'd
Out of the bowels of the harmless earth,
Which many a good tall fellow had destroy'd
So cowardly; and but for these vile guns,
He would himself have been a soldier.
This bald unjointed chat of his, my lord,
I answer'd indirectly, as I said;
And I beseech you, let not his report
Come current for an accusation
Betwixt my love and your high majesty.

Blunt. The circumstance consider'd, good my lord,
    Whate'er Lord Harry Percy then had said
    To such a person and in such a place,
    At such a time, with all the rest re-told,
    May reasonably die and never rise
    To do him wrong, or any way impeach
    What then he said, so he unsay it now.

King. Why, yet he doth deny his prisoners,
    But with proviso and exception,
    That we at our own charge shall ransom straight
    His brother-in-law, the foolish Mortimer;
    Who, on my soul, hath wilfully betray'd
    The lives of those that he did lead to fight
    Against that great magician, damn'd Glendower,
    Whose daughter, as we hear, the Earl of March
    Hath lately married. Shall our coffers, then,
    Be emptied to redeem a traitor home?
    Shall we buy treason? and indent with fears,
    When they have lost and forfeited themselves?
    No, on the barren mountains let him starve;
    For I shall never hold that man my friend
    Whose tongue shall ask me for one penny cost
    To ransom home revolted Mortimer.

Hotspur. Revolted Mortimer!
    He never did fall off, my sovereign liege,
    But by the chance of war: to prove that true
    Needs no more but one tongue for all those wounds,
    Those mouthed wounds, which valiantly he took,
    When on the gentle Severn's sedgy bank,
    In single opposition, hand to hand,
    He did confound the best part of an hour
    In changing hardiment with great Glendower:

Three times they breathed and three times did they drink,
Upon agreement, of swift Severn's flood;
Who then, affrighted with their bloody looks,
Ran fearfully among the trembling reeds,
And hid his crisp head in the hollow bank
Bloodstained with these valiant combatants.
Never did base and rotten policy
Colour her working with such deadly wounds;
Nor never could the noble Mortimer
Receive so many, and all willingly:
Then let not him be slander'd with revolt.

King. Thou dost belie him, Percy, thou dost belie him;
He never did encounter with Glendower:
I tell thee,
He durst as well have met the devil alone
As Owen Glendower for an enemy.
Art thou not ashamed? But, sirrah, henceforth
Let me not hear you speak of Mortimer:
Send me your prisoners with the speediest means,
Or you shall hear in such a kind from me
As will displease you. My Lord Northumberland,
We license your departure with your son.
Send us your prisoners, or you will hear of it.

                    Exeunt King Henry, Blunt, *and train.*

Hotspur. An if the devil come and roar for them,
I will not send them: I will after straight
And tell him so; for I will ease my heart,
Albeit I make a hazard of my head.

Northumberland. What, drunk with choler? stay and pause a while:
Here comes your uncle.

                    Re-enter Worcester

Hotspur.   Speak of Mortimer!
   'Zounds, I will speak of him; and let my soul
   Want mercy, if I do not join with him:
   Yea, on his part I'll empty all these veins,
   And shed my dear blood drop by drop in the dust,
   But I will lift the down-trod Mortimer
   As high in the air as this unthankful king,
   As this ingrate and canker'd Bolingbroke.

Northumberland. Brother, the king hath made your nephew mad.

Worcester. Who struck this heat up after I was gone?

Hotspur. He will, forsooth, have all my prisoners;
   And when I urged the ransom once again
   Of my wife's brother, then his cheek look'd pale,
   And on my face he turn'd an eye of death,
   Trembling even at the name of Mortimer.

Worcester. I cannot blame him: was not he proclaim'd,
   By Richard that dead is, the next of blood?

Northumberland. He was; I heard the proclamation:
   And then it was when the unhappy king—
   Whose wrongs in us God pardon!—did set forth
   Upon his Irish expedition;
   From whence he intercepted did return
   To be deposed and shortly murdered.

Worcester. And for whose death we in the world's wide mouth
   Live scandalized and foully spoken of.

Hotspur. But, soft, I pray you; did King Richard then
   Proclaim my brother Edmund Mortimer
   Heir to the crown?

Northumberland.   He did; myself did hear it.

Hotspur. Nay, then I cannot blame his cousin king,
   That wish'd him on the barren mountains starve.

But shall it be, that you, that set the crown
Upon the head of this forgetful man,
And for his sake wear the detested blot
Of murderous subornation, shall it be,
That you a world of curses undergo,
Being the agents, or base second means,
The cords, the ladder, or the hangman rather?
O, pardon me that I descend so low,
To show the line and the predicament
Wherein you range under this subtle king;
Shall it for shame be spoken in these days,
Or fill up chronicles in time to come,
That men of your nobility and power
Did gage them both in an unjust behalf,
As both of you—God pardon it!—have done,
To put down Richard, that sweet lovely rose,
And plant this thorn, this canker, Bolingbroke?
And shall it in more shame be further spoken,
That you are fool'd, discarded and shook off
By him for whom these shames ye underwent?
No; yet time serves wherein you may redeem
Your banish'd honours, and restore yourselves
Into the good thoughts of the world again,
Revenge the jeering and disdain'd contempt
Of this proud king, who studies day and night
To answer all the debt he owes to you
Even with the bloody payment of your deaths:
Therefore, I say,—

Worcester.   Peace, cousin, say no more:
And now I will unclasp a secret book,
And to your quick-conceiving discontents
I'll read you matter deep and dangerous,

As full of peril and adventurous spirit
As to o'er-walk a current roaring loud
On the unsteadfast footing of a spear.

Hotspur. If he fall in, good night! or sink or swim:
Send danger from the east unto the west,
So honour cross it from the north to south,
And let them grapple: O, the blood more stirs
To rouse a lion than to start a hare!

Northumberland. Imagination of some great exploit
Drives him beyond the bounds of patience.

Hotspur. By heaven, methinks it were an easy leap,
To pluck bright honour from the pale-faced moon,
Or dive into the bottom of the deep,
Where fathom-line could never touch the ground,
And pluck up drowned honour by the locks;
So he that doth redeem her thence might wear
Without corrival all her dignities:
But out upon this half-faced fellowship!

Worcester. He apprehends a world of figures here,
But not the form of what he should attend.
Good cousin, give me audience for a while.

Hotspur. I cry you mercy.

Worcester.   Those same noble Scots
That are your prisoners,—

Hotspur.   I'll keep them all;
By God, he shall not have a Scot of them;
No, if a Scot would save his soul, he shall not:
I'll keep them, by this hand.

Worcester.   You start away
And lend no ear unto my purposes.
Those prisoners you shall keep.

Hotspur.   Nay, I will; that's flat:
  He said he would not ransom Mortimer;
  Forbad my tongue to speak of Mortimer;
  But I will find him when he lies asleep,
  And in his ear I'll holla 'Mortimer!'
  Nay, I'll have a starling shall be taught to speak
  Nothing but 'Mortimer,' and give it him,
  To keep his anger still in motion.

Worcester. Hear you, cousin; a word.

Hotspur. All studies here I solemnly defy,
  Save how to gall and pinch this Bolingbroke:
  And that same sword-and-buckler Prince of Wales,
  But that I think his father loves him not
  And would be glad he met with some mischance,
  I would have him poison'd with a pot of ale.

Worcester. Farewell, kinsman: I'll talk to you
  When you are better temper'd to attend.

Northumberland. Why, what a wasp-stung and impatient fool
  Art thou to break into this woman's mood,
  Tying thine ear to no tongue but thine own!

Hotspur. Why, look you, I am whipp'd and scourged with rods,
  Nettled, and stung with pismires, when I hear
  Of this vile politician, Bolingbroke.
  In Richard's time,—what do you call the place?—
  A plague upon it, it is in Gloucestershire;
  'Twas where the madcap duke his uncle kept,
  His uncle York; where I first bow'd my knee
  Unto this king of smiles, this Bolingbroke,—
  'Sblood!—When you and he came back from Ravenspurgh.

Northumberland. At Berkley-castle.

Hotspur. You say true:

Why, what a candy deal of courtesy
This fawning greyhound then did proffer me!
Look, 'when his infant fortune came to age,'
And 'gentle Harry Percy,' and 'kind cousin;'
O, the devil take such cozeners! God forgive me!
Good uncle, tell your tale; I have done.

Worcester. Nay, if you have not, to it again;
We will stay your leisure.

Hotspur.   I have done, i' faith.

Worcester. Then once more to your Scottish prisoners.
Deliver them up without their ransom straight,
And make the Douglas' son your only mean
For powers in Scotland; which, for divers reasons
Which I shall send you written, be assured,
Will easily be granted. You, my lord,

                                        To Northumberland.

Your son in Scotland being thus employ'd,
Shall secretly into the bosom creep
Of that same noble prelate, well beloved,
The archbishop.

Hotspur. Of York, is it not?

Worcester. True; who bears hard
His brother's death at Bristol, the Lord Scroop.
I speak not this in estimation,
As what I think might be, but what I know
Is ruminated, plotted and set down,
And only stays but to behold the face
Of that occasion that shall bring it on.

Hotspur. I smell it: upon my life, it will do well.

Northumberland. Before the game is a-foot, thou still let'st slip.

Hotspur. Why, it cannot choose but be a noble plot:
    And then the power of Scotland and of York,
    To join with Mortimer, ha?

Worcester.   And so they shall.

Hotspur. In faith, it is exeedingly well aim'd.

Worcester. And 'tis no little reason bids us speed,
    To save our heads by raising of a head;
    For, bear ourselves as even as we can,
    The king will always think him in our debt,
    And think we think ourselves unsatisfied,
    Till he hath found a time to pay us home:
    And see already how he doth begin
    To make us strangers to his looks of love.

Hotspur. He does, he does: we'll be revenged on him.

Worcester. Cousin, farewell: no further go in this
    Than I by letters shall direct your course.
    When time is ripe, which will be suddenly,
    I'll steal to Glendower and Lord Mortimer;
    Where you and Douglas and our powers at once,
    As I will fashion it, shall happily meet,
    To bear our fortunes in our own strong arms,
    Which now we hold at much uncertainty.

Northumberland. Farewell, good brother: we shall thrive, I trust.

Hotspur. Uncle, adieu: O, let the hours be short
    Till fields and blows and groans applaud our sport!

                              Exeunt.

act 2

scene 1. [*Rochester. An inn yard*]

Enter a Carrier *with a lantern in his hand*

First Carrier. Heigh-ho! an it be not four by the day, I'll be hanged: Charles' wain is over the new chimney, and yet our horse not packed. What, ostler!

Ostler. [*Within*] Anon, anon.

First Carrier. I prithee, Tom, beat Cut's saddle, put a few flocks in the point; poor jade is wrung in the withers out of all cess.

Enter another Carrier

Second Carrier. Peas and beans are as dank here as a dog, and that is the next way to give poor jades the bots: this house is turned upside down since Robin Ostler died.

First Carrier. Poor fellow, never joyed since the price of oats rose; it was the death of him.

Second Carrier. I think this be the most villanous house in all London road for fleas: I am stung like a tench.

First Carrier. Like a tench! by the mass, there is ne'er a king christen could be better bit than I have been since the first cock.

Second Carrier. Why, they will allow us ne'er a jordan, and then we leak in your chimney; and your chamber-lie breeds fleas like a loach.

First Carrier. What, ostler! come away and be hanged! come away.

Second Carrier. I have a gammon of bacon and two razes of ginger, to be delivered as far as Charing-cross.

First Carrier. God's body! the turkeys in my pannier are quite starved. What, ostler! A plague on thee! hast thou never an eye in thy head? canst not hear? An 'twere not as good deed as drink, to break the pate on thee, I am a very villain. Come, and be hanged! hast no faith in thee?

Enter Gadshill

Gadshill. Good morrow, carriers. What's o'clock?

First Carrier. I think it be two o'clock.

Gadshill. I prithee, lend me thy lantern, to see my gelding in the stable.

First Carrier. Nay, by God, soft; I know a trick worth two of that, i' faith.

Gadshill. I pray thee, lend me thine.

Second Carrier. Ay, when? canst tell? Lend me thy lantern, quoth he? marry, I'll see thee hanged first.

Gadshill. Sirrah carrier, what time do you mean to come to London?

Second Carrier. Time enough to go to bed with a candle, I warrant thee. Come, neighbour Mugs, we'll call up the gentlemen: they will along with company, for they have great charge.

Exeunt Carriers.

Gadshill. What, ho! chamberlain!

Chamberlain. [*Within*] At hand, quoth pick-purse.

Gadshill. That's even as fair as—at hand, quoth the chamberlain; for thou variest no more from picking of purses than giving direction doth from labouring; thou layest the plot how.

Enter Chamberlain

Chamberlain. Good morrow, Master Gadshill. It holds current that I told you yesternight: there's a franklin in the wild of Kent hath brought three hundred marks with him in gold: I heard him tell it to one of his company last night at supper; a kind of auditor; one that hath abundance of charge too, God knows what. They are up already, and call for eggs and butter: they will away presently.

Gadshill. Sirrah, if they meet not with Saint Nicholas' clerks, I'll give thee this neck.

Chamberlain. No, I'll none of it: I pray thee, keep that for the hangman; for I know thou worshippest Saint Nicholas as truly as a man of falsehood may.

Gadshill. What talkest thou to me of the hangman? if I hang, I'll make a fat pair of gallows; for if I hang, old Sir John hangs with me, and thou knowest he is no starveling. Tut! there are other Trojans that thou dreamest not of, the which for sport sake are content to do the profession some grace; that would, if matters should be looked into, for their own credit sake, make all whole. I am joined with no foot landrakers, no long-staff sixpenny strikers, none of these mad mustachio purple-hued malt-worms; but with nobility and tranquillity, burgomasters and great oneyers, such as can hold in, such as will strike sooner than speak, and speak sooner than drink, and drink sooner than pray: and yet, 'zounds, I lie; for they pray continually to their saint, the commonwealth; or rather, not pray to her, but prey on her, for they ride up and down on her and make her their boots.

Chamberlain. What, the commonwealth their boots? will she hold out water in foul way?

Gadshill. She will, she will; justice hath liquored her. We steal as in a castle, cock-sure; we have the receipt of fern-seed, we walk invisible.

Chamberlain. Nay, by my faith, I think you are more beholding to the night than to fern-seed for your walking invisible.

Gadshill. Give me thy hand: thou shalt have a share in our purchase, as I am a true man.

Chamberlain. Nay, rather let me have it, as you are a false thief.

Gadshill. Go to; 'homo' is a common name to all men. Bid the ostler bring my gelding out of the stable. Farewell, you muddy knave.

Exeunt.

scene 2. [*The highway, near* Gadshill]

Enter Prince Henry *and* Poins

Poins. Come, shelter, shelter: I have removed Falstaff's horse, and he frets like a gummed velvet.

Prince. Stand close.

Enter Falstaff

Falstaff. Poins! Poins, and be hanged! Poins!

Prince. Peace, ye fat-kidneyed rascal! what a brawling dost thou keep!

Falstaff. Where's Poins, Hal?

Prince. He is walked up to the top of the hill: I'll go seek him.

Falstaff. I am accursed to rob in that thief's company: the rascal hath removed my horse, and tied him I know not where. If I travel but four foot by the squier further afoot, I shall break my wind. Well, I doubt not but to die a fair death for all this, if I 'scape hanging for killing that rogue. I have forsworn his company hourly any time this two and twenty years, and yet I am bewitched with the rogue's company. If the rascal have not given me medicines to make me love him, I'll be hanged; it could not be else; I have drunk medicines. Poins! Hal! a plague upon you both! Bardolph! Peto! I'll starve ere I'll rob a foot further. An 'twere not as good a deed as drink, to turn true man and to leave these rogues, I am the veriest varlet that ever chewed with a tooth. Eight yards of uneven ground is threescore and ten miles afoot with me; and the stony-hearted villains know it well enough: a plague upon it when thieves cannot be true one to another! [*They whistle*] Whew! A plague upon you all! Give me my horse, you rogues; give me my horse, and be hanged!

Prince. Peace, ye fat-guts! lie down; lay thine ear close to the ground and list if thou canst hear the tread of travellers.

Falstaff. Have you any levers to lift me up again, being down? 'Sblood, I'll not bear mine own flesh so far afoot again for all the coin in thy father's exchequer. What a plague mean ye to colt me thus?

Prince. Thou liest; thou art not colted, thou art uncolted.

Falstaff. I prithee, good Prince Hal, help me to my horse, good king's son.

Prince. Out, ye rogue! shall I be your ostler?

Falstaff. Go hang thyself in thine own heir-apparent garters! If I be ta'en, I'll peach for this. An I have not ballads made on you all and sung to filthy tunes, let a cup of sack be my poison: when a jest is so forward, and afoot too! I hate it.

    Enter Gadshill, Bardolph *and* Peto *with him*

Gadshill. Stand.

Falstaff. So I do, against my will.

Poins. O, 'tis our setter: I know his voice. Bardolph, what news?

Bardolph. Case ye, case ye; on with your vizards: there's money of the king's coming down the hill; 'tis going to the king's exchequer.

Falstaff. You lie, ye rogue; 'tis going to the king's tavern.

Gadshill. There's enough to make us all.

Falstaff. To be hanged.

Prince. Sirs, you four shall front them in the narrow lane; Ned Poins and I will walk lower: if they 'scape from your encounter, then they light on us.

Peto. How many be there of them?

Gadshill. Some eight or ten.

Falstaff. 'Zounds, will they not rob us?

Prince. What, a coward, Sir John Paunch?

Falstaff. Indeed, I am not John of Gaunt, your grandfather; but yet no coward, Hal.

Prince. Well, we leave that to the proof.

Poins. Sirrah Jack, thy horse stands behind the hedge: when thou needest him, there thou shalt find him. Farewell, and stand fast.

Falstaff. Now cannot I strike him, if I should be hanged.

Prince. Ned, where are our disguises?

Poins. Here, hard by: stand close.

Exeunt Prince *and* Poins.

Falstaff. Now, my masters, happy man be his dole, say I: every man to his business.

Enter the Travellers

First Traveller. Come, neighbour: the boy shall lead our horses down the hill; we'll walk afoot awhile, and ease our legs.

Thieves. Stand!

Travellers. Jesus bless us!

Falstaff. Strike, down with them, cut the villains' throats: ah! whoreson caterpillars! bacon-fed knaves! they hate us youth: down with them; fleece them.

Travellers. O, we are undone, both we and ours for ever!

Falstaff. Hang ye, gorbellied knaves, are ye undone? No, ye fat chuffs; I would your store were here! On, bacons, on! What, ye knaves! young men must live. You are grandjurors, are ye? we'll jure ye, 'faith.

> *Here they rob them and bind them. Exeunt.*
> *Re-enter* Prince Henry *and* Poins *disguised.*

Prince. The thieves have bound the true men. Now could thou and I rob the thieves and go merrily to London, it would be argument for a week, laughter for a month and a good jest for ever.

Poins. Stand close; I hear them coming.

Enter the Thieves *again*

Falstaff. Come, my masters, let us share, and then to horse before day. An the Prince and Poins be not two arrant cowards, there's no equity stirring: there's no more valour in that Poins than in a wild-duck.

Prince. Your money!

Poins. Villains! [*As they are sharing, the* Prince *and* Poins *set upon them; they all run away; and* Falstaff, *after a blow or two, runs away too, leaving the booty behind them*]

Prince. Got with much ease. Now merrily to horse:

The thieves are all scatter'd and possess'd with fear
So strongly that they dare not meet each other;
Each takes his fellow for an officer.
Away, good Ned. Falstaff sweats to death,
And lards the lean earth as he walks along:
Were't not for laughing, I should pity him.

Poins. How the fat rogue roar'd!

Exeunt.

scene 3. [*Warkworth Castle*]

Enter Hotspur *solus, reading a letter*

Hotspur. 'But, for mine own part, my lord, I could be well contented to be there, in respect of the love I bear your house.'
He could be contented: why is he not, then? In respect of the
love he bears our house: he shows in this, he loves his own
barn better than he loves our house. Let me see some more.
'The purpose you undertake is dangerous;'—why, that's
certain: 'tis dangerous to take a cold, to sleep, to drink; but I
tell you, my lord fool, out of this nettle, danger, we pluck
this flower, safety. 'The purpose you undertake is dangerous;
the friends you have named uncertain; the time itself un-
sorted; and your whole plot too light for the counterpoise of
so great an opposition.' Say you so, say you so? I say unto
you again, you are a shallow cowardly hind, and you lie.
What a lack-brain is this! By the Lord, our plot is a good plot
as ever was laid; our friends true and constant: a good plot,
good friends, and full of expectation; an excellent plot, very
good friends. What a frosty-spirited rogue is this! Why, my
lord of York commends the plot and the general course of
the action. 'Zounds, an I were now by this rascal, I could
brain him with his lady's fan. Is there not my father, my

uncle, and myself? Lord Edmund Mortimer, my lord of York, and Owen Glendower? is there not besides the Douglas? have I not all their letters to meet me in arms by the ninth of the next month? and are they not some of them set forward already? What a pagan rascal is this! an infidel! Ha! you shall see now in very sincerity of fear and cold heart, will he to the king, and lay open all our proceedings. O, I could divide myself, and go to buffets, for moving such a dish of skim milk with so honourable an action! Hang him! let him tell the king: we are prepared. I will set forward to-night.

Enter Lady Percy

How now, Kate! I must leave you within these two hours.

Lady Percy. O, my good lord, why are you thus alone?
For what offence have I this fortnight been
A banish'd woman from my Harry's bed?
Tell me, sweet lord, what is't that takes from thee
Thy stomach, pleasure, and thy golden sleep?
Why dost thou bend thine eyes upon the earth,
And start so often when thou sit'st alone?
Why hast thou lost the fresh blood in thy cheeks,
And given my treasures and my rights of thee
To thick-eyed musing and cursed melancholy?
In thy faint slumbers I by thee have watch'd,
And heard thee murmur tales of iron wars;
Speak terms of manage to thy bounding steed;
Cry 'Courage! to the field!' And thou hast talk'd
Of sallies and retires, of trenches, tents,
Of palisadoes, frontiers, parapets,
Of basilisks, of cannon, culverin,
Of prisoners' ransom, and of soldiers slain,
And all the currents of a heady fight.
Thy spirit within thee hath been so at war

And thus hath so bestirr'd thee in thy sleep,
That beads of sweat have stood upon thy brow,
Like bubbles in a late-disturbed stream;
And in thy face strange motions have appear'd,
Such as we see when men restrain their breath
On some great sudden hest. O, what portents are these?
Some heavy business hath my lord in hand,
And I must know it, else he loves me not.

Hotspur. What, ho!

Enter Servant

Is Gilliams with the packet gone?

Servant. He is, my lord, an hour ago.

Hotspur. Hath Butler brought those horses from the sheriff?

Servant. One horse, my lord, he brought even now.

Hotspur. What horse? a roan, a crop-ear, is it not?

Servant. It is, my lord.

Hotspur.　　　　　　That roan shall be my throne.
　Well, I will back him straight: O esperance!
　Bid Butler lead him forth into the park.

Exit Servant.

Lady Percy. But hear you, my lord.

Hotspur. What say'st thou, my lady?

Lady Percy. What is it carries you away?

Hotspur. Why, my horse, my love, my horse.

Lady Percy. Out, you mad-headed ape!
　A weasel hath not such a deal of spleen
　As you are toss'd with. In faith,
　I'll know your business, Harry, that I will.
　I fear my brother Mortimer doth stir

About his title, and hath sent for you
To line his enterprize: but if you go—

Hotspur. So far afoot, I shall be weary, love.

Lady Percy. Come, come, you paraquito, answer me
Directly unto this question that I ask:
In faith, I'll break thy little finger, Harry,
And if thou wilt not tell me all things true.

Hotspur. Away,
Away, you trifler! Love! I love thee not,
I care not for thee, Kate: this is no world
To play with mammets and to tilt with lips:
We must have bloody noses and crack'd crowns,
And pass them current too. God's me, my horse!
What say'st thou, Kate? what wouldst thou have with me?

Lady Percy. Do you not love me? do you not, indeed?
Well, do not then; for since you love me not,
I will not love myself. Do you not love me?
Nay, tell me if you speak in jest or no.

Hotspur. Come, wilt thou see me ride?
And when I am o' horseback, I will swear
I love thee infinitely. But hark you, Kate;
I must not have you henceforth question me
Whither I go, nor reason whereabout:
Whither I must, I must; and, to conclude,
This evening must I leave you, gentle Kate.
I know you wise, but yet no farther wise
Than Harry Percy's wife: constant you are,
But yet a woman: and for secrecy,
No lady closer; for I well believe
Thou wilt not utter what thou dost not know;
And so far will I trust thee, gentle Kate.

Lady Percy. How! so far?

Hotspur. Not an inch further. But hark you, Kate:
   Whither I go, thither shall you go too;
   To-day will I set forth, to-morrow you.
   Will this content you, Kate?

Lady Percy.   It must of force.

                                        Exeunt.

scene 4.   [*The Boar's-Head Tavern in Eastcheap*]

Enter the Prince, *and* Poins

Prince. Ned, prithee, come out of that fat room, and lend me thy
   hand to laugh a little.

Poins. Where hast been, Hal?

Prince. With three or four loggerheads amongst three or
   fourscore hogsheads. I have sounded the very base-string of
   humility. Sirrah, I am sworn brother to a leash of drawers;
   and can call them all by their christen names, as Tom, Dick,
   and Francis. They take it already upon their salvation, that
   though I be but Prince of Wales, yet I am the king of courtesy; and tell me flatly I am no proud Jack, like Falstaff, but a
   Corinthian, a lad of mettle, a good boy (by the Lord, so they
   call me!), and when I am king of England, I shall command
   all the good lads in Eastcheap. They call drinking deep, dye-
   ing scarlet; and when you breathe in your watering, they cry
   'hem!' and bid you play it off. To conclude, I am so good a
   proficient in one quarter of an hour, that I can drink with
   any tinker in his own language during my life. I tell thee,
   Ned, thou hast lost much honour, that thou wert not with
   me in this action. But, sweet Ned,—to sweeten which name

of Ned, I give thee this pennyworth of sugar, clapped even now into my hand by an under-skinker, one that never spake other English in his life than 'Eight shillings and sixpence,' and 'You are welcome,' with this shrill addition, 'Anon, anon, sir! Score a pint of bastard in the Half-moon,' or so. But, Ned, to drive away the time till Falstaff come, I prithee, do thou stand in some by-room, while I question my puny drawer to what end he gave me the sugar; and do thou never leave calling 'Francis,' that his tale to me may be nothing but 'Anon.' Step aside, and I'll show thee a precedent.

Poins. Francis!

Prince. Thou art perfect.

Poins. Francis!

Exit Poins.

Enter Francis

Francis. Anon, anon, sir. Look down into the Pomgarnet, Ralph.

Prince. Come hither, Francis.

Francis. My lord?

Prince. How long hast thou to serve, Francis?

Francis. Forsooth, five years, and as much as to—

Poins. [*Within*] Francis!

Francis. Anon, anon, sir.

Prince. Five year! by'r lady, a long lease for the clinking of pewter. But, Francis, darest thou be so valiant as to play the coward with thy indenture and show it a fair pair of heels and run from it?

Francis. O Lord, sir, I'll be sworn upon all the books in England, I could find in my heart.

Poins. [*Within*] Francis!

Francis. Anon, sir.

Prince. How old art thou, Francis?

Francis. Let me see—about Michaelmas next I shall be—

Poins. [*Within*] Francis!

Francis. Anon, sir. Pray stay a little, my lord.

Prince. Nay, but hark you, Francis: for the sugar thou gavest me, 'twas a pennyworth, was't not?

Francis. O Lord, I would it had been two!

Prince. I will give thee for it a thousand pound: ask me when thou wilt, and thou shalt have it.

Poins. [*Within*] Francis!

Francis. Anon, anon.

Prince. Anon, Francis? No, Francis; but to-morrow, Francis; or Francis, o' Thursday; or indeed, Francis, when thou wilt. But, Francis!

Francis. My lord?

Prince. Wilt thou rob this leathern jerkin, crystal-button, not-pated, agate-ring, puke-stocking, caddis-garter, smooth-tongue, Spanish-pouch,—

Francis. O lord, sir, who do you mean?

Prince. Why, then, your brown bastard is your only drink; for look you, Francis, your white canvas doublet will sully: in Barbary, sir, it cannot come to so much.

Francis. What, sir?

Poins. [*Within*] Francis!

Prince. Away, you rogue! dost thou not hear them call?

> *Here they both call him; the* Drawer *stands amazed,*
> *not knowing which way to go.*

Enter Vintner

Vintner. What, standest thou still, and hearest such a calling? Look to the guests within. [*Exit* Francis] My lord, old Sir John, with half-a-dozen more, are at the door: shall I let them in?

Prince. Let them alone awhile, and then open the door. [*Exit* Vintner] Poins!

Re-enter Poins

Poins. Anon, anon, sir.

Prince. Sirrah, Falstaff and the rest of the thieves are at the door: shall we be merry?

Poins. As merry as crickets, my lad. But hark ye; what cunning match have you made with this jest of the drawer? come, what's the issue?

Prince. I am now of all humours that have showed themselves humours since the old days of goodman Adam to the pupil age of this present twelve o'clock at midnight.

Re-enter Francis. What's o'clock, Francis?

Francis. Anon, anon, sir.

Exit.

Prince. That ever this fellow should have fewer words than a parrot, and yet the son of a woman! His industry is up-stairs and down-stairs; his eloquence the parcel of a reckoning. I am not yet of Percy's mind, the Hotspur of the north; he that kills me some six or seven dozen of Scots at a breakfast, washes his hands, and says to his wife 'Fie upon this quiet life! I want work.' 'O my sweet Harry,' says she, 'how many hast thou killed to-day?' 'Give my roan horse a drench,' says he; and answers 'Some fourteen,' an hour after; 'a trifle, a trifle.' I prithee, call in Falstaff: I'll play Percy, and that damned brawn shall play Dame Mortimer his wife. '*Rivo!*' says the drunkard. Call in ribs, call in tallow.

> *Enter* Falstaff, Gadshill, Bardolph, *and* Peto; Francis
> *following with wine*

Poins. Welcome, Jack: where hast thou been?

Falstaff. A plague of all cowards, I say, and a vengeance too! marry, and amen! Give me a cup of sack, boy. Ere I lead this life long, I'll sew nether stocks and mend them and foot them too. A plague of all cowards! Give me a cup of sack, rogue. *Is there no virtue extant?*

> *He drinks.*

Prince. Didst thou never see Titan kiss a dish of butter? pitiful-hearted Titan, that melted at the sweet tale of the sun's! if thou didst, then behold that compound.

Falstaff. You rogue, here's lime in this sack too: there is nothing but roguery to be found in villanous man: yet a coward is worse than a cup of sack with lime in it. A villanous coward! Go thy ways, old Jack; die when thou wilt, if manhood, good manhood, be not forgot upon the face of the earth, then am I a shotten herring. There lives not three good men unhanged in England; and one of them is fat, and grows old: God help the while! a bad world, I say. I would I were a weaver; I could sing psalms or any thing. A plague of all cowards, I say still.

Prince. How now, wool-sack! what mutter you?

Falstaff. A king's son! If I do not beat thee out of thy kingdom with a dagger of lath, and drive all thy subjects afore thee like a flock of wild-geese, I'll never wear hair on my face more. You Prince of Wales!

Prince. Why, you whoreson round man, what's the matter?

Falstaff. Are not you a coward? answer me to that: and Poins there?

Poins. 'Zounds, ye fat paunch, an ye call me coward, by the Lord, I'll stab thee.

Falstaff. I call thee coward! I'll see thee damned ere I call thee coward: but I would give a thousand pound I could run as fast as thou canst. You are straight enough in the shoulders, you care not who sees your back: call you that backing of your friends? A plague upon such backing! give me them that will face me. Give me a cup of sack: I am a rogue, if I drunk to-day.

Prince. O villain! thy lips are scarce wiped since thou drunkest last.

Falstaff. All's one for that. [*He drinks*] A plague of all cowards, still say I.

Prince. What's the matter?

Falstaff. What's the matter! there be four of us here have ta'en a thousand pound this day morning.

Prince. Where is it, Jack? where is it?

Falstaff. Where is it! taken from us it is: a hundred upon poor four of us.

Prince. What, a hundred, man?

Falstaff. I am a rogue, if I were not at half-sword with a dozen of them two hours together. I have 'scaped by miracle. I am eight times thrust through the doublet, four through the hose; my buckler cut through and through; my sword hacked like a hand-saw—*ecce signum*! I never dealt better since I was a man: all would not do. A plague of all cowards! Let them speak: if they speak more or less than truth, they are villains and the sons of darkness.

Prince. Speak, sirs; how was it?

Gadshill. We four set upon some dozen—

Falstaff. Sixteen at least, my lord.

Gadshill. And bound them.

Peto. No, no, they were not bound.

Falstaff. You rogue, they were bound, every man of them; or I am a Jew else, an Ebrew Jew.

Gadshill. As we were sharing, some six or seven fresh men set upon us—

Falstaff. And unbound the rest, and then come in the other.

Prince. What, fought you with them all?

Falstaff. All! I know not what you call all; but if I fought not with fifty of them, I am a bunch of radish: if there were not two or three and fifty upon poor old Jack, then am I no two-legged creature.

Prince. Pray God you have not murdered some of them.

Falstaff. Nay, that's past praying for: I have peppered two of them; two I am sure I have paid, two rogues in buckram suits. I tell thee what, Hal, if I tell thee a lie, spit in my face, call me horse. Thou knowest my old ward; here I lay, and thus I bore my point. Four rogues in buckram let drive at me—

Prince. What, four? thou saidst but two even now.

Falstaff. Four, Hal; I told thee four.

Poins. Ay, ay, he said four.

Falstaff. These four came all a-front, and mainly thrust at me. I made me no more ado but took all their seven points in my target, thus.

Prince. Seven? why, there were but four even now.

Falstaff. In buckram?

Poins. Ay, four, in buckram suits.

Falstaff. Seven, by these hilts, or I am a villain else.

Prince. Prithee, let him alone; we shall have more anon.

Falstaff. Dost thou hear me, Hal?

Prince. Ay, and mark thee too, Jack.

Falstaff. Do so, for it is worth the listening to. These nine in buckram that I told thee of,—

Prince. So, two more already.

Falstaff. Their points being broken,—

Poins. Down fell their hose.

Falstaff. Began to give me ground: but I followed me close, came in foot and hand; and with a thought seven of the eleven I paid.

Prince. O monstrous! eleven buckram men grown out of two!

Falstaff. But, as the devil would have it, three misbegotten knaves in Kendal green came at my back and let drive at me; for it was so dark, Hal, that thou couldst not see thy hand.

Prince. These lies are like their father that begets them; gross as a mountain, open, palpable. Why, thou clay-brained guts, thou knotty-pated fool, thou whoreson, obscene, greasy tallow-catch,—

Falstaff. What, art thou mad? art thou mad? is not the truth the truth?

Prince. Why, how couldst thou know these men in Kendal green, when it was so dark thou couldst not see thy hand? come, tell us your reason: what sayest thou to this?

Poins. Come, your reason, Jack, your reason.

Falstaff. What, upon compulsion? 'Zounds, an I were at the strappado, or all the racks in the world, I would not tell you on compulsion. Give you a reason on compulsion! if reasons were as plentiful as blackberries, I would give no man a reason upon compulsion, I.

Prince. I'll be no longer guilty of this sin; this sanguine coward, this bed-presser, this horse-back-breaker, this huge hill of flesh,—

Falstaff. 'Sblood, you starveling, you eelskin, you dried neat's tongue, you bull's pizzle, you stock-fish! O for breath to utter what is like thee! you tailor's-yard, you sheath, you bow-case, you vile standing tuck,—

Prince. Well, breathe a while, and then to it again: and when thou hast tired thyself in base comparisons, hear me speak but this.

Poins. Mark, Jack.

Prince. We two saw you four set on four and bound them, and were masters of their wealth. Mark now, how a plain tale shall put you down. Then did we two set on you four; and, with a word, out-faced you from your prize, and have it; yea, and can show it you here in the house: and, Falstaff, you carried your guts away as nimbly, with as quick dexterity, and roared for mercy, and still run and roared, as ever I heard bull-calf. What a slave art thou, to hack thy sword as thou hast done, and then say it was in fight! What trick, what device, what starting-hole, canst thou now find out to hide thee from this open and apparent shame?

Poins. Come, let's hear, Jack; what trick hast thou now?

Falstaff. By the Lord, I knew ye as well as he that made ye. Why, hear you, my masters: was it for me to kill the heir-apparent? should I turn upon the true prince? why, thou knowest I am as valiant as Hercules: but beware instinct; the lion will not touch the true prince. Instinct is a great matter; I was now a coward on instinct. I shall think the better of myself and thee during my life; I for a valiant lion, and thou for a true prince. But, by the Lord, lads, I am glad you have the money. Hostess, clap to the doors: watch to-night, pray to-morrow. Gallants, lads, boys, hearts of gold, all the titles of good fellowship come to you! What, shall we be merry? shall we have a play extempore?

Prince. Content; and the argument shall be thy running away.

Falstaff. Ah, no more of that, Hal, an thou lovest me!

Enter Hostess

Hostess. O Jesu, my lord the prince!

Prince. How now, my lady the hostess! what sayest thou to me?

Hostess. Marry, my lord, there is a nobleman of the court at door would speak with you: he says he comes from your father.

Prince. Give him as much as will make him a royal man, and send him back again to my mother.

Falstaff. What manner of man is he?

Hostess. An old man.

Falstaff. What doth gravity out of his bed at midnight? Shall I give him his answer?

Prince. Prithee, do, Jack.

Falstaff. Faith, and I'll *send him packing.*

Exit.

Prince. Now, sirs: by'r lady, you fought fair; so did you, Peto; so did you, Bardolph: you are lions too, you ran away upon instinct, you will not touch the true prince; no, fie!

Bardolph. Faith, I ran when I saw others run.

Prince. Faith, tell me now in earnest, how came Falstaff's sword so hacked?

Peto. Why, he hacked it with his dagger, and said he would swear truth out of England but he would make you believe it was done in fight, and persuaded us to do the like.

Bardolph. Yea, and to tickle our noses with spear-grass to make them bleed, and then to beslubber our garments with it and swear it was the blood of true men. I did that I did not this seven year before, I blushed to hear his monstrous devices.

Prince. O villain, thou stolest a cup of sack eighteen years ago, and wert taken with the manner, and ever since thou hast blushed extempore. Thou hadst fire and sword on thy side, and yet thou rannest away: what instinct hadst thou for it?

Bardolph. My lord, do you see these meteors? do you behold these exhalations?

Prince. I do.

Bardolph. What think you they portend?

Prince. Hot livers and cold purses.

Bardolph. Choler, my lord, if rightly taken.

Prince. No, if rightly taken, halter.

Re-enter Falstaff

Here comes lean Jack, here comes bare-bone. How now, my sweet creature of bombast! How long is't ago, Jack, since thou sawest thine own knee?

Falstaff. My own knee! when I was about thy years, Hal, I was not an eagle's talon in the waist; I could have crept into any alderman's thumb-ring: a plague of sighing and grief! it blows a man up like a bladder. There's villanous news abroad: here was Sir John Bracy from your father; you must to the court in the morning. That same mad fellow of the north, Percy, and he of Wales, that gave Amamon the basti-nado, and made Lucifer cuckold, and swore the devil his true liegeman upon the cross of a Welsh hook—what a plague call you him?

Poins. O, Glendower.

Falstaff. Owen, Owen, the same; and his son-in-law Mortimer, and old Northumberland, and that sprightly Scot of Scots, Douglas, that runs o' horseback up a hill perpendicular,—

Prince. He that rides at high speed and with his pistol kills a sparrow flying.

Falstaff. You have hit it.

Prince. So did he never the sparrow.

Falstaff. Well, that rascal hath good mettle in him; he will not run.

Prince. Why, what a rascal art thou then, to praise him so for running!

Falstaff. O' horseback, ye cuckoo; but afoot he will not budge a foot.

Prince. Yes, Jack, upon instinct.

Falstaff. I grant ye, upon instinct. Well, he is there too, and one Mordake, and a thousand blue-caps more: Worcester is stolen away to-night; thy father's beard is turned white with the news: you may buy land now as cheap as stinking mackerel.

Prince. Why, then, it is like, if there come a hot June and this civil buffeting hold, we shall buy maidenheads as they buy hob-nails, by the hundreds.

Falstaff. By the mass, lad, thou sayest true; it is like we shall have good trading that way. But tell me, Hal, art not thou horrible afeard? thou being heir-apparent, could the world pick thee out three such enemies again as that fiend Douglas, that spirit Percy, and that devil Glendower? art thou not horribly afraid? doth not thy blood thrill at it?

Prince. Not a whit, i' faith; I lack some of thy instinct.

Falstaff. Well, thou wilt be horribly chid to-morrow when thou comest to thy father: if thou love me, practise an answer.

Prince. Do thou stand for my father, and examine me upon the particulars of my life.

Falstaff. Shall I? content: this chair shall be my state, this dagger my sceptre, and this cushion my crown.

Prince. Thy state is taken for a joined-stool, thy golden sceptre for a leaden dagger, and thy precious rich crown for a pitiful bald crown!

Falstaff. Well, an the fire of grace be not quite out of thee, now shalt thou be moved. Give me a cup of sack to make my eyes look red, that it may be thought I have wept; for I must speak in passion, and I will do it in King Cambyses' vein.

Prince. Well, here is my leg.

Falstaff. And here is my speech. Stand aside, nobility.

Hostess. O Jesu, this is excellent sport, i' faith!

Falstaff. Weep not, sweet queen; for trickling tears are vain.

Hostess. O, the father, how he holds his countenance!

Falstaff. For God's sake, lords, convey my tristful queen;
For tears do stop the flood-gates of her eyes.

Hostess. O Jesu, he doth it as like one of these harlotry players as ever I see!

Falstaff. Peace, good pint-pot; peace, good tickle-brain. Harry, I do not only marvel where thou spendest thy time, but also how thou art accompanied: for though the camomile, the more it is trodden on the faster it grows, yet youth, the more it is wasted the sooner it wears. That thou art my son, I have partly thy mother's word, partly my own opinion, but chiefly a villanous trick of thine eye, and a foolish hanging of thy nether lip, that doth warrant me. If then thou be son to me, here lies the point; why, being son to me, art thou so pointed at? Shall the blessed sun of heaven prove a micher and eat blackberries? a question not to be asked. Shall the son of England prove a thief and take purses? a question to be asked. There is a thing, Harry, which thou hast often heard of, and it is known to many in our land by the name of pitch: this pitch, as ancient writers do report, doth defile; so doth the company thou keepest: for, Harry, now I do not speak to thee in drink but in tears, not in pleasure but in passion, not in words only, but in woes also: and yet there is a virtuous man whom I have often noted in thy company, but I know not his name.

Prince. What manner of man, an it like your majesty?

Falstaff. A goodly portly man, i' faith, and a corpulent; of a cheerful look, a pleasing eye, and a most noble carriage; and, as I think, his age some fifty, or, by'r lady, inclining to three score; and now I remember me, his name is Falstaff: if that man should be lewdly given, he deceiveth me; for, Harry, I see virtue in his looks. If then the tree may be known by the fruit, as the fruit by the tree, then, peremptorily I speak it, there is virtue in that Falstaff: him keep with, the rest banish. And tell me now, thou naughty varlet, tell me, where hast thou been this month?

Prince. Dost thou speak like a king? Do thou stand for me, and I'll play my father.

Falstaff. Depose me? if thou dost it half so gravely, so majestically, both in word and matter, hang me up by the heels for a rabbit-sucker or a poulter's hare.

Prince. Well, here I am set.

Falstaff. And here I stand: judge, my masters.

Prince. Now, Harry, whence come you?

Falstaff. My noble lord, from Eastcheap.

Prince. The complaints I hear of thee are grievous.

Falstaff. 'Sblood, my lord, they are false: nay, I'll tickle ye for a young prince, i' faith.

Prince. Swearest thou, ungracious boy? henceforth ne'er look on me. Thou art violently carried away from grace: there is a devil haunts thee in the likeness of an old fat man; a tun of man is thy companion. Why dost thou converse with that trunk of humours, that bolting-hutch of beastliness, that swollen parcel of dropsies, that huge bombard of sack, that stuffed cloak-bag of guts, that roasted Manningtree ox with the pudding in his belly, that reverend vice, that grey iniquity, that father ruffian, that vanity in years? Wherein is he good, but to taste sack and drink it? wherein neat and cleanly, but to carve a capon and eat it? wherein cunning, but in craft? wherein crafty, but in villany? wherein villanous, but in all things? wherein worthy, but in nothing?

Falstaff. I would your grace would take me with you whom means your grace?

Prince. *That villanous abominable misleader of youth,* Falstaff, that old white-bearded Satan.

Falstaff. My lord, the man I know.

Prince. I know thou dost.

Falstaff. But to say I know more harm in him than in myself, were to say more than I know. That he is old, the more the pity, his white hairs do witness it; but that he is, saving your reverence, a whoremaster, that I utterly deny. If sack and sugar be a fault, God help the wicked! if to be old and merry be a sin, then many an old host that I know is damned: if to be fat be to be hated, then Pharaoh's lean kine are to be loved. No, my good lord; banish Peto, banish Bardolph, banish Poins: but for sweet Jack Falstaff, kind Jack Falstaff, true Jack Falstaff, valiant Jack Falstaff, and therefore more valiant, being, as he is, old Jack Falstaff, banish not him thy Harry's company, banish not him thy Harry's company: *banish plump Jack, and banish all the world.*

Prince. I do, I will.

                                           A knocking heard.

Exeunt Hostess, Francis, *and* Bardolph.
Re-enter Bardolph, *running*

Bardolph. O, my lord, my lord! the sheriff with a most monstrous watch is at the door.

Falstaff. Out, ye rogue! Play out the play: I have much to say in the behalf of that Falstaff.

Re-enter the Hostess

Hostess. O Jesu, my lord, my lord!—

Prince. Heigh, heigh! the devil rides upon a fiddlestick: what's the matter?

Hostess. The sheriff and all the watch are at the door: they are come to search the house. Shall I let them in?

Falstaff. Dost thou hear, Hal? never call a true piece of gold a counterfeit: *thou art essentially mad, without seeming so.*

Prince. And thou a natural coward, without instinct.

Falstaff. I deny your major: if you will deny the sheriff, so; if not, let him enter: if I become not a cart as well as another man, a plague on my bringing up! I hope I shall as soon be strangled with a halter as another.

Prince. Go, hide thee behind the arras: the rest walk up above. Now, my masters, for a true face and good conscience.

Falstaff. Both which I have had: but their date is out, and therefore I'll hide me.

Prince. Call in the sheriff.

Exeunt all except the Prince *and* Peto.

Enter Sheriff *and the* Carrier

Now, master sheriff, what is your will with me?

Sheriff. First, pardon me, my lord. A hue and cry
Hath follow'd certain men unto this house.

Prince. What men?

Sheriff. One of them is well known, my gracious lord,

A gross fat man.

Carrier.   As fat as butter.

Prince. The man, I do assure you, is not here;
For I myself at this time have employ'd him.
And, sheriff, I will engage my word to thee
That I will, by to-morrow dinner-time,
Send him to answer thee, or any man,
For any thing he shall be charged withal:
And so let me entreat you leave the house.

Sheriff. I will, my lord. There are two gentlemen
Have in this robbery lost three hundred marks.

Prince. It may be so: if he have robb'd these men,
He shall be answerable; and so farewell.

Sheriff. Good night, my noble lord.

Prince. I think it is good morrow, is it not?

Sheriff. Indeed, my lord, I think it be two o'clock.

Exeunt Sheriff *and* Carrier.

Prince. This oily rascal is known as well as Paul's.
Go, call him forth.

Peto. Falstaff!—Fast asleep behind the arras, and snorting like a
horse.

Prince. Hark, how hard he fetches breath. Search his pockets.
[*He searcheth his pockets, and findeth certain papers*]
What hast thou found?

Peto. Nothing but papers, my lord.

Prince. Let's see what they be: read them.

Peto [*Reads*] Item, A capon, ... 2s. 2d.
    Item, Sauce, ... 4d.
    Item, Sack, two gallons, ... 5s. 8d.
    Item, Anchovies and sack after supper, 2s. 6d.
    Item, Bread, ... ob.

Prince. O monstrous! but one half-pennyworth of bread to this
intolerable deal of sack! What there is else, keep close; we'll
read it at more advantage: there let him sleep till day. I'll to
the court in the morning. We must all to the wars, and thy
place shall be honourable. I'll procure this fat rogue a charge
of foot; and I know his death will be a march of twelve-
score. The money shall be paid back again with advantage.
Be with me betimes in the morning; and so, good morrow,
Peto.

Peto. Good morrow, good my lord.

                Exeunt.

act 3

scene 1. [*Bangor. The* Archdeacon's *house*]

Enter Hotspur, Worcester, Mortimer, *and* Glendower

Mortimer. These promises are fair, the parties sure.
  And our induction full of prosperous hope.

Hotspur. Lord Mortimer, and cousin Glendower,
  Will you sit down?
  And uncle Worcester: a plague upon it!
  I have forgot the map.

Glendower.   No, here it is.
  Sit, cousin Percy; sit, good cousin Hotspur,
  For by that name as oft as Lancaster
  Doth speak of you, his cheek looks pale, and with
  A rising sigh he wisheth you in heaven.

Hotspur. And you in hell, as oft as he hears Owen Glendower
  spoke of.

Glendower. I cannot blame him: at my nativity
  The front of heaven was full of fiery shapes,
  Of burning cressets; and at my birth

The frame and huge foundation of the earth
Shaked like a coward.

Hotspur. Why, so it would have done at the same season, if your
mother's cat had but kittened, though yourself had never
been born.

Glendower. I say the earth did shake when I was born.

Hotspur. And I say the earth was not of my mind,
If you suppose as fearing you it shook.

Glendower. The heavens were all on fire, the earth did tremble.

Hotspur. O, then the earth shook to see the heavens on fire,
And not in fear of your nativity.
Diseased nature oftentimes breaks forth
In strange eruptions; oft the teeming earth
Is with a kind of colic pinch'd and vex'd
By the imprisoning of unruly wind.
Within her womb; which, for enlargement striving,
Shakes the old beldam earth and topples down
Steeples and moss-grown towers. At your birth
Our grandam earth, having this distemperature,
In passion shook.

Glendower.   Cousin, of many men
I do not bear these crossings. Give me leave
To tell you once again that at my birth
The front of heaven was full of fiery shapes,
The goats ran from the mountains, and the herds
Were strangely clamorous to the frighted fields.
These signs have mark'd me extraordinary;
And all the courses of my life do show
I am not in the roll of common men.
Where is he living, clipp'd in with the sea
That chides the banks of England, Scotland, Wales,

Which calls me pupil, or hath read to me?
And bring him out that is but woman's son
Can trace me in the tedious ways of art,
And hold me pace in deep experiments.

Hotspur. I think there's no man speaks better Welsh.
I'll to dinner.

Mortimer. Peace, cousin Percy; you will make him mad.

Glendower. I can call spirits from the vasty deep.

Hotspur. Why, so can I, or so can any man;
But will they come when you do call for them?

Glendower. Why, I can teach you, cousin, to command
The devil.

Hotspur. And I can teach thee, coz, to shame the devil
By telling truth: tell truth, and shame the devil.
If thou have power to raise him, bring him hither,
And I'll be sworn I have power to shame him hence.
O, while you live, tell truth, and shame the devil!

Mortimer. Come, come, no more of this unprofitable chat.

Glendower. Three times hath Henry Bolingbroke made head
Against my power; thrice from the banks of Wye
And sandy-bottom'd Severn have I sent him
Bootless home and weather-beaten back.

Hotspur. Home without boots, and in foul weather too!
How 'scapes he agues, in the devil's name?

Glendower. Come, here is the map: shall we divide our right
According to our threefold order ta'en?

Mortimer. The archdeacon hath divided it
Into three limits very equally:
England, from Trent and Severn hitherto,
By south and east is to my part assign'd:

All westward, Wales beyond the Severn shore,
And all the fertile land within that bound,
To Owen Glendower: and, dear coz, to you
The remnant northward, lying off from Trent.
And our indentures tripartite are drawn;
Which being sealed interchangeably,
A business that this night may execute,
To-morrow, cousin Percy, you and I
And my good Lord of Worcester will set forth
To meet your father and the Scottish power,
As is appointed us, at Shrewsbury.
My father Glendower is not ready yet,
Nor shall we need his help these fourteen days.

[*To Glendower*]
Within that space you may have drawn together
Your tenants, friends, and neighbouring gentlemen.

Glendower. A shorter time shall send me to you, lords:
And in my conduct shall your ladies come;
From whom you now must steal and take no leave,
For there will be a world of water shed
Upon the parting of your wives and you.

Hotspur. Methinks my moiety, north from Burton here,
In quantity equals not one of yours:
See how this river comes me cranking in,
And cuts me from the best of all my land
A huge half-moon, a monstrous cantle out.
I'll have the current in this place damm'd up;
And here the smug and silver Trent shall run
In a new channel, fair and evenly;
It shall not wind with such a deep indent,
To rob me of so rich a bottom here.

Glendower. Not wind? it shall, it must; you see it doth.

Mortimer. Yea, but
    Mark how he bears his course, and runs me up
    With like advantage on the other side;
    Gelding the opposed continent as much
    As on the other side it takes from you.

Worcester. Yea, but a little charge will trench him here,
    And on this north side win this cape of land;
    And then he runs straight and even.

Hotspur. I'll have it so: a little charge will do it.

Glendower. I'll not have it alter'd.

Hotspur.   Will not you?

Glendower. No, nor you shall not.

Hotspur.   Who shall say me nay?

Glendower. Why, that will I.

Hotspur. Let me not understand you, then; speak it in Welsh.

Glendower. I can speak English, lord, as well as you;
    For I was train'd up in the English court;
    Where, being but young, I framed to the harp
    Many an English ditty lovely well,
    And gave the tongue a helpful ornament,
    A virtue that was never seen in you.

Hotspur. Marry,
    And I am glad of it with all my heart:
    I had rather be a kitten and cry mew
    Than one of these same metre ballad-mongers;
    I had rather hear a brazen canstick turn'd,
    Or a dry wheel grate on the axle-tree;
    And that would set my teeth nothing on edge,
    Nothing so much as mincing poetry:
    'Tis like the forced gait of a shuffling nag.

Glendower. Come, you shall have Trent turn'd.

Hotspur. I do not care: I'll give thrice so much land
    To any well-deserving friend;
    But in the way of bargain, mark ye me,
    I'll cavil on the ninth part of a hair.
    Are the indentures drawn? shall we be gone?

Glendower. The moon shines fair; you may away by night:
    I'll haste the writer, and withal
    Break with your wives of your departure hence:
    I am afraid my daughter will run mad,
    So much she doteth on her Mortimer.

                                                Exit.

Mortimer. Fie, cousin Percy! how you cross my father!

Hotspur. I cannot choose: sometime he angers me
    With telling me of the moldwarp and the ant,
    Of the dreamer Merlin and his prophecies,
    And of a dragon and a finless fish,
    A clip-wing'd griffin and a moulten raven,
    A couching lion and a ramping cat,
    And such a deal of skimble-skamble stuff
    As puts me from my faith. I tell you what,—
    He held me last night at least nine hours
    In reckoning up the several devils' names
    That were his lackeys: I cried 'hum,' and 'well, go to,'
    But mark'd him not a word. O, he is as tedious
    As a tired horse, a railing wife;
    Worse than a smoky house: I had rather live
    With cheese and garlic in a windmill, far,
    Than feed on cates and have him talk to me
    In any summer-house in Christendom.

Mortimer. In faith, he is a worthy gentleman,

Exceedingly well read, and profited
In strange concealments; valiant as a lion,
And wondrous affable, and as bountiful
As mines of India. Shall I tell you, cousin?
He holds your temper in a high respect,
And curbs himself even of his natural scope
When you come 'cross his humour; faith, he does:
I warrant you, that man is not alive
Might so have tempted him as you have done,
Without the taste of danger and reproof:
But do not use it oft, let me entreat you.

Worcester. In faith, my lord, you are too wilful-blame;
And since your coming hither have done enough
To put him quite besides his patience.
You must needs learn, lord, to amend this fault:
Though sometimes it show greatness, courage, blood,—
And that's the dearest grace it renders you,—
Yet oftentimes it doth present harsh rage,
Defect of manners, want of government,
Pride, haughtiness, opinion and disdain:
The least of which haunting a nobleman
Loseth men's hearts, and leaves behind a stain
Upon the beauty of all parts besides,
Beguiling them of commendation.

Hotspur. Well, I am school'd: good manners be your speed!
Here come our wives, and let us take our leave.

Re-enter Glendower with the Ladies

Mortimer. This is the deadly spite that angers me;
My wife can speak no English, I no Welsh.

Glendower. My daughter weeps: she will not part with you;
She'll be a soldier too, she'll to the wars.

Mortimer. Good father, tell her that she and my aunt Percy
 Shall follow in your conduct speedily.
 Glendower *speaks to her in Welsh, and she answers him in the same.*

Glendower. She is desperate here; a peevish self-will'd harlotry,
 one that no persuasion can do good upon.

The Lady speaks in Welsh.

Mortimer. I understand thy looks: that pretty Welsh
 Which thou pour'st down from these swelling heavens
 I am too perfect in; and, but for shame,
 In such a parley should I answer thee.

The Lady speaks again in Welsh.

 I understand thy kisses and thou mine,
 And that's a feeling disputation:
 But I will never be a truant, love,
 Till I have learn'd thy language; for thy tongue
 Makes Welsh as sweet as ditties highly penn'd,
 Sung by a fair queen in a summer's bower,
 With ravishing division, to her lute.

Glendower. Nay, if you melt, then will she run mad.

The Lady speaks again in Welsh.

Mortimer. O, I am ignorance itself in this!

Glendower. She bids you on the wanton rushes lay you down
 And rest your gentle head upon her lap,
 And she will sing the song that pleaseth you,
 And on your eyelids crown the god of sleep,
 Charming your blood with pleasing heaviness,
 Making such difference 'twixt wake and sleep
 As is the difference betwixt day and night
 The hour before the heavenly-harness'd team
 Begins his golden progress in the east.

Mortimer. With all my heart I'll sit and hear her sing:

By that time will our book, I think, be drawn.

Glendower. Do so;
　And those musicians that shall play to you
　Hang in the air a thousand leagues from hence,
　And straight they shall be here: sit, and attend.

Hotspur. Come, Kate, thou art perfect in lying down: come,
　quick, quick, that I may lay my head in thy lap.

Lady Percy. Go, ye giddy goose.

　　　　　　　　　　　　　　　　　The music plays.

Hotspur. Now I perceive the devil understands Welsh;
　And 'tis no marvel he is so humorous.
　By'r lady, he is a good musician.

Lady Percy. Then should you be nothing but musical, for you
　are altogether governed by humours. Lie still, ye thief, and
　hear the lady sing in Welsh.

Hotspur. I had rather hear Lady, my brach, howl in Irish.

Lady Percy. Wouldst thou have thy head broken?

Hotspur. No.

Lady Percy. Then be still.

Hotspur. Neither; 'tis a woman's fault.

Lady Percy. Now God help thee!

Hotspur. To the Welsh lady's bed.

Lady Percy. What's that?

Hotspur. Peace! she sings.

　　　　　　　　　Here the Lady *sings a Welsh song.*

Hotspur. Come, Kate, I'll have your song too.

Lady Percy. Not mine, in good sooth.

Hotspur. Not yours, in good sooth! Heart! you swear like a
　comfit-maker's wife. 'Not you, in good sooth,' and 'as true as

I live,' and 'as God shall mend me,' and 'as sure as day,'
And givest such sarcenet surety for thy oaths,
As if thou never walk'st further than Finsbury.
Swear me, Kate, like a lady as thou art,
A good mouth-filling oath, and leave 'in sooth,'
And such protest of pepper-gingerbread,
To velvet-guards and Sunday-citizens.
Come, sing.

Lady Percy. I will not sing.

Hotspur. 'Tis the next way to turn tailor, or be red-breast
teacher. An the indentures be drawn, I'll away within these
two hours; and so, come in when ye will.

Exit.

Glendower. Come, come, Lord Mortimer; you are as slow
As hot Lord Percy is on fire to go.
But this our book is drawn; we'll but seal,
And then to horse immediately.

Mortimer. With all my heart.

Exeunt.

scene 2. [*London. The palace*]

Enter the King, Prince of Wales, *and others*

King. Lords, give us leave; the Prince of Wales and I
Must have some private conference: but be near at hand,
For we shall presently have need of you.

Exeunt Lords.

I know not whether God will have it so,
For some displeasing service I have done,
That, in his secret doom, out of my blood
He'll breed revengement and a scourge for me;

But thou dost in thy passages of life
Make me believe that thou art only mark'd
For the hot vengeance and the rod of heaven
To punish my mistreadings. Tell me else,
Could such inordinate and low desires,
Such poor, such bare, such lewd, such mean attempts,
Such barren pleasures, rude society,
As thou art match'd withal and grafted to,
Accompany the greatness of thy blood,
And hold their level with thy princely heart?

Prince. So please your majesty, I would I could
Quit all offences with as clear excuse
As well as I am doubtless I can purge
Myself of many I am charged withal:
Yet such extenuation let me beg,
As, in reproof of many tales devised,
Which oft the ear of greatness needs must hear,
By smiling pick-thanks and base newsmongers,
I may, for some things true, wherein my youth
Hath faulty wander'd and irregular,
Find pardon on my true submission.

King. God pardon thee! yet let me wonder, Harry,
At thy affections, which do hold a wing
Quite from the flight of all thy ancestors.
Thy place in council thou hast rudely lost,
Which by thy younger brother is supplied,
And art almost an alien to the hearts
Of all the court and princes of my blood:
The hope and expectation of thy time
Is ruin'd, and the soul of every man
Prophetically doth forethink thy fall.
Had I so lavish of my presence been,

So common-hackney'd in the eyes of men,
So stale and cheap to vulgar company,
Opinion, that did help me to the crown,
Had still kept loyal to possession,
And left me in reputeless banishment,
A fellow of no mark nor likelihood.
By being seldom seen, I could not stir
But like a comet I was wonder'd at;
That men would tell their children 'This is he;'
Others would say 'Where, which is Bolingbroke?'
And then I stole all courtesy from heaven,
And dress'd myself in such humility
That I did pluck allegiance from men's hearts,
Loud shouts and salutations from their mouths,
Even in the presence of the crowned king.
Thus did I keep my person fresh and new;
My presence, like a robe pontifical,
Ne'er seen but wonder'd at: and so my state,
Seldom but sumptuous, showed like a feast,
And wan by rareness such solemnity.
The skipping king, he ambled up and down,
With shallow jesters and rash bavin wits,
Soon kindled and soon burnt; carded his state,
Mingled his royalty with capering fools,
Had his great name profaned with their scorns,
And gave his countenance, against his name,
To laugh at gibing boys, and stand the push
Of every beardless vain comparative,
Grew a companion to the common streets,
Enfeoff'd himself to popularity;
That, being daily swallow'd by men's eyes,
They surfeited with honey and began
To loathe the taste of sweetness, whereof a little

More than a little is by much too much.
So when he had occasion to be seen,
He was but as the cuckoo is in June,
Heard, not regarded; seen, but with such eyes
As, sick and blunted with community,
Afford no extraordinary gaze,
Such as is bent on sun-like majesty
When it shines seldom in admiring eyes;
But rather drowzed and hung their eyelids down,
Slept in his face and render'd such aspect
As cloudy men use to their adversaries,
Being with his presence glutted, gorged and full.
And in that very line, Harry, standest thou;
For thou hast lost thy princely privilege
With vile participation: not an eye
But is a-weary of thy common sight,
Save mine, which hath desired to see thee more;
Which now doth that I would not have it do,
Make blind itself with foolish tenderness.

Prince. I shall hereafter, my thrice gracious lord,
Be more myself.

King.   For all the world
As thou art to this hour was Richard then
When I from France set foot at Ravenspurgh,
And even as I was then is Percy now.
Now, by my sceptre and my soul to boot,
He hath more worthy interest to the state
Than thou the shadow of succession;
For of no right, nor colour like to right,
He doth fill fields with harness in the realm,
Turns head against the lion's armed jaws,
And, being no more in debt to years than thou,

Leads ancient lords and reverend bishops on
To bloody battles and to bruising arms.
What never-dying honour hath he got
Against renowned Douglas! whose high deeds,
Whose hot incursions and great name in arms
Holds from all soldiers chief majority
And military title capital
Through all the kingdoms that acknowledge Christ:
Thrice hath this Hotspur, Mars in swathling clothes,
This infant warrior, in his enterprizes
Discomfited great Douglas, ta'en him once,
Enlarged him and made a friend of him,
To fill the mouth of deep defiance up,
And shake the peace and safety of our throne.
And what say you to this? Percy, Northumberland,
The Archbishop's grace of York, Douglas, Mortimer,
Capitulate against us and are up.
But wherefore do I tell these news to thee?
Why, Harry, do I tell thee of my foes,
Which art my near'st and dearest enemy?
Thou that art like enough, through vassal fear,
Base inclination and the start of spleen,
To fight against me under Percy's pay,
To dog his heels and curtsy at his frowns,
To show how much thou art degenerate.

Prince. Do not think so; you shall not find it so:
And God forgive them that so much have sway'd
Your majesty's good thoughts away from me!
I will redeem all this on Percy's head,
And in the closing of some glorious day
Be bold to tell you that I am your son;
When I will wear a garment all of blood,

And stain my favours in a bloody mask,
Which, wash'd away, shall scour my shame with it:
And that shall be the day, whene'er it lights,
That this same child of honour and renown,
This gallant Hotspur, this all-praised knight,
And your unthought-of Harry chance to meet.
For every honour sitting on his helm,
Would they were multitudes, and on my head
My shames redoubled! for the time will come,
That I shall make this northern youth exchange
His glorious deeds for my indignities.
Percy is but my factor, good my lord,
To engross up glorious deeds on my behalf;
And I will call him to so strict account,
That he shall render every glory up,
Yea, even the slightest worship of his time,
Or I will tear the reckoning from his heart.
This, in the name of God, I promise here:
The which if He be pleased I shall perform,
I do beseech your majesty may salve
The long-grown wounds of my intemperance:
If not, the end of life cancels all bands;
And I will die a hundred thousand deaths
Ere break the smallest parcel of this vow.

King. A hundred thousand rebels die in this:
Thou shalt have charge and sovereign trust herein.

Enter Blunt

How now, good Blunt? thy looks are full of speed.

Blunt. So hath the business that I come to speak of.
Lord Mortimer of Scotland hath sent word
That Douglas and the English rebels met
The eleventh of this month at Shrewsbury:

A mighty and a fearful head they are,
If promises be kept on every hand,
As ever offer'd foul play in a state.

King. The Earl of Westmoreland set forth to-day;
With him my son, Lord John of Lancaster;
For this advertisement is five days old:
On Wednesday next, Harry, you shall set forward;
On Thursday we ourselves will march: our meeting
Is Bridgenorth: and, Harry, you shall march
Through Gloucestershire; by which account,
Our business valued, some twelve days hence
Our general forces at Bridgenorth shall meet.
Our hands are full of bussiness: let's away;
Advantage feeds him fat, while men delay.

Exeunt.

scene 3. [*Boar's-Head Tavern in Eastcheap*]

Enter Falstaff *and* Bardolph

Falstaff. Bardolph, am I not fallen away vilely since this last action? do I not bate? do I not dwindle? Why, my skin hangs about me like an old lady's loose gown; I am withered like an old apple-john. Well, I'll repent, and that suddenly, while I am in some liking; I shall be out of heart shortly, and then I shall have no strength to repent. An I have not forgotten what the inside of a church is made of, I am a peppercorn, a brewer's horse: the inside of a church! Company, villanous company, hath been the spoil of me.

Bardolph. Sir John, you are so fretful, you cannot live long.

Falstaff. Why, there is it: come sing me a bawdy song; make me merry. I was as virtuously given as a gentleman need to be;

virtuous enough; *swore little; diced not above seven times a week; went to a bawdy-house not above once in a quarter—of an hour;* paid money that I borrowed, three or four times; lived well, and in good compass: and now I live out of all order, out of all compass.

Bardolph. Why, you are so fat, Sir John, that you must needs be out of all compass, out of all reasonable compass, Sir John.

Falstaff. Do thou amend thy face, and I'll amend my life: thou art our admiral, thou bearest the lantern in the poop, but 'tis in the nose of thee; thou art the Knight of the Burning Lamp.

Bardolph. Why, Sir John, my face does you no harm.

Falstaff. No, I'll be sworn; I make as good use of it as many a man doth of a Death's-head or a *memento mori:* I never see thy face but I think upon hell-fire, and Dives that lived in purple; for there he is in his robes, burning, burning. If thou wert any way given to virtue, I would swear by thy face; my oath should be, 'By this fire, that's God's angel:' but thou art altogether given over; and wert indeed, but for the light in thy face, the son of utter darkness. When thou rannest up Gadshill in the night to catch my horse, if I did not think thou hadst been an *ignis fatuus* or a ball of wildfire, there's no purchase in money. O, thou art a perpetual triumph, an everlasting bonfire-light! Thou hast saved me a thousand marks in links and torches, walking with thee in he night betwixt tavern and tavern: but the sack that thou hast drunk me would have bought me lights as good cheap at the dearest chandler's in Europe. I have maintained that salamander of yours with fire any time this two and thirty years; God reward me for it!

Bardolph. 'Sblood, I would my face were in your belly!

Falstaff. God-a-mercy! so should I be sure to be heart burnt.

Enter Hostess

How now, Dame Partlet the hen! have you inquired yet who picked my pocket?

Hostess. Why, Sir John, what do you think, Sir John? do you think I keep thieves in my house? I have searched, I have inquired, so has my husband, man by man, boy by boy, servant by servant: the tithe of a hair was never lost in my house before.

Falstaff. Ye lie, hostess: Bardolph was shaved, and lost many a hair; and I'll be sworn my pocket was picked. Go to, you are a woman, go.

Hostess. Who, I? no; I defy thee: God's light, I was never called so in mine own house before.

Falstaff. Go to, I know you well enough.

Hostess. No, Sir John; you do not know me, Sir John. I know you, Sir John: you owe me money, Sir John; and now you pick a quarrel to beguile me of it: I bought you a dozen of shirts to your back.

Falstaff. Dowlas, filthy dowlas: I have given them away to bakers' wives, and they have made bolters of them.

Hostess. Now, as I am a true woman, holland of eight shillings an ell. You owe money here besides, Sir John, for your diet and by-drinkings, and money lent you, four and twenty pound.

Falstaff. He had his part of it; let him pay.

Hostess. He? alas, he is poor; he hath nothing.

Falstaff. How! poor? look upon his face; what call you rich? let them coin his nose, let them coin his cheeks: I'll not pay a denier. What, will you make a younker of me? shall I not *take mine ease in mine inn* but I shall have my pocket picked? I have lost a seal-ring of my grandfather's worth forty mark.

Hostess. O Jesu, I have heard the prince tell him, I know not
how oft, that that ring was copper!

Falstaff. How! the prince is a Jack, a sneak-cup: 'sblood, an he
were here, I would cudgel him like a dog, if he would say so.
Enter the Prince, *marching, and* Falstaff *meets them playing on his
truncheon like a fife*

How now, lad! is the wind in that door, i' faith? must we all
march?

Bardolph. Yea, two and two, Newgate fashion.

Hostess. My lord, I pray you, hear me.

Prince. What sayest thou, Mistress Quickly? How doth thy husband? I love him well; he is an honest man.

Hostess. Good my lord, hear me.

Falstaff. Prithee, let her alone, and list to me.

Prince. What sayest thou, Jack?

Falstaff. The other night I fell asleep here behind the arras, and
had my pocket picked: this house is turned bawdy-house;
they pick pockets.

Prince. What didst thou lose, Jack?

Falstaff. Wilt thou believe me, Hal? three or four bonds of forty
pound a-piece, and a seal-ring of my grandfather's.

Prince. A trifle, some eight-penny matter.

Hostess. So I told him, my lord; and I said I heard your grace say
so: and, my lord, he speaks most vilely of you, like a foul-
mouthed man as he is; and said he would cudgel you.

Prince. What! he did not?

Hostess. There's neither faith, truth, nor womanhood in me else.

Falstaff. There's no more faith in thee than in a stewed prune;
nor no more truth in thee than in a drawn fox; and for

womanhood, Maid Marian may be the deputy's wife of the ward to thee. Go, you thing, go.

Hostess. Say, what thing? what thing?

Falstaff. What thing! why, a thing to thank God on.

Hostess. I am no thing to thank God on, I would thou shouldst know it; I am an honest man's wife: and, setting thy knighthood aside, thou art a knave to call me so.

Falstaff. Setting thy womanhood aside, thou art a beast to say otherwise.

Hostess. Say, what beast, thou knave, thou?

Falstaff. What beast! why, an otter.

Prince. An otter, Sir John! why an otter?

Falstaff. Why, she's neither fish nor flesh; a man knows not where to have her.

Hostess. Thou art an unjust man in saying so: thou or any man knows where to have me, thou knave, thou!

Prince. Thou sayest true, hostess; and he slanders thee most grossly.

Hostess. So he doth you, my lord; and said this other day you ought him a thousand pound.

Prince. Sirrah, do I owe you a thousand pound?

Falstaff. A thousand pound, Hal! a million: thy love is worth a million: thou owest me thy love.

Hostess. Nay, my lord, he called you Jack, and said he would cudgel you.

Falstaff. Did I, Bardolph?

Bardolph. Indeed, Sir John, you said so.

Falstaff. Yea, if he said my ring was copper.

Prince. I say 'tis copper: darest thou be as good as thy word now?

Falstaff. Why, Hal, thou knowest, as thou art but man, I dare: but as thou art prince, I fear thee as I fear the roaring of the lion's whelp.

Prince. And why not as the lion?

Falstaff. The king himself is to be feared as the lion: dost thou think I'll fear thee as I fear thy father? nay, an I do, I pray God my girdle break.

Prince. O, if it should, how would thy guts fall about thy knees! But, sirrah, there's no room for faith, truth, nor honesty in this bosom of thine; it is all filled up with guts and midriff. Charge an honest woman with picking thy pocket! why, thou whoreson, impudent, embossed rascal, if there were anything in thy pocket but tavern-reckonings, memorandums of bawdy-houses, and one poor penny-worth of sugar-candy to make thee long-winded, if thy pocket were enriched with any other injuries but these, I am a villain: and yet you will stand to it; you will not pocket up wrong: art thou not ashamed?

Falstaff. Dost thou hear, Hal? thou knowest *in the state of inno-cency Adam fell; and what should poor Jack Falstaff do in the days of villany?* Thou seest I have more flesh than another man; and therefore more frailty. You confess then, you picked my pocket?

Prince. It appears so by the story.

Falstaff. Hostess, I forgive thee: go, make ready breakfast; love thy husband, look to thy servants, cherish thy guests: thou shalt find me tractable to any honest reason: thou seest I am pacified still. Nay, prithee, be gone. [*Exit* Hostess] Now, Hal, to the news at court: for the robbery, lad, how is that answered?

Prince. O, my sweet beef, I must still be good angel to thee: the money is paid back again.

Falstaff. O, I do not like that paying back; 'tis a double labour.

Prince. I am good friends with my father, and may do any thing.

Falstaff. Rob me the exchequer the first thing thou doest, and do it with unwashed hands too.

Bardolph. Do, my lord.

Prince. I have procured thee, Jack, a charge of foot.

Falstaff. I would it had been of horse. Where shall I find one that can steal well? O for a fine thief, of the age of two and twenty or thereabouts! I am heinously unprovided. Well, God be thanked for these rebels, they offend none but the virtuous: I laud them, I praise them.

Prince. Bardolph!

Bardolph. My lord?

Prince. Go bear this letter to Lord John of Lancaster, to my brother John; this to my Lord of Westmoreland. [*Exit* Bardolph] Go, Peto, to horse, to horse; for thou and I have thirty miles to ride yet ere dinner time. [*Exit* Peto] Jack, meet me to-morrow in the Temple hall at two o'clock in the afternoon.
There shalt thou know thy charge, and there receive
Money and order for their furniture.
The land is burning; Percy stands on high;
And either we or they must lower lie.

Exit.

Falstaff. Rare words! brave world! Hostess, my breakfast, come!
O, I could wish this tavern were my drum!

Exit.

act 4

[*The rebel camp near Shrewsbury*]

Enter Hotspur, Worcester, *and* Douglas

Hotspur. Well said, my noble Scot: if speaking truth
   In this fine age were not thought flattery,
   Such attribution should the Douglas have,
   As not a soldier of this season's stamp
   Should go so general current through the world.
   By God, I cannot flatter; I do defy
   The tongues of soothers; but a braver place
   In my heart's love hath no man than yourself:
   Nay, task me to my word; approve me, lord.

Douglas. Thou art the king of honour:
   No man so potent breathes upon the ground
   But I will beard him.

Hotspur.   Do so, and 'tis well.

           Enter a Messenger *with letters*

What letters hast thou there?—I can but thank you.

Messenger. These letters come from your father.

Hotspur. Letters from him! why comes he not himself?

Messenger. He cannot come, my lord; he is grievous sick.

Hotspur. 'Zounds! how has he the leisure to be sick
    In such a justling time? Who leads his power?
    Under whose government come they along?

Messenger. His letters bear his mind, not I, my lord.

Worcester. I prithee, tell me, doth he keep his bed?

Messenger. He did, my lord, four days ere I set forth;
    And at the time of my departure thence
    He was much fear'd by his physicians.

Worcester. I would the state of time had first been whole,
    Ere he by sickness had been visited:
    His health was never better worth than now.

Hotspur. Sick now? droop now? this sickness doth infect
    The very life-blood of our enterprise;
    'Tis catching hither, even to our camp.
    He writes me here, that inward sickness—
    And that his friends by deputation could not
    So soon be drawn, nor did he think it meet
    To lay so dangerous and dear a trust
    On any soul removed but on his own.
    Yet doth he give us bold advertisement,
    That with our small conjunction we should on,
    To see how fortune is disposed to us;
    For, as he writes, *there is no quailing now,*
    Because the king is certainly possess'd
    Of all our purposes. What say you to it?

Worcester. Your father's sickness is a maim to us.

Hotspur. A perilous gash, a very limb lopp'd off:
    And yet, in faith, it is not; his present want
    Seems more than we shall find it: were it good

To set the exact wealth of all our states
All at one cast? to set so rich a main
On the nice hazard of one doubtful hour?
It were not good; for therein should we read
The very bottom and the soul of hope,
The very list, the very utmost bound
Of all our fortunes.

Douglas.   Faith, and so we should;
Where now remains a sweet reversion:
We may boldly spend upon the hope of what
Is to come in:
A comfort of retirement lives in this.

Hotspur. A rendezvous, a home to fly unto,
If that the devil and mischance look big
Upon the maidenhead of our affairs.

Worcester. But yet I would your father had been here.
The quality and hair of our attempt
Brooks no division: it will be thought
By some that know not why he is away,
That wisdom, loyalty and mere dislike
Of our proceedings kept the earl from hence:
And think how such an apprehension
May turn the tide of fearful faction,
And breed a kind of question in our cause;
For well you know we of the offering side
Must keep aloof from strict arbitrement,
And stop all sight-holes, every loop from whence
The eye of reason may pry in upon us:
This absence of your father's draws a curtain,
That shows the ignorant a kind of fear
Before not dreamt of.

Hotspur.   You strain too far.

I rather of his absence make this use:
It lends a lustre and more great opinion,
A larger dare to our great enterprise,
Than if the earl were here; for men must think,
If we without his help can make a head
To push against a kingdom, with his help
We shall o'erturn it topsy-turvy down.
Yet all goes well, yet all our joints are whole.

Douglas. As heart can think: there is not such a word
Spoke of in Scotland as this term of fear.

Enter Sir Richard Vernon

Hotspur. My cousin Vernon! welcome, by my soul.

Vernon. Pray God my news be worth a welcome, lord.
The Earl of Westmoreland, seven thousand strong,
Is marching hitherwards; with him Prince John.

Hotspur. No harm: what more?

Vernon.   And further, I have learn'd,
The king himself in person is set forth,
Or hitherwards intended speedily,
With strong and mighty preparation.

Hotspur. He shall be welcome too. Where is his son,
The nimble-footed madcap Prince of Wales,
And his comrades, that *daff'd the world aside,*
And bid it pass?

Vernon.   All furnish'd, all in arms;
All plumed like estridges that with the wind
Baited like eagles having lately bathed;
Glittering in golden coats, like images;
As full of spirit as the month of May,
And gorgeous as the sun at midsummer;
Wanton as youthful goats, wild as young bulls.

I saw young Harry, with his beaver on,
His cushes on his thighs, gallantly arm'd,
Rise from the ground like feather'd Mercury,
And vaulted with such ease into his seat,
As if an angel dropp'd down from the clouds,
To turn and wind a fiery Pegasus,
And witch the world with noble horsemanship.

Hotspur. No more, no more: worse than the sun in March,
This praise doth nourish agues. Let them come;
They come like sacrifices in their trim,
And to the fire-eyed maid of smoky war
All hot and bleeding will we offer them:
The mailed Mars shall on his altar sit
Up to the ears in blood. I am on fire
To hear this rich reprisal is so nigh
And yet not ours. Come, let me taste my horse,
Who is to bear me like a thunderbolt
Against the bosom of the Prince of Wales:
Harry to Harry shall, hot horse to horse,
Meet and ne'er part till one drop down a corse.
O that Glendower were come!

Vernon.   There is more news:
I learn'd in Worcester, as I rode along,
He cannot draw his power this fourteen days.

Douglas. That's the worst tidings that I hear of yet.

Worcester. Ay, by my faith, that bears a frosty sound.

Hotspur. What may the king's whole battle reach unto?

Vernon. To thirty thousand.

Hotspur.   Forty let it be:
My father and Glendower being both away,
The powers of us may serve so great a day.

Come, let us take a muster speedily:
Doomsday is near; die all, die merrily.

Douglas. Talk not of dying: I am out of fear
Of death or death's hand for this one half year.

Exeunt.

scene 2. [*A public road near Coventry*]

Enter Falstaff *and* Bardolph

Falstaff. Bardolph, get thee before to Coventry; fill me a bottle
of sack: our soldiers shall march through; we'll to Sutton
Co'fil' to-night.

Bardolph. Will you give me money, captain?

Falstaff. Lay out, lay out.

Bardolph. This bottle makes an angel.

Falstaff. An if it do, take it for thy labour; and if it make twenty,
take them all; I'll answer the coinage. Bid my lieutenant Peto
meet me at town's end.

Bardolph. I will, captain: farewell.

Exit.

Falstaff. If I be not ashamed of my soldiers, I am a soused gur-
net. I have misused the king's press damnably. I have got, in
exchange of a hundred and fifty soldiers, three hundred and
odd pounds. I press me none but good householders,
yeomen's sons; inquire me out contracted bachelors, such as
had been asked twice on the banns; such a commodity of
warm slaves, as had as lief hear the devil as a drum; such as
fear the report of a caliver worse than a struck fowl or a hurt
wild-duck. I pressed me none but such toasts-and-butter,
with hearts in their bellies no bigger than pins'-heads, and

they have bought out their services; and now my whole
charge consists of ancients, corporals, lieutenants, gentlemen
of companies, slaves as ragged as Lazarus in the painted cloth,
where the glutton's dogs licked his sores; and such as indeed
were never soldiers, but discarded unjust serving-men,
younger sons to younger brothers, revolted tapsters, and
ostlers trade-fallen; the cankers of a calm world and a long
peace, ten times more dishonourable ragged than an old fazed
ancient: and such have I, to fill up the rooms of them that
have bought out their services, that you would think that I
had a hundred and fifty tattered prodigals lately come from
swine-keeping, from eating draff and husks. A mad fellow
met me on the way and told me I had unloaded all the gibbets and pressed the dead bodies. No eye hath seen such
scarecrows. I'll not march through Coventry with them,
that's flat: nay, and the villains march wide betwixt the legs, as
if they had gyves on; for indeed I had the most of them out
of prison. There's but a shirt and a half in all my company;
and the half shirt is two napkins tacked together and thrown
over the shoulders like a herald's coat without sleeves; and the
shirt, to say the truth, stolen from my host at Saint Alban's, or
the red-nose innkeeper of Daventry. But that's all one; they'll
find linen enough on every hedge.

Enter the Prince *and* Westmoreland

Prince. How now, blown Jack! how now, quilt!

Falstaff. What, Hal! how now, mad wag! what a devil dost thou
in Warwickshire? My good Lord of Westmoreland, I cry you
mercy: I thought your honour had already been at Shrewsbury.

Westmoreland. Faith, Sir John, 'tis more than time that I were
there, and you too; but my powers are there already. The
king, I can tell you, looks for us all: we must away all night.

Falstaff. Tut, never fear me: I am as vigilant as a cat to steal cream.

Prince. I think, to steal cream indeed, for thy theft hath already made thee butter. But tell me, Jack, whose fellows are these that come after?

Falstaff. Mine, Hal, mine.

Prince. I did never see such pitiful rascals.

Falstaff. Tut, tut; good enough to toss; food for powder, food for powder; they'll fill a pit as well as better: tush, man, mortal men, mortal men.

Westmoreland. Ay, but, Sir John, methinks they are exceeding poor and bare, too beggarly.

Falstaff. Faith, for their poverty, I know not where they had that; and for their bareness, I am sure they never learned that of me.

Prince. No, I'll be sworn; unless you call three fingers on the ribs bare. But, sirrah, make haste: Percy is already in the field.

Falstaff. What, is the king encamped?

Westmoreland. He is, Sir John: I fear we shall stay too long.

Falstaff. Well,
To the latter end of a fray and the beginning of a feast
Fits a dull fighter and a keen guest.

Exeunt.

scene 3. [*The rebel camp near Shrewsbury*]

Enter Hotspur, Worcester, Douglas, *and* Vernon

Hotspur. We'll fight with him to-night.

Worcester.   It may not be.

Douglas. You give him then advantage.

Vernon.   Not a whit.

Hotspur. Why say you so? looks he not for supply?

Vernon. So do we.

Hotspur.   His is certain, ours is doubtful.

Worcester. Good cousin, be advised; stir not to-night.

Vernon. Do not, my lord.

Douglas.   You do not counsel well:
    You speak it out of fear and cold heart.

Vernon. Do me no slander, Douglas: by my life,
    And I dare well maintain it with my life,
    If well-respected honour bid me on,
    I hold as little counsel with weak fear
    As you, my lord, or any Scot that this day lives:
    Let it be seen to-morrow in the battle
    Which of us fears.

Douglas.   Yea, or to-night.

Vernon.   Content.

Hotspur. To-night, say I.

Vernon. Come, come, it may not be. I wonder much,
    Being men of such great leading as you are,
    That you foresee not what impediments
    Drag back our expedition: certain horse
    Of my cousin Vernon's are not yet come up:
    Your uncle Worcester's horse came but to-day;
    And now their pride and mettle is asleep,
    Their courage with hard labour tame and dull,
    That not a horse is half the half of himself.

Hotspur. So are the horses of the enemy

In general, journey-bated and brought low:
The better part of ours are full of rest.

Worcester. The number of the king exceedeth ours:
For God's sake, cousin, stay till all come in.

The trumpet sounds a parley.

Enter Sir Walter Blunt

Blunt. I come with gracious offers from the king,
If you vouchsafe me hearing and respect.

Hotspur. Welcome, Sir Walter Blunt; and would to God
You were of our determination!
Some of us love you well; and even those some
Envy your great deservings and good name,
Because you are not of our quality,
But stand against us like an enemy.

Blunt. And God defend but still I should stand so,
So long as out of limit and true rule
You stand against anointed majesty.
But to my charge. The king hath sent to know
The nature of your griefs, and whereupon
You conjure from the breast of civil peace
Such bold hostility, teaching his duteous land
Audacious cruelty. If that the king
Have any way your good deserts forgot,
Which he confesseth to be manifold,
He bids you name your griefs; and with all speed
You shall have your desires with interest,
And pardon absolute for yourself and these
Herein misled by your suggestion.

Hotspur. The king is kind; and well we know the king
Knows at what time to promise, when to pay.

My father and my uncle and myself
Did give him that same royalty he wears;
And when he was not six and twenty strong,
Sick in the world's regard, wretched and low,
A poor unminded outlaw sneaking home,
My father gave him welcome to the shore;
And when he heard him swear and vow to God
He came but to be Duke of Lancaster,
To sue his livery and beg his peace,
With tears of innocency and terms of zeal,
My father, in kind heart and pity moved,
Swore him assistance and perform'd it too.
Now when the lords and barons of the realm
Perceived Northumberland did lean to him,
The more and less came in with cap and knee;
Met him in boroughs, cities, villages,
Attended him on bridges, stood in lanes,
Laid gifts before him, proffer'd him their oaths,
Gave him their heirs, as pages follow'd him
Even at the heels in golden multitudes.
He presently, as greatness knows itself,
Steps me a little higher than his vow
Made to my father, while his blood was poor,
Upon the naked shore at Ravenspurgh;
And now, forsooth, takes on him to reform
Some certain edicts and some strait decrees
That lie too heavy on the commonwealth,
Cries out upon abuses, seems to weep
Over his country's wrongs; and by this face,
This seeming brow of justice, did he win
The hearts of all that he did angle for;
Proceeded further; cut me off the heads

Of all the favourites that the absent king
In deputation left behind him here,
When he was personal in the Irish war.

Blunt. Tut, I came not to hear this.

Hotspur.   Then to the point.
In short time after, he deposed the king;
Soon after that, deprived him of his life;
And in the neck of that, task'd the whole state;
To make that worse, suffer'd his kinsman March,
Who is, if every owner were well placed,
Indeed his king, to be engaged in Wales,
There without ransom to lie forfeited;
Disgraced me in my happy victories,
Sought to entrap me by intelligence;
Rated mine uncle from the council-board;
In rage dismiss'd my father from the court;
Broke oath on oath, committed wrong on wrong,
And in conclusion drove us to seek out
This head of safety, and withal to pry
Into his title, the which we find
Too indirect for long continuance.

Blunt. Shall I return this answer to the king?

Hotspur. Not so, Sir Walter: we'll withdraw a while.
Go to the king; and let there be impawn'd
Some surety for a safe return again,
And in the morning early shall mine uncle
Bring him our purposes: and so farewell.

Blunt. I would you would accept of grace and love.

Hotspur. And may be so we shall.

Blunt.   Pray God you do.

                                                          Exeunt.

scene 4. [*York. The* Archbishop's *palace*]

Enter the Archbishop of York *and* Sir Michael

Archbishop. Hie, good Sir Michael; bear this sealed brief
   With winged haste to the lord marshal;
   This to my cousin Scroop, and all the rest
   To whom they are directed. If you knew
   How much they do import, you would make haste.

Sir Michael. My good lord,
   I guess their tenour.

Archbishop.   Like enough you do.
   To-morrow, good Sir Michael, is a day
   Wherein the fortune of ten thousand men
   Must bide the touch; for, sir, at Shrewsbury,
   As I am truly given to understand,
   The king with mighty and quick-raised power
   Meets with Lord Harry: and I fear, Sir Michael,
   What with the sickness of Northumberland,
   Whose power was in the first proportion,
   And what with Owen Glendower's absence thence,
   Who with them was a rated sinew too
   And comes not in, o'er-ruled by prophecies,
   I fear the power of Percy is too weak
   To wage an instant trial with the king.

Sir Michael. Why, my good lord, you need not fear;
   There is Douglas and Lord Mortimer.

Archbishop. No, Mortimer is not there.

Sir Michael. But there is Mordake, Vernon, Lord Harry Percy,
   And there is my Lord of Worcester and a head
   Of gallant warriors, noble gentlemen.

Archbishop. And so there is: but yet the king hath drawn
   The special head of all the land together:
   The Prince of Wales, Lord John of Lancaster,
   The noble Westmoreland and warlike Blunt;
   And many mo corrivals and dear men
   Of estimation and command in arms.

Sir Michael. Doubt not, my lord, they shall be well opposed.

Archbishop. I hope no less, yet needful 'tis to fear;
   And, to prevent the worst, Sir Michael, speed:
   For if Lord Percy thrive not, ere the king
   Dismiss his power, he means to visit us,
   For he hath heard of our confederacy,
   And 'tis but wisdom to make strong against him:
   Therefore make haste. I must go write again
   To other friends; and so farewell, Sir Michael.

                                                    Exeunt.

act 5

scene 1. [*The* King's *camp near Shrewsbury*]

Enter the King, Prince of Wales, Lord John of
Lancaster, Sir Walter Blunt, *and* Falstaff

King. How bloodily the sun begins to peer
    Above yon busky hill! the day looks pale
    At his distemperature.

Prince.   The southern wind
    Doth play the trumpet to his purposes,
    And by his hollow whistling in the leaves
    Foretells a tempest and a blustering day.

King. Then with the losers let it sympathise,
    For nothing can seem foul to those that win.

                                The trumpet sounds.

Enter Worcester *and* Vernon.
    How now, my Lord of Worcester! 'tis not well
    That you and I should meet upon such terms
    As now we meet. You have deceived our trust,
    And made us doff our easy robes of peace,

To crush our old limbs in ungentle steel:
This is not well, my lord, this is not well.
What say you to it? will you again unknit
This churlish knot of all–abhorred war?
And move in that obedient orb again
Where you did give a fair and natural light,
And be no more an exhaled meteor,
A prodigy of fear, and a portent
Of broached mischief to the unborn times?

Worcester. Hear me, my liege:
For mine own part, I could be well content
To entertain the lag-end of my life
With quiet hours; for, I do protest,
I have not sought the day of this dislike.

King. You have not sought it! how comes it, then?

Falstaff. Rebellion lay in his way, and he found it.

Prince. Peace, chewet, peace!

Worcester. It pleased your majesty to turn your looks
Of favour from myself and all our house;
And yet I must remember you, my lord,
We were the first and dearest of your friends.
For you my staff of office did I break
In Richard's time; and posted day and night
To meet you on the way, and kiss your hand,
When yet you were in place and in account
Nothing so strong and fortunate as I.
It was myself, my brother, and his son,
That brought you home, and boldly did outdare
The dangers of the time. You swore to us,
And you did swear that oath at Doncaster,
That you did nothing purpose 'gainst the state;
Nor claim no further than your new-fall'n right,

The seat of Gaunt, dukedom of Lancaster:
To this we swore our aid. But in short space
It rain'd down fortune showering on your head;
And such a flood of greatness fell on you,
What with our help, what with the absent king,
What with the injuries of a wanton time,
The seeming sufferances that you had borne,
And the contrarious winds that held the king
So long in his unlucky Irish wars
That all in England did repute him dead:
And from this swarm of fair advantages
You took occasion to be quickly woo'd
To gripe the general sway into your hand;
Forgot your oath to us at Doncaster;
And being fed by us you used us so
As that ungentle gull, the cuckoo's bird,
Useth the sparrow; did oppress our nest;
Grew by our feeding to so great a bulk
That even our love durst not come near your sight
For fear of swallowing; but with nimble wing
We were enforced, for safety sake, to fly
Out of your sight and raise this present head;
Whereby we stand opposed by such means
As you yourself have forged against yourself,
By unkind usage, dangerous countenance,
And violation of all faith and troth
Sworn to us in your younger enterprise.

King. These things indeed you have articulate,
Proclaim'd at market-crosses, read in churches,
To face the garment of rebellion
With some fine colour that may please the eye
Of fickle changelings and poor discontents,
Which gape and rub the elbow at the news

Of hurlyburly innovation:
And never yet did insurrection want
Such water-colours to impaint his cause;
Nor moody beggars, starving for a time
Of pellmell havoc and confusion.

Prince. In both your armies there is many a soul
Shall pay full dearly for this encounter,
If once they join in trial. Tell your nephew,
The Prince of Wales doth join with all the world
In praise of Henry Percy: by my hopes,
This present enterprise set off his head,
I do not think a braver gentleman,
More active-valiant or more valiant-young,
More daring or more bold, is now alive
To grace this latter age with noble deeds.
For my part, I may speak it to my shame,
I have a truant been to chivalry;
And so I hear he doth account me too;
Yet this before my father's majesty—
I am content that he shall take the odds
Of his great name and estimation,
And will, to save the blood on either side,
Try fortune with him in a single fight.

King. And, Prince of Wales, so dare we venture thee,
Albeit considerations infinite
Do make against it. No, good Worcester, no,
We love our people well; even those we love
That are misled upon your cousin's part;
And, will they take the offer of our grace,
Both he and they and you, yea, every man
Shall be my friend again and I'll be his:
So tell your cousin, and bring me word

What he will do: but if he will not yield,
Rebuke and dread correction wait on us
And they shall do their office. So, be gone;
We will not now be troubled with reply:
We offer fair; take it advisedly.

> *Exeunt* Worcester *and* Vernon.

Prince. It will not be accepted, on my life:
The Douglas and the Hotspur both together
Are confident against the world in arms.

King. Hence, therefore, every leader to his charge;
For, on their answer, will we set on them:
And God befriend us, as our cause is just!

> *Exeunt all but the* Prince of Wales *and* Falstaff.

Falstaff. Hal, if thou see me down in the battle, and bestride
me, so; 'tis a point of friendship.

Prince. Nothing but a colossus can do thee that friendship.
Say thy prayers, and farewell.

Falstaff. I would 'twere bed-time, Hal, and all well.

Prince. Why, thou owest God a death.

> *Exit.*

Falstaff. 'Tis not due yet; I would be loath to pay him before his
day. What need I be so forward with him that calls not on
me? Well, 'tis no matter; honour pricks me on. Yea, but how
if honour prick me off when I come on? how then? Can
honour set to a leg? no: or an arm? no: or take away the grief
of a wound? no. Honour hath no skill in surgery, then? no.
What is honour? a word. What is in that word honour? what
is that honour? air. A trim reckoning! Who hath it? he that
died o' Wednesday. Doth he feel it? no. Doth he hear it? no.
'Tis insensible, then? yea, to the dead. But will it not live
with the living? no. Why? detraction will not suffer it.

Therefore I'll none of it. Honour is a mere scutcheon: and so
ends my catechism.

Exit.

scene 2. [*The rebel camp*]

Enter Worcester *and* Vernon

Worcester. O, no, my nephew must not know, Sir Richard,
The liberal and kind offer of the king.

Vernon. 'Twere best he did.

Worcester.   Then are we all undone.
It is not possible, it cannot be,
The king should keep his word in loving us:
He will suspect us still, and find a time
To punish this offence in other faults:
Suspicion all our lives shall be stuck full of eyes;
For treason is but trusted like the fox,
Who, ne'er so tame, so cherish'd and lock'd up,
Will have a wild trick of his ancestors.
Look how we can, or sad or merrily,
Interpretation will misquote our looks,
And we shall feed like oxen at a stall,
The better cherish'd, still the nearer death.
My nephew's trespass may be well forgot;
It hath the excuse of youth and heat of blood;
And an adopted name of privilege,
A hare-brain'd Hotspur, govern'd by a spleen:
All his offences live upon my head
And on his father's; we did train him on,
And, his corruption being ta'en from us,
We, as the spring of all, shall pay for all.

Therefore, good cousin, let not Harry know,
In any case, the offer of the king.

Vernon. Deliver what you will; I'll say 'tis so.
Here comes your cousin.

Enter Hotspur *and* Douglas

Hotspur. My uncle is return'd:
Deliver up my Lord of Westmoreland.
Uncle, what news?

Worcester. The king will bid you battle presently.

Douglas. Defy him by the Lord of Westmoreland.

Hotspur. Lord Douglas, go you and tell him so.

Douglas. Marry, and shall, and very willingly.   *Exit.*

Worcester. There is no seeming mercy in the king.

Hotspur. Did you beg any? God forbid!

Worcester. I told him gently of our grievances,
Of his oath-breaking; which he mended thus,
By now forswearing that he is forsworn:
He calls us rebels, traitors; and will scourge
With haughty arms this hateful name in us.

Re-enter Douglas

Douglas. Arm, gentlemen; to arms! for I have thrown
A brave defiance in King Henry's teeth,
And Westmoreland, that was engaged, did bear it;
Which cannot choose but bring him quickly on.

Worcester. The Prince of Wales stepp'd forth before the king,
And, nephew, challenged you to single fight.

Hotspur. O, would the quarrel lay upon our heads,
And that no man might draw short breath to-day
But I and Harry Monmouth! Tell me, tell me,
How show'd his tasking? seem'd it in contempt?

Vernon. No, by my soul; I never in my life
    Did hear a challenge urged more modestly,
    Unless a brother should a brother dare
    To gentle exercise and proof of arms.
    He gave you all the duties of a man;
    Trimm'd up your praises with a princely tongue,
    Spoke your deservings like a chronicle,
    Making you ever better than his praise
    By still dispraising praise valued with you;
    And, which became him like a prince indeed,
    He made a blushing cital of himself;
    And chid his truant youth with such a grace
    As if he master'd there a double spirit
    Of teaching and of learning instantly.
    There did he pause: but let me tell the world,
    If he outlive the envy of this day,
    England did never owe so sweet a hope,
    So much misconstrued in his wantonness.

Hotspur. Cousin, I think thou art enamoured
    On his follies: never did I hear
    Of any prince so wild a libertie.
    But be he as he will, yet once ere night
    I will embrace him with a soldier's arm,
    That he shall shrink under my courtesy.
    Arm, arm with speed: and, fellows, soldiers, friends,
    Better consider what you have to do
    Than I, that have not well the gift of tongue,
    Can lift your blood up with persuasion.
               Enter a Messenger

Messenger. My lord, here are letters for you.

Hotspur. I cannot read them now.
    O gentlemen, the time of life is short!

To spend that shortness basely were too long,
If life did ride upon a dial's point,
Still ending at the arrival of an hour.
An if we live, we live to tread on kings;
If die, brave death, when princes die with us!
Now, for our consciences, the arms are fair,
When the intent of bearing them is just.

     Enter another Messenger

Messenger. My lord, prepare; the king comes on apace.

Hotspur. I thank him, that he cuts me from my tale,
For I profess not talking; only this—
Let each man do his best: and here draw I
A sword, whose temper I intend to stain
With the best blood that I can meet withal
In the adventure of this perilous day.
Now, Esperance! Percy! and set on.
Sound all the lofty instruments of war,
And by that music let us all embrace;
For, heaven to earth, some of us never shall
A second time do such a courtesy.

    The trumpets sound. They embrace, and exeunt.

scene 3. [*Plain between the camps*]

  The King *enters with his power. Alarum to the battle.*
   Then enter Douglas *and* Sir Walter Blunt

Blunt. What is thy name, that in the battle thus
 Thou crossest me? what honour dost thou seek
 Upon my head?

Douglas.   Know then, my name is Douglas;
 And I do haunt thee in the battle thus,
 Because some tell me that thou art a king.

Blunt. They tell thee true.

Douglas. The Lord of Stafford dear to–day hath bought
    Thy likeness; for instead of thee, King Harry,
    This sword hath ended him: so shall it thee,
    Unless thou yield thee as my prisoner.

Blunt. I was not born a yielder, thou proud Scot;
    And thou shalt find a king that will revenge
    Lord Stafford's death.

They fight. Douglas *kills* Blunt.

Enter Hotspur

Hotspur. O Douglas, hadst thou fought at Holmedon thus,
    I never had triumph'd upon a Scot.

Douglas. All's done, all's won; here breathless lies the king.

Hotspur. Where?

Douglas. Here.

Hotspur. This, Douglas? no: I know this face full well:
    A gallant knight he was, his name was Blunt;
    Semblably furnish'd like the king himself.

Douglas. A fool go with thy soul, whither it goes!
    A borrowed title hast thou bought too dear:
    Why didst thou tell me that thou wert a king?

Hotspur. The king hath many marching in his coats.

Douglas. Now, by my sword, I will kill all his coats;
    I'll murder all his wardrobe, piece by piece,
    Until I meet the king.

Hotspur.   Up, and away!
    Our soldiers stand full fairly for the day.

Exeunt.

Alarum. Enter Falstaff, *solus*

Falstaff. Though I could 'scape shot-free at London, I fear the shot here; here's no scoring but upon the pate. Soft! who are you? Sir Walter Blunt: there's honour for you! here's no vanity! I am as hot as molten lead, and as heavy too: God keep lead out of me! I need no more weight than mine own bowels. I have led my ragamuffins where they are peppered: there's not three of my hundred and fifty left alive; and they are for the town's end, to beg during life. But who comes here?

Enter the Prince

Prince. What, stand'st thou idle here? lend me thy sword:
Many a nobleman lies stark and stiff
Under the hoofs of vaunting enemies,
Whose deaths are yet unrevenged: I prithee, lend
me thy sword.

Falstaff. O Hal, I prithee, give me leave to breathe a while. Turk Gregory never did such deeds in arms as I have done this day. I have paid Percy, I have made him sure.

Prince. He is, indeed; and living to kill thee. I prithee, lend me thy sword.

Falstaff. Nay, before God, Hal, if Percy be alive, thou get'st not my sword; but take my pistol, if thou wilt.

Prince. Give it me: what, is it in the case?

Falstaff. Ay, Hal; 'tis hot, 'tis hot; there's that will sack a city.

The Prince *draws it out, and finds it to be a bottle of sack.*

Prince. What, is it a time to jest and dally now?

He throws the bottle at him. Exit.

Falstaff. Well, if Percy be alive, I'll pierce him. If he do come in my way, so: if he do not, if I come in his willingly, let him

make a carbonado of me. I like not such grinning honour as
Sir Walter hath: give me life: which if I can save, so; if not,
honour comes unlooked for, and there's an end.

Exit.

scene 4. [*Another part of the field*]

Alarum. Excursions. Enter the King, *the* Prince, Lord John of
Lancaster, *and* Earl of Westmoreland

King. I prithee,
 Harry, withdraw thyself; thou bleed'st too much.
 Lord John of Lancaster, go you with him.

Lancaster. Not I, my lord, unless I did bleed too.

Prince. I beseech your majesty, make up,
 Lest your retirement do amaze your friends.

King. I will do so.
 My Lord of Westmoreland, lead him to his tent.

Westmoreland. Come, my lord, I'll lead you to your tent.

Prince. Lead me, my lord? I do not need your help:
 And God forbid a shallow scratch should drive
 The Prince of Wales from such a field as this,
 Where stain'd nobility lies trodden on,
 And rebels' arms triumph in massacres!

Lancaster. We breathe too long: come, cousin Westmoreland,
 Our duty this way lies; for God's sake, come.

Exeunt Prince John *and* Westmoreland.

Prince. By God, thou hast deceived me, Lancaster;
 I did not think thee lord of such a spirit:
 Before, I loved thee as a brother, John;
 But now, I do respect thee as my soul.

King. I saw him hold Lord Percy at the point,
  With lustier maintenance than I did look for
  Of such an ungrown warrior.

Prince.   O, this boy
  Lends mettle to us all!

                                    Exit.

Enter Douglas

Douglas. Another king! they grow like Hydra's heads:
  I am the Douglas, fatal to all those
  That wear those colours on them: what art thou,
  That counterfeit'st the person of a king?

King. The king himself; who, Douglas, grieves at heart
  So many of his shadows thou hast met
  And not the very king. I have two boys
  Seek Percy and thyself about the field:
  But, seeing thou fall'st on me so luckily,
  I will assay thee: so, defend thyself.

Douglas. I fear thou art another counterfeit;
  And yet, in faith, thou bear'st thee like a king:
  But mine I am sure thou art, who'er thou be,
  And thus I win thee.

    They fight; the King *being in danger, re-enter* Prince of Wales.

Prince. Hold up thy head, vile Scot, or thou art like
  Never to hold it up again! the spirits
  Of valiant Shirley, Stafford, Blunt, are in my arms:
  It is the Prince of Wales that threatens thee;
  Who never promiseth but he means to pay.

                    They fight: Douglas *flies*.

Cheerly, my lord: how fares your grace?
  Sir Nicholas Gawsey hath for succour sent,
  And so hath Clifton: I'll to Clifton straight.

King. Stay, and breathe a while:
    Thou hast redeem'd thy lost opinion,
    And show'd thou makest some tender of my life,
    In this fair rescue thou hast brought to me.

Prince. O God! they did me too much injury
    That ever said I hearken'd for your death.
    If it were so, I might have let alone
    The insulting hand of Douglas over you,
    Which would have been as speedy in your end
    As all the poisonous potions in the world,
    And saved the treacherous labour of your son.

King. Make up to Clifton: I'll to Sir Nicholas Gawsey.

                    Exit.

Enter Hotspur

Hotspur. If I mistake not, thou art Harry Monmouth.

Prince. Thou speak'st as if I would deny my name.

Hotspur. My name is Harry Percy.

Prince.   Why, then I see
    A very valiant rebel of the name.
    I am the Prince of Wales; and think not, Percy,
    To share with me in glory any more:
    Two stars keep not their motion in one sphere;
    Nor can one England brook a double reign,
    Of Harry Percy and the Prince of Wales.

Hotspur. Nor shall it, Harry; for the hour is come
    To end the one of us; and would to God
    Thy name in arms were now as great as mine!

Prince. I'll make it greater ere I part from thee;
    And all the budding honours on thy crest
    I'll crop, to make a garland for my head.

Hotspur. I can no longer brook thy vanities.

They fight.

Enter Falstaff

Falstaff. Well said, Hal! to it, Hal! Nay, you shall find no
    boy's play here, I can tell you.
    Re-enter Douglas; *he fights with* Falstaff, *who falls down as if he
    were dead, and exit* Douglas. Hotspur *is wounded, and falls*

Hotspur. O, Harry, thou hast robb'd me of my youth!
    I better brook the loss of brittle life
    Than those proud titles thou hast won of me;
    They wound my thoughts worse than thy sword my flesh:
    But thought's the slave of life, and life time's fool;
    And time, that takes survey of all the world,
    Must have a stop. O, I could prophesy,
    But that the earthy and cold hand of death
    Lies on my tongue: no, Percy, thou art dust,
    And food for—

Dies.

Prince. For worms, brave Percy: fare thee well, great heart!
    Ill-weaved ambition, how much art thou shrunk!
    When that this body did contain a spirit,
    A kingdom for it was too small a bound;
    But now two paces of the vilest earth
    Is room enough: this earth that bears thee dead
    Bears not alive so stout a gentleman.
    If thou wert sensible of courtesy,
    I should not make so dear a show of zeal:
    But let my favours hide thy mangled face;
    And, even in thy behalf, I'll thank myself
    For doing these fair rites of tenderness.
    Adieu, and take thy praise with thee to heaven!

Thy ignominy sleep with thee in the grave,
But not remember'd in thy epitaph!

He spieth Falstaff *on the ground.*

What, old acquaintance! could not all this flesh
Keep in a little life? Poor Jack, farewell!
I could have better spared a better man:
O, I should have a heavy miss of thee,
If I were much in love with vanity!
Death hath not struck so fat a deer to-day,
Though many dearer, in this bloody fray.
Embowell'd will I see thee by and by:
Till then in blood by noble Percy lie.

Exit.

Falstaff. [*Rising up*] Embowelled! if thou embowel me to-day,
I'll give you leave to powder me and eat me too to-morrow.
'Sblood, 'twas time to counterfeit, or that hot termagant
Scot had paid me scot and lot too. Counterfeit? I lie, I am
no counterfeit: to die, is to be a counterfeit; for he is but
the counterfeit of a man who hath not the life of a man:
but to counterfeit dying, when a man thereby liveth, is
to be no counterfeit, but the true and perfect image of
life indeed. The better part of valour is discretion; in the
which better part I have saved my life. 'Zounds, I am
afraid of this gunpowder Percy, though be dead: how, if
he should counterfeit too, and rise? by my faith, I am
afraid he would prove the better counterfeit. Therefore
I'll make him sure; yea, and I'll swear I killed him. Why
may he not rise as well as I? Nothing confutes me but
eyes, and nobody sees me. Therefore, sirrah [*stabbing
him*], with a new wound in your thigh, come you along
with me.

Takes up Hotspur *on his back.*

Re-enter the Prince of Wales *and* Lord John of
Lancaster

Prince. Come, brother John; full bravely hast thou flesh'd
Thy maiden sword.

Lancaster. But, soft! whom have we here?
Did you not tell me this fat man was dead?

Prince. I did; I saw him dead,
Breathless and bleeding on the ground. Art thou alive?
Or is it fantasy that plays upon our eyesight?
I prithee, speak; we will not trust our eyes
Without our ears: thou art not what thou seem'st.

Falstaff. No, that's certain; I am not a double man: but if I be
not Jack Falstaff, then am I a Jack. There is Percy [*throwing the
body down*]: if your father will do me any honour, so; if not,
let him kill the next Percy himself. I look to be either earl or
duke, I can assure you.

Prince. Why, Percy I killed myself, and saw thee dead.

Falstaff. Didst thou? Lord, Lord, how this world is given to lying! I grant you I was down and out of breath; and so was he:
but we rose both at an instant, and fought a long hour by
Shrewsbury clock. If I may be believed, so; if not, let them
that should reward valour bear the sin upon their own heads.
I'll take it upon my death, I gave him this wound in the
thigh: if the man were alive, and would deny it, 'zounds, I
would make him eat a piece of my sword.

Lancaster. This is the strangest tale that ever I heard.

Prince. This is the strangest fellow, brother John.
Come, bring your luggage nobly on your back:
For my part, if a lie may do thee grace,
I'll gild it with the happiest terms I have.

A retreat is sounded.

The trumpet sounds retreat; the day is ours.
Come, brother, let us to the highest of the field,
To see what friends are living, who are dead.

> *Exeunt* Prince of Wales *and* Lancaster.

Falstaff. I'll follow, as they say, for reward. He that rewards
me, God reward him! If I do grow great, I'll grow less; for
I'll purge, and leave sack, and live cleanly as a nobleman
should do.

> *Exit.*

scene 5.   [*Another part of the field*]

The trumpets sound. Enter the King, Prince of Wales, Lord John
of Lancaster, Earl of Westmoreland, *with* Worcester *and*
Vernon *prisoners*

King. Thus ever did rebellion find rebuke.
Ill-spirited Worcester! did not we send grace,
Pardon and terms of love to all of you?
And wouldst thou turn our offers contrary?
Misuse the tenour of thy kinsman's trust?
Three knights upon our party slain to-day,
A noble earl and many a creature else
Had been alive this hour,
If like a Christian thou hadst truly borne
Betwixt our armies true intelligence.

Worcester. What I have done my safety urged me to;
And I embrace this fortune patiently,
Since not to be avoided it falls on me.

King. Bear Worcester to the death, and Vernon too:
Other offenders we will pause upon.

> *Exeunt* Worcester *and* Vernon, *guarded.*

How goes the field?

Prince. The noble Scot, Lord Douglas, when he saw
    The fortune of the day quite turn'd from him,
    The noble Percy slain, and all his men
    Upon the foot of fear, fled with the rest;
    And falling from a hill, he was so bruised
    That the pursuers took him. At my tent
    The Douglas is; and I beseech your grace
    I may dispose of him.

King.   With all my heart.

Prince. Then, brother John of Lancaster, to you
    This honourable bounty shall belong:

    Go to the Douglas, and deliver him
    Up to his pleasure, ransomless and free:
    His valours shown upon our crests to-day
    Hath taught us how to cherish such high deeds
    Even in the bosom of our adversaries.

Lancaster. I thank your grace for this high courtesy,
    Which I shall give away immediately.

King. Then this remains, that we divide our power.
    You, son John, and my cousin Westmoreland
    Towards York shall bend you with your dearest speed,
    To meet Northumberland and the prelate Scroop,
    Who, as we hear, are busily in arms:
    Myself and you, son Harry, will towards Wales,
    To fight with Glendower and the Earl of March.
    Rebellion in this land shall lose his sway,
    Meeting the check of such another day:
    And since this business so fair is done,
    Let us not leave till all our own be won.

                                   Exeunt.

william shakespeare

henry IV

part two

synopsis

The first reports from the Shrewsbury field of battle which come to the Earl of Northumberland are of the entire success of the rebellion against King Henry, but he finally hears the sad truth of the death of his son Hotspur at the hands of the Prince of Wales and the complete defeat of the insurgent forces, together with the tidings that the King has ordered an army under Prince John of Lancaster and the Earl of Westmoreland to proceed against the Archbishop of York and himself.

In a towering rage which his retainers strive to calm, Northumberland makes plans to join his forces with those of the Archbishop, and the prelate, warned by Hotspur's recklessness, ponders the chances of battle with his followers, *Hastings* and *Mowbray,* son of the King's old enemy, the banished Duke of Norfolk, but determines to oppose the royal army in Yorkshire, in view of Henry's forces being divided on three fronts, against the French, the Welsh and the rebels, and in confident expectation of reinforcements from Northumberland.

The Earl's wife and daughter-in-law, Hotspur's widow, urge

him, however, to let his allies prove their own strength, and at length prevail upon him to take refuge for a time in Scotland from his enemies, while King Henry, ill both in body and soul, gives up the Welsh campaign and returns with the Prince of Wales to London after dispatching a large additional force against the rebels.

Meanwhile, Sir John Falstaff, commissioned by the King to enlist soldiers on his way north to join Prince John's army, is lingering in London with his old associates at the Boar's-Head Tavern. He barely escapes arrest for debt at the instance of the Hostess, Mistress Quickly, but with his usual effrontery capitalizes on his present employment and borrows still more money from the stupid woman to continue his drunken roistering in which the Prince and his companion Poins join, disguised as waiters upon Falstaff's table. Messengers arriving from Westminster with news of important dispatches from the north quickly restore the Prince to his sense of duty, and he hurries away to be in attendance on his sick father. Falstaff is haled to his job by army officers, and journeying to Gloucestershire to the home of his friend, Justice Shallow, the fat rascal fills his purse by allowing the able-bodied recruits he has selected for the northern army to buy themselves off, while he retains the weaklings for the King's service.

In the rebel camp in Yorkshire, the Archbishop of York, Mowbray and Hastings receive the cold regrets of Northumberland that he cannot join them, but feeling that they are sufficiently strong they prepare for battle as the royal forces approach. Instead of hazarding an engagement, Prince John sends the Earl of Westmoreland to parley with the insurgents in Gaultree Forest, and asks for a presentation of their alleged grievances which the Prince later promises on his sacred word of honor to have redressed upon the immediate disbandment of both armies. The rebels take him at his word and dismiss their forces, whereupon the cold-blooded, perjured Prince arrests for high treason and condemns

to death the Archbishop and his associates, with the dastardly assertion that he had pledged nothing but the redress of grievances, and, having given secret instructions to his own army to
remain intact, he orders them to pursue and slaughter the scattered insurgents.

At Westminster, Henry's counsellor, the Earl of Warwick, en-
deavors to ease the mind of the sleepless, conscience-stricken
King by assuring him of the ultimate success of his armies, and
of the death of his enemy Glendower, the powerful Welsh warrior, but the monarch's sick thoughts travel back to Richard's
deposition and to the days of his old friendship with Northumberland. Apathetically, he receives the tidings the messengers
bring, one by one, of the overthrow of Northumberland by the
Sheriff of Yorkshire and the routing of the Archbishop of York's
rebel army. Past hope and comfort, the King falls into a deep stu-
por which deceives the Prince of Wales watching alone at his
bedside, and, thinking his father dead, he carries the crown to an
adjoining room where he may mourn in solitude. Awakening
and finding his crown gone, Henry accuses his son of desiring his
death, and it is only through the pleading of the Prince, coupled
with Warwick's testimony of his genuine grief, that the two are
reconciled. The dying King advises his son to avert further do-
mestic rebellions by engaging in foreign wars, and is carried to
breathe his last in the Jerusalem Chamber at Westminster and
thus fulfil a prophecy that he would die in Jerusalem.

Again sponging on his friends in Gloucestershire, Falstaff hears
of the King's death, calls for his horse and proceeds posthaste to
London for the coronation of his old friend, Prince Hal, promis-
ing all his companions knighthoods, dignities and riches, and to
Justice Shallow any office in the land that he may choose. But the
onetime wastrel Prince, already approved as a levelheaded, effi-
cient soldier, and now putting duty to the state before all other
considerations, rebukes Falstaff publicly and orders his arrest and

banishment, at the same time arranging for his maintenance for life. He appoints as one of his advisers the same Lord Chief-Justice who once committed him to jail when as Prince Hal he struck the judge in the face for sentencing to imprisonment one of his riotous companions. And, crowned King as Henry V, he calls Parliament to discuss the invasion of France.

historical data

The Second Part of *Henry IV* continues history from 1403 to the King's death and the accession of Henry V in 1413. Its sources are the same as those from which Part One was derived, Shakespeare, in this instance, leaning rather more heavily upon *The Famous Victories of Henry the Fifth* for episodes in his narrative.

As was the case in the Induction to *The Taming of the Shrew,* Part Two contains many references to familiar places and persons with whom the dramatist was acquainted. The character of Falstaff is further developed, and a touch of pathos added in the contrast of his old age with his riotous manner of living. Shallow and Silence, the country justices, appear to have been invented solely as foils for Sir John.

As no reference is made on the title page of the first quarto edition of the First Part to any sequel, it seems evident that Part Two, which is an epilogue to *The Historie of Henry IV,* was not written until after the publication of the first part. Ben Jonson mentions "Justice Silence" in his *Every Man out of his Humor,* acted in 1599, so the date of composition of this play may be fixed with reasonable certainty as 1598.

dramatis personæ

Rumour, *the Presenter*.

King Henry *the Fourth*.

Henry, Prince of Wales, *after-*
wards King Henry V.,

Thomas, Duke of Clarence, } *his sons*.

Prince John of Lancaster,

Prince Humphrey of Gloucester,

Earl of Warwick.

Earl of Westmoreland.

Earl of Surrey.

Gower.

Harcourt.

Blunt.

Lord Chief Justice *of the King's Bench*.

A Servant *of the Chief Justice*.

Earl of Northumberland.

Scroop, *Archbishop of York*.

Lord Mowbray.

Lord Hastings.

Lord Bardolph.

Sir John Colevile.

Travers and Morton, *retainers of Northumberland*.

Sir John Falstaff.

His Page.

Bardolph.

Pistol.

Poins.

Peto.

Shallow, } *country justices*.
Silence,

Davy, *servant to Shallow*.

Mouldy, Shadow, Wart, Feeble, *and* Bullcalf, *recruits*.

Fang *and* Snare, *sheriff's officers*.

Lady Northumberland.

Lady Percy.

Mistress Quickly, *hostess of a tavern in Eastcheap*.

Doll Tearsheet.

Lords *and* Attendants; Porter, Drawers, Beadles, Grooms, &
c. A Dancer, *speaker of the epilogue*.

Scene: England.

induction

Enter Rumour, *painted full of tongues*

Rumour. Open your ears; for which of you will stop
    The vent of hearing when loud Rumour speaks?
    I, from the orient to the drooping west,
    Making the wind my post-horse, still unfold
    The acts commenced on this ball of earth:
    Upon my tongues continual slanders ride,
    The which in every language I pronounce,
    Stuffing the ears of men with false reports.
    I speak of peace, while covert enmity
    Under the smile of safety wounds the world:
    And who but Rumour, who but only I,
    Make fearful musters and prepared defence,
    Whiles the big year, swoln with some other grief,
    Is thought with child by the stern tyrant war,
    And no such matter? Rumour is a pipe
    Blown by surmises, jealousies, conjectures,
    And of so easy and so plain a stop

That the blunt monster with uncounted heads,
The still-discordant wavering multitude,
Can play upon it. But what need I thus
My well-known body to anatomize
Among my household? Why is Rumour here?
I run before King Harry's victory;
Who in a bloody field by Shrewsbury
Hath beaten down young Hotspur and his troops,
Quenching the flame of bold rebellion
Even with the rebels' blood. But what mean I
To speak so true at first? my office is
To noise abroad that Harry Monmouth fell
Under the wrath of noble Hotspur's sword,
And that the king before the Douglas' rage
Stoop'd his anointed head as low as death.
This have I rumour'd through the peasant towns
Between that royal field of Shrewsbury
And this worm-eaten hold of ragged stone,
Where Hotspur's father, old Northumberland,
Lies crafty-sick: the posts come tiring on,
And not a man of them brings other news
Than they have learn'd of me: from Rumour's tongues
They bring smooth comforts false, worse than true wrongs.

Exit.

act 1

scene 1. [*The same*]

Enter Lord Bardolph

Lord Bardolph. Who keeps the gate here, ho?
The Porter opens the gate

Where is the earl?

Porter. What shall I say you are?

Lord Bardolph. Tell thou the earl
   That the Lord Bardolph doth attend him here.

Porter. His lordship is walk'd forth into the orchard:
   Please it your honour, knock but at the gate,
   And he himself will answer.
Enter Northumberland

Lord Bardolph.   Here comes the earl.

Exit Porter.

Northumberland. What news, Lord Bardolph? every minute now
   Should be the father of some stratagem:
   The times are wild; contention, like a horse
   Full of high feeding, madly hath broke loose
   And bears down all before him.

Lord Bardolph.   Noble earl,
  I bring you certain news from Shrewsbury.

Northumberland. Good, an God will!

Lord Bardolph.   As good as heart can wish:
  The king is almost wounded to the death;
  And, in the fortune of my lord your son,
  Prince Harry slain outright; and both the Blunts
  Kill'd by the hand of Douglas; young Prince John
  And Westmoreland and Stafford fled the field;
  And Harry Monmouth's brawn, the hulk Sir John,
  Is prisoner to your son: O, such a day,
  So fought, so follow'd and so fairly won,
  Came not till now to dignify the times,
  Since Cæsar's fortunes!

Northumberland.   How is this derived?
  Saw you the field? came you from Shrewsbury?

Lord Bardolph. I spake with one, my lord, that came from thence,
  A gentleman well bred and of good name,
  That freely render'd me these news for true.

Northumberland. Here comes my servant Travers, whom I sent
  On Tuesday last to listen after news.
                    Enter Travers

Lord Bardolph. My lord, I over-rode him on the way;
  And he is furnish'd with no certainties
  More than he haply may retail from me.

Northumberland. Now, Travers, what good tidings comes
  with you?

Travers. My lord, Sir John Umfrevile turn'd me back
  With joyful tidings; and, being better horsed,
  Out-rode me. After him came spurring hard
  A gentleman, almost forspent with speed,

That stopp'd by me to breathe his bloodied horse.
He ask'd the way to Chester; and of him
I did demand what news from Shrewsbury:
He told me that rebellion had bad luck,
And that young Harry Percy's spur was cold.
With that, he gave his able horse the head,
And bending forward struck his armed heels
Against the panting sides of his poor jade
Up to the rowel-head, and starting so
He seem'd in running to devour the way,
Staying no longer question.

Northumberland.   Ha? Again:
Said he young Harry Percy's spur was cold?
Of Hotspur Coldspur? that rebellion
Had met ill luck?

Lord Bardolph.   My lord, I'll tell you what;
If my young lord your son have not the day,
Upon mine honour, for a silken point
I'll give my barony: never talk of it.

Northumberland. Why should that gentleman that rode by
Travers
Give then such instances of loss?

Lord Bardolph.   Who, he?
He was some hilding fellow that had stolen
The horse he rode on, and, upon my life,
Spoke at a venture. Look, here comes more news.

                  Enter Morton

Northumberland. Yea, this man's brow, like to a title-leaf,
Foretells the nature of a tragic volume:
So looks the strond whereon the imperious flood
Hath left a witness'd usurpation.
Say, Morton, didst thou come from Shrewsbury?

Morton. I ran from Shrewsbury, my noble lord;
    Where hateful death put on his ugliest mask
    To fright our party.

Northumberland.   How doth my son and brother?
    Thou tremblest; and the whiteness in thy cheek
    Is apter than thy tongue to tell thy errand.
    Even such a man, so faint, so spiritless,
    So dull, so dead in look, so woe-begone,
    Drew Priam's curtain in the dead of night,
    And would have told him half his Troy was burnt;
    But Priam found the fire ere he his tongue,
    And I my Percy's death ere thou report'st it.
    This thou wouldst say, 'Your son did thus and thus;
    Your brother thus: so fought the noble Douglas:'
    Stopping my greedy ear with their bold deeds:
    But in the end, to stop my ear indeed,
    Thou hast a sigh to blow away this praise,
    Ending with 'Brother, son, and all are dead.'

Morton. Douglas is living, and your brother, yet;
    But, for my lord your son,—

Northumberland.   Why, he is dead.
    See what a ready tongue suspicion hath!
    He that but fears the thing he would not know
    Hath by instinct knowledge from others' eyes
    That what he fear'd is chanced. Yet speak, Morton;
    Tell thou an earl his divination lies,
    And I will take it as a sweet disgrace,
    And make thee rich for doing me such wrong.

Morton. You are too great to be by me gainsaid:
    Your spirit is too true, your fears too certain.

Northumberland. Yet, for all this, say not that Percy's dead.
    I see a strange confession in thine eye:

Thou shakest thy head, and hold'st it fear or sin
To speak a truth. If he be slain, say so;
The tongue offends not that reports his death:
And he doth sin that doth belie the dead,
Not he which says the dead is not alive.
Yet the first bringer of unwelcome news
Hath but a losing office, and his tongue
Sounds ever after as a sullen bell,
Remember'd tolling a departing friend.

Lord Bardolph. I cannot think, my lord, your son is dead.

Morton. I am sorry I should force you to believe
That which I would to God I had not seen;
But these mine eyes saw him in bloody state,
Rendering faint quittance, wearied and outbreathed,
To Harry Monmouth; whose swift wrath beat down
The never-daunted Percy to the earth,
From whence with life he never more sprung up.
In few, his death, whose spirit lent a fire
Even to the dullest peasant in his camp,
Being bruited once, took fire and heat away
From the best-temper'd courage in his troops;
For from his metal was his party steel'd;
Which once in him abated, all the rest
Turn'd on themselves, like dull and heavy lead:
And as the thing that's heavy in itself,
Upon enforcement flies with greatest speed,
So did our men, heavy in Hotspur's loss,
Lend to this weight such lightness with their fear
That arrows fled not swifter toward their aim
Than did our soldiers, aiming at their safety,
Fly from the field. Then was that noble Worcester
Too soon ta'en prisoner; and that furious Scot,

The bloody Douglas, whose well-labouring sword
Had three times slain the appearance of the king,
'Gan vail his stomach and did grace the shame
Of those that turn'd their backs, and in his flight,
Stumbling in fear, was took. The sum of all
Is that the king hath won, and hath sent out
A speedy power to encounter you, my lord,
Under the conduct of young Lancaster
And Westmoreland. This is the news at full.

Northumberland. For this I shall have time enough to mourn.
In poison there is physic; and these news,
Having been well, that would have made me sick,
Being sick, have in some measure made me well:
And as the wretch, whose fever-weaken'd joints,
Like strengthless hinges, buckle under life,
Impatient of his fit, breaks like a fire
Out of his keeper's arms, even so my limbs,
Weaken'd with grief, being now enraged with grief,
Are thrice themselves. Hence, therefore, thou nice crutch!
A scaly gauntlet now with joints of steel
Must glove this hand: and hence, thou sickly coif!
Thou art a guard too wanton for the head
Which princes, flesh'd with conquest, aim to hit.
Now bind my brows with iron; and approach
The ragged'st hour that time and spite dare bring
To frown upon the enraged Northumberland!
Let heaven kiss earth! now let not Nature's hand
Keep the wild flood confined! let order die!
And let this world no longer be a stage
To feed contention in a lingering act;
But let one spirit of the first-born Cain
Reign in all bosoms, that, each heart being set

On bloody courses, the rude scene may end,
And darkness be the burier of the dead!

Lord Bardolph. This strained passion doth you wrong, my lord.

Morton. Sweet earl, divorce not wisdom from your honour,
The lives of all your loving complices
Lean on your health; the which, if you give o'er
To stormy passion, must perforce decay.
You cast the event of war, my noble lord,
And summ'd the account of chance, before you said
'Let us make head.' It was your presurmise,
That, in the dole of blows, your son might drop:
You knew he walk'd o'er perils, on an edge,
More likely to fall in than to get o'er;
You were advised his flesh was capable
Of wounds and scars, and that his forward spirit
Would lift him where most trade of danger ranged:
Yet did you say 'Go forth;' and none of this,
Though strongly apprehended, could restrain
The stiff-borne action: what hath then befallen,
Or what hath this bold enterprise brought forth,
More than that being which was like to be?

Lord Bardolph. We all that are engaged to this loss
Knew that we ventured on such dangerous seas
That if we wrought out life 'twas ten to one;
And yet we ventured, for the gain proposed
Choked the respect of likely peril fear'd;
And since we are o'erset, venture again.
Come, we will all put forth, body and goods.

Morton. 'Tis more than time: and my most noble lord,
I hear for certain, and dare speak the truth,
The gentle Archbishop of York is up

With well–appointed powers: he is a man
Who with a double surety binds his followers.
My lord your son had only but the corpse,
But shadows and the shows of men, to fight;
For that same word, rebellion, did divide
The action of their bodies from their souls;
And they did fight with queasiness, constrain'd,
As men drink potions, that their weapons only
Seem'd on our side; but, for their spirits and souls,
This word, rebellion, it had froze them up,
As fish are in a pond. But now the bishop
Turns insurrection to religion:
Supposed sincere and holy in his thoughts,
He's followed both with body and with mind;
And doth enlarge his rising with the blood
Of fair King Richard, scraped from Pomfret stones;
Derives from heaven his quarrel and his cause;
Tells them he doth bestride a bleeding land,
Gasping for life under great Bolingbroke;
And more and less do flock to follow him.

Northumberland. I knew of this before; but, to speak truth,
This present grief had wiped it from my mind.
Go in with me; and counsel every man
The aptest way for safety and revenge:
Get posts and letters, and make friends with speed:
Never so few, and never yet more need.

            Exeunt.

scene 2. [*London. A street*]

Enter Falstaff, *with his* Page *bearing his sword and buckler*

Falstaff. Sirrah, you giant, what says the doctor to my water?

Page. He said, sir, the water itself was a good healthy water; but, for the party that owed it, he might have moe diseases than he knew for.

Falstaff. Men of all sorts take a pride to gird at me: the brain of this foolish-compounded clay, man, is not able to invent any thing that tends to laughter, more than I invent or is invented on me: I am not only witty in myself, but the cause that wit is in other men. I do here walk before thee like a sow that hath overwhelmed all her litter but one. If the prince put thee into my service for any other reason than to set me off, why then I have no judgement. Thou whoreson mandrake, thou art fitter to be worn in my cap than to wait at my heels. I was never manned with an agate till now: but I will inset you neither in gold nor silver, but in vile apparel, and send you back again to your master for a jewel,—the juvenal, the prince your master, whose chin is not yet fledge. I will sooner have a beard grow in the palm of my hand than he shall get one off his cheek; and yet he will not stick to say his face is a face-royal: God may finish it when he will, 'tis not a hair amiss yet: he may keep it still at a face-royal, for a barber shall never earn sixpence out of it; and yet he'll be crowing as if he had writ man ever since his father was a bachelor. He may keep his own grace, but he's almost out of mine, I can assure him. What said Master Dombledon about the satin for my short cloak and my slops?

Page. He said, sir, you should procure him better assurance than

Bardolph: he would not take his bond and yours, he liked not the security.

Falstaff. Let him be damned, like the glutton! pray God his tongue be hotter! A whoreson Achitophel! a rascally yea-forsooth knave! to bear a gentleman in hand, and then stand upon security! The whoreson smooth-pates do now wear nothing but high shoes and bunches of keys at their girdles; and if a man is through with them in honest taking up, then they must stand upon security. I had as lief they would put ratsbane in my mouth as offer to stop it with security. I looked a' should have sent me two and twenty yards of satin, as I am a true knight, and he sends me security. Well, he may sleep in security; for he hath the horn of abundance, and the lightness of his wife shines through it: and yet cannot he see, though he have his own lanthorn to light him. Where's Bardolph?

Page. He's gone into Smithfield to buy your worship a horse.

Falstaff. I bought him in Paul's, and he'll buy me a horse in Smithfield: an I could get me but a wife in the stews, I were manned, horsed, and wived.

Enter the Lord Chief Justice *and* Servant

Page. Sir, here comes the nobleman that committed the prince for striking him about Bardolph.

Falstaff. Wait close; I will not see him.

Chief Justice. What's he that goes there?

Servant. Falstaff, an't please your lordship.

Chief Justice. He that was in question for the robbery?

Servant. He, my lord: but he hath since done good service at Shrewsbury; and, as I hear, is now going with some charge to the Lord John of Lancaster.

Chief Justice. What, to York? Call him back again.

Servant. Sir John Falstaff!

Falstaff. Boy, tell him I am deaf.

Page. You must speak louder; my master is deaf.

Chief Justice. I am sure he is, to the hearing of any thing good. Go, pluck him by the elbow; I must speak with him.

Servant. Sir John!

Falstaff. What! a young knave, and begging! Is there not wars? is there not employment? doth not the king lack subjects? do not the rebels need soldiers? Though it be a shame to be on any side but one, it is worse shame to beg than to be on the worst side, were it worse than the name of rebellion can tell how to make it.

Servant. You mistake me, sir.

Falstaff. Why, sir, did I say you were an honest man? setting my knighthood and my soldiership aside, I had lied in my throat, if I had said so.

Servant. I pray you, sir, then set your knighthood and your sol-diership aside; and give me leave to tell you, you lie in your throat, if you say I am any other than an honest man.

Falstaff. I give thee leave to tell me so? I lay aside that which grows to me? If thou gettest any leave of me, hang me; if thou takest leave, thou wert better be hanged. You hunt counter: hence! avaunt!

Servant. Sir, my lord would speak with you.

Chief Justice. Sir John Falstaff, a word with you.

Falstaff. My good lord! God give your lordship good time of day. I am glad to see your lordship abroad: I heard say your lordship was sick: I hope your lordship goes abroad by advice.

Your lordship, though not clean past your youth, hath yet some smack of age in you, some relish of the saltness of time; and I most humbly beseech your lordship to have a reverend care of your health.

Chief Justice. Sir John, I sent for you before your expedition to Shrewsbury.

Falstaff. An't please your lordship, I hear his majesty is returned with some discomfort from Wales.

Chief Justice. I talk not of his majesty: you would not come when I sent for you.

Falstaff. And I hear, moreover, his highness is fallen into this same whoreson apoplexy.

Chief Justice. Well, God mend him! I pray you, let me speak with you.

Falstaff. This apoplexy is, as I take it, a kind of lethargy, an't please your lordship; a kind of sleeping in the blood, a whoreson tingling.

Chief Justice. What tell you me of it? be it as it is.

Falstaff. It hath it original from much grief, from study and perturbation of the brain: I have read the cause of his effects in Galen: it is a kind of deafness.

Chief Justice. I think you are fallen into the disease; for you hear not what I say to you.

Falstaff. Very well, my lord, very well: rather, an't please you, it is the disease of not listening, the malady of not marking, that I am troubled withal.

Chief Justice. To punish you by the heels would amend the attention of your ears; and I care not if I do become your physician.

Falstaff. I am as poor as Job, my lord, but not so patient: your lordship may minister the potion of imprisonment to me in respect of poverty; but how I should be your patient to follow your prescriptions, the wise may make some dram of a scruple, or indeed a scruple itself.

Chief Justice. I sent for you, when there were matters against you for your life, to come speak with me.

Falstaff. As I was then advised by my learned counsel in the laws of this land-service, I did not come.

Chief Justice. Well, the truth is, Sir John, you live in great infamy.

Falstaff. He that buckles him in my belt cannot live in less.

Chief Justice. Your means are very slender, and your waste is great.

Falstaff. I would it were otherwise; I would my means were greater, and my waist slenderer.

Chief Justice. You have misled the youthful prince.

Falstaff. The young prince hath misled me: I am the fellow with the great belly, and he my dog.

Chief Justice. Well, I am loath to gall a new-healed wound: your day's service at Shrewsbury hath a little gilded over your night's exploit on Gadshill: you may thank the unquiet time for your quiet o'er-posting that action.

Falstaff. My lord?

Chief Justice. But since all is well, keep it so: wake not a sleeping wolf.

Falstaff. To wake a wolf is as bad as to smell a fox.

Chief Justice. What! you are as a candle, the better part burnt out.

Falstaff. A wassail candle, my lord, all tallow: if I did say of wax, my growth would approve the truth.

Chief Justice. There is not a white hair on your face but should have his effect of gravity.

Falstaff. His effect of gravy, gravy, gravy.

Chief Justice. You follow the young prince up and down, like his ill angel.

Falstaff. Not so, my lord; your ill angel is light; but I hope he that looks upon me will take me without weighing: and yet, in some respects, I grant, I cannot go: I cannot tell. Virtue is of so little regard in these costermonger times that true valour is turned bear-herd: pregnancy is made a tapster, and hath his quick wit wasted in giving reckonings: all the other gifts appertinent to man, as the malice of this age shapes them, are not worth a gooseberry. You that are old consider not the capacities of us that are young; you do measure the heat of our livers with the bitterness of your galls: and we that are in the vaward of our youth, I must confess, are wags too.

Chief Justice. Do you set down your name in the scroll of youth, that are written down old with all the characters of age? Have you not a moist eye? a dry hand? a yellow cheek? a white beard? a decreasing leg? an increasing belly? is not your voice broken? your wind short? your chin double? your wit single? and every part about you blasted with antiquity? and will you yet call yourself young? Fie, fie, fie, Sir John!

Falstaff. My lord, I was born about three of the clock in the afternoon, with a white head and something a round belly. For my voice, I have lost it with halloing and singing of anthems. To approve my youth further, I will not: the truth is, I am only old in judgement and understanding; and he that will caper with me for a thousand marks, let him lend me the money, and have at him. For the box of the ear that the prince gave you, he gave it like a rude prince, and you took it like a sensible lord. I have checked him for it, and the young lion repents; [*Aside*] marry, not in ashes and sackcloth, but in new silk and old sack.

Chief Justice. Well, God send the prince a better companion!

Falstaff. God send the companion a better prince! I cannot rid my hands of him.

Chief Justice. Well, the king hath severed you and Prince Harry: I hear you are going with Lord John of Lancaster against the Archbishop and the Earl of Northumberland.

Falstaff. Yea; I thank your pretty sweet wit for it. But look you pray, all you that kiss my lady Peace at home, that our armies join not in a hot day; for, by the Lord, I take but two shirts out with me, and I mean not to sweat extraordinarily: if it be a hot day, and I brandish any thing but a bottle, I would I might never spit white again. There is not a dangerous action can peep out his head, but I am thrust upon it: well, I cannot last ever: but it was alway yet the trick of our English nation, if they have a good thing, to make it too common. If ye will needs say I am an old man, you should give me rest. I would to God my name were not so terrible to the enemy as it is: I were better to be eaten to death with a rust than to be scoured to nothing with perpetual motion.

Chief Justice. Well, be honest, be honest; and God bless your expedition!

Falstaff. Will your lordship lend me a thousand pound to furnish me forth?

Chief Justice. Not a penny, not a penny; you are too impatient to bear crosses. Fare you well: commend me to my cousin Westmoreland.

Exeunt Chief Justice *and* Servant.

Falstaff. If I do, fillip me with a three-man beetle. A man can no more separate age and covetousness than a' can part young

limbs and lechery: but the gout galls the one, and the pox
pinches the other; and so both the degrees prevent my curses.
Boy!

Page. Sir?

Falstaff. What money is in my purse?

Page. Seven groats and two pence.

Falstaff. I can get no remedy against this consumption of the
purse: borrowing only lingers and lingers it out, but the disease is incurable. Go bear this letter to my Lord of Lancaster;
this to the prince; this to the Earl of Westmoreland; and this
to old Mistress Ursula, whom I have weekly sworn to marry
since I perceived the first white hair on my chin. About it:
you know where to find me. [*Exit* Page] A pox of this gout!
or, a gout of this pox! for the one or the other plays the
rogue with my great toe. 'Tis no matter if I do halt; I have
the wars for my colour, and my pension shall seem the more
reasonable. A good wit will make use of any thing: I will
turn diseases to commodity.

Exit.

scene 3.   [*York. The* Archbishop's *palace*]

Enter the Archbishop, *the* Lords Hastings, Mowbray, *and* Bardolph

Archbishop. Thus have you heard our cause and known our
      means;
    And, my most noble friends, I pray you all,
    Speak plainly your opinions of our hopes:
    And first, lord marshal, what say you to it?

Mowbray. I well allow the occasion of our arms;
    But gladly would be better satisfied
    How in our means we should advance ourselves

To look with forehead bold and big enough
Upon the power and puissance of the king.

Hastings. Our present musters grow upon the file
To five and twenty thousand men of choice;
And our supplies live largely in the hope
Of great Northumberland, whose bosom burns
With an incensed fire of injuries.

Lord Bardolph. The question then, Lord Hastings, standeth thus;
Whether our present five and twenty thousand
May hold up head without Northumberland?

Hastings. With him, we may.

Lord Bardolph.   Yea, marry, there's the point:
But if without him we be thought too feeble,
My judgement is, we should not step too far
Till we had his assistance by the hand;
For in a theme so bloody-faced as this
Conjecture, expectation, and surmise
Of aids incertain should not be admitted.

Archbishop. 'Tis very true, Lord Bardolph; for indeed
It was young Hotspur's case at Shrewsbury.

Lord Bardolph. It was, my lord; who lined himself with hope,
Eating the air on promise of supply,
Flattering himself in project of a power
Much smaller than the smallest of his thoughts:
And so, with great imagination
Proper to madmen, led his powers to death,
And winking leap'd into destruction.

Hastings. But, by your leave, it never yet did hurt
To lay down likelihoods and forms of hope.

Lord Bardolph. Yes, if this present quality of war,
Indeed the instant action: a cause on foot,

Lives so in hope, as in an early spring
We see the appearing buds; which to prove fruit,
Hope gives not so much warrant as despair
That frosts will bite them. When we mean to build,
We first survey the plot, then draw the model;
And when we see the figure of the house,
Then must we rate the cost of the erection;
Which if we find outweighs ability,
What do we then but draw anew the model
In fewer offices, or at least desist
To build at all? Much more, in this great work,
Which is almost to pluck a kingdom down
And set another up, should we survey
The plot of situation and the model,
Consent upon a sure foundation,
Question surveyors, know our own estate,
How able such a work to undergo,
To weigh against his opposite; or else
We fortify in paper and in figures,
Using the names of men instead of men:
Like one that draws the model of a house
Beyond his power to build it; who, half through,
Gives o'er and leaves his part-created cost
A naked subject to the weeping clouds,
And waste for churlish winter's tyranny.

Hastings. Grant that our hopes, yet likely of fair birth,
   Should be still-born, and that we now possess'd
   The utmost man of expectation,
   I think we are a body strong enough,
   Even as we are, to equal with the king.

Lord Bardolph. What, is the king but five and twenty thousand?

Hastings. To us no more; nay, not so much, Lord Bardolph.

For his divisions, as the times do brawl,
Are in three heads: one power against the French,
And one against Glendower; perforce a third
Must take up us: so is the unfirm king
In three divided; and his coffers sound
With hollow poverty and emptiness.

Archbishop. That he should draw his several strengths together
And come against us in full puissance,
Need not be dreaded.

Hastings.   If he should do so,
He leaves his back unarm'd; the French and Welsh
Baying him at the heels: never fear that.

Lord Bardolph. Who is it like should lead his forces hither?

Hastings. The Duke of Lancaster and Westmoreland;
Against the Welsh, himself and Harry Monmouth:
But who is substituted 'gainst the French,
I have no certain notice.

Archbishop.   Let us on,
And publish the occasion of our arms.
The commonwealth is sick of their own choice;
Their over-greedy love hath surfeited:
An habitation giddy and unsure
Hath he that buildeth on the vulgar heart.
O thou fond many, with what loud applause
Didst thou beat heaven with blessing Bolingbroke,
Before he was what thou wouldst have him be!
And being now trimm'd in thine own desires,
Thou, beastly feeder, art so full of him,
That thou provokst thyself to cast him up.
So, so, thou common dog, didst thou disgorge
Thy glutton bosom of the royal Richard;
And now thou wouldst eat thy dead vomit up,

And howl'st to find it. What trust is in these times?
They that, when Richard lived, would have him die,
Are now become enamour'd on his grave:
Thou, that threw'st dust upon his goodly head
When through proud London he came sighing on
After the admired heels of Bolingbroke,
Criest now 'O earth, yield us that king again,
And take thou this!' O thoughts of men accursed!
Past and to come seems best; things present, worst.

Mowbray. Shall we go draw our numbers, and set on?

Hastings. We are time's subjects, and time bids be gone.

Exeunt.

act 2

scene 1. [*London. A street*]

Enter Hostess, Fang *and his* Boy *with her, and* Snare *following*

Hostess. Master Fang, have you entered the action?

Fang. It is entered.

Hostess. Where's your yeoman? Is 't a lusty yeoman? will a' stand to 't?

Fang. Sirrah, where's Snare?

Hostess. O Lord, ay! good Master Snare.

Snare. Here, here.

Fang. Snare, we must arrest Sir John Falstaff.

Hostess. Yea, good Master Snare; I have entered him and all.

Snare. It may chance cost some of us our lives, for he will stab.

Hostess. Alas the day! take heed of him; he stabbed me in mine own house, most beastly in good faith, he cares not what mischief he does, if his weapon be out: he will foin like any devil; he will spare neither man, woman, nor child.

Fang. If I can close with him, I care not for his thrust.

Hostess. No, nor I neither: I'll be at your elbow.

Fang. An I but fist him once; an a' come but within my vice,—

Hostess. I am undone by his going; I warrant you, he's an infinitive thing upon my score. Good Master Fang, hold him sure: good Master Snare, let him not 'scape. A' comes continuantly to Pie-corner—saving your manhoods—to buy a saddle; and he is indited to dinner to the Lubber's-head in Lumbert street, to Master Smooth's the silkman: I pray ye, since my exion is entered and my case so openly known to the world, let him be brought in to his answer. A hundred mark is a long one for a poor lone woman to bear: and I have borne, and borne, and borne; and have been fubbed off, and fubbed off, and fubbed off, from this day to that day, that it is a shame to be thought on. There is no honesty in such dealing; unless a woman should be made an ass and a beast, to bear every knave's wrong. Yonder he comes; and that arrant malmsey-nose knave, Bardolph, with him. Do your offices, do your offices: Master Fang and Master Snare, do me, do me, do me your offices.

Enter Falstaff, Page, *and* Bardolph

Falstaff. How now! whose mare's dead? what's the matter?

Fang. Sir John, I arrest you at the suit of Mistress Quickly.

Falstaff. Away, varlets! Draw, Bardolph: cut me off the villain's head: throw the quean in the channel.

Hostess. Throw me in the channel! I'll throw thee in the channel. Wilt thou? wilt thou? thou bastardly rogue! Murder, murder! Ah, thou honey-suckle villain! wilt thou kill God's officers and the king's? Ah, thou honey-seed rogue! thou art a honey-seed, a man-queller, and a woman-queller.

Falstaff. Keep them off, Bardolph.

Fang. A rescue! a rescue!

Hostess. Good people, bring a rescue or two. Thou wo't, wo't thou? thou wo't, wo't ta? do, do, thou rogue! do, thou hempseed!

Page. Away, you scullion! you rampallian! you fustilarian! I'll tickle your catastrophe.

   Enter the Lord Chief Justice, *and his men*

Chief Justice. What is the matter? keep the peace here, ho!

Hostess. Good my lord, be good to me. I beseech you, stand to me.

Chief Justice. How now, Sir John! what are you brawling here? Doth this become your place, your time and business? You should have been well on your way to York. Stand from him, fellow: wherefore hang'st upon him?

Hostess. O my most worshipful lord, an 't please your grace, I am a poor widow of Eastcheap, and he is arrested at my suit.

Chief Justice. For what sum?

Hostess. It is more than for some, my lord; it is for all, all I have. He hath eaten me out of house and home; he hath put all my substance into that fat belly of his: but I will have some of it out again, or I will ride thee o' nights like the mare.

Falstaff. I think I am as like to ride the mare, if I have any vantage of ground to get up.

Chief Justice. How comes this, Sir John? Fie! what man of good temper would endure this tempest of exclamation? Are you not ashamed to enforce a poor widow to so rough a course to come by her own?

Falstaff. What is the gross sum that I owe thee?

Hostess. Marry, if thou wert an honest man, thyself and the

money too. Thou didst swear to me upon a parcel-gilt gob-
let, sitting in my Dolphin-chamber, at the round table, by a
sea-coal fire, upon Wednesday in Wheeson week, when the
prince broke thy head for liking his father to a singing-man
of Windsor, thou didst swear to me then, as I was washing
thy wound, to marry me and make me my lady thy wife.
Canst thou deny it? Did not goodwife Keech, the butcher's
wife, come in then and call me gossip Quickly? coming in to
borrow a mess of vinegar; telling us she had a good dish of
prawns; whereby thou didst desire to eat some; whereby I
told thee they were ill for a green wound? And didst thou
not, when she was gone down stairs, desire me to be no more
so familiarity with such poor people; saying that ere long
they should call me madam? And didst thou not kiss me and
bid me fetch thee thirty shillings? I put thee now to thy
book-oath: deny it, if thou canst.

Falstaff. My lord, this is a poor mad soul; and she says up and
down the town that her eldest son is like you: she hath been
in good case, and the truth is, poverty hath distracted her. But
for these foolish officers, I beseech you I may have redress
against them.

Chief Justice. Sir John, Sir John, I am well acquainted with your
manner of wrenching the true cause the false way. It is not a
confident brow, nor the throng of words that come with
such more than impudent sauciness from you, can thrust me
from a level consideration: you have, as it appears to me, prac-
tised upon the easy-yielding spirit of this woman, and made
her serve your uses both in purse and in person.

Hostess. Yea, in truth, my lord.

Chief Justice. Pray thee, peace. Pay her the debt you owe her, and
unpay the villany you have done her: the one you may do
with sterling money, and the other with current repentance.

Falstaff. My lord, I will not undergo this sneap without reply.
You call honourable boldness impudent sauciness: if a man
will make curtsy and say nothing, he is virtuous: no, my lord,
my humble duty remembered, I will not be your suitor. I say
to you, I do desire deliverance from these officers, being
upon hasty employment in the king's affairs.

Chief Justice. You speak as having power to do wrong: but answer
in the effect of your reputation, and satisfy the poor woman.

Falstaff. Come hither, hostess.

Enter Gower

Chief Justice. Now, Master Gower, what news?

Gower. The king, my lord, and Harry Prince of Wales
Are near at hand: the rest the paper tells.

Falstaff. As I am a gentleman.

Hostess. Faith, you said so before.

Falstaff. As I am a gentleman. Come, no more words of it.

Hostess. By this heavenly ground I tread on, I must be fain to
pawn both my plate and the tapestry of my dining-
chambers.

Falstaff. Glasses, glasses, is the only drinking: and for thy walls, a
pretty slight drollery, or the story of the Prodigal, or the German hunting in water-work, is worth a thousand of these
bed-hangings and these fly-bitten tapestries. Let it be ten
pound, if thou canst. Come, an 'twere not for thy humours,
there's not a better wench in England. Go, wash thy face, and
draw the action. Come, thou must not be in this humour
with me; dost not know me? come, come, I know thou wast
set on to this.

Hostess. Pray thee, Sir John, let it be but twenty nobles: i' faith, I
am loath to pawn my plate, so God save me, la!

Falstaff. Let it alone; I'll make other shift: you'll be a fool still.

Hostess. Well, you shall have it, though I pawn my gown. I hope you'll come to supper. You'll pay me all together?

Falstaff. Will I live? [*To* Bardolph] Go, with her, with her; hook on, hook on.

Hostess. Will you have Doll Tearsheet meet you at supper?

Falstaff. No more words; let's have her.

Exeunt Hostess, Bardolph, Officers, *and* Boy.

Chief Justice. I have heard better news.

Falstaff. What's the news, my lord?

Chief Justice. Where lay the king tonight?

Gower. At Basingstoke, my lord.

Falstaff. I hope, my lord, all's well: what is the news, my lord?

Chief Justice. Come all his forces back?

Gower. No; fifteen hundred foot, five hundred horse,
    Are march'd up to my Lord of Lancaster,
    Against Northumberland and the Archbishop.

Falstaff. Comes the king back from Wales, my noble lord?

Chief Justice. You shall have letters of me presently:
    Come, go along with me, good Master Gower.

Falstaff. My lord!

Chief Justice. What's the matter?

Falstaff. Master Gower, shall I entreat you with me to dinner?

Gower. I must wait upon my good lord here; I thank you, good
    Sir John.

Chief Justice. Sir John, you loiter here too long, being you are to
    take soldiers up in counties as you go.

Falstaff. Will you sup with me, Master Gower?

Chief Justice. What foolish master taught you these manners, Sir John?

Falstaff. Master Gower, if they become me not, he was a fool that taught them me. This is the right fencing grace, my lord; tap for tap, and so part fair.

Chief Justice. Now the Lord lighten thee! thou art a great fool.

Exeunt.

scene 2. [*London. The Prince's room*]

Enter Prince Henry *and* Poins

Prince. Before God, I am exceeding weary.

Poins. Is 't come to that? I had thought weariness durst not have attached one of so high blood.

Prince. Faith, it does me; though it discolours the complexion of my greatness to acknowledge it. Doth it not show vilely in me to desire small beer?

Poins. Why, a prince should not be so loosely studied as to remember so weak a composition.

Prince. Belike then my appetite was not princely got; for, by my troth, I do now remember the poor creature, small beer. But, indeed, these humble considerations make me out of love with my greatness. What a disgrace is it to me to remember thy name! or to know thy face to-morrow! or to take note how many pair of silk stockings thou hast, viz. these, and those that were thy peach-coloured ones! or to bear the inventory of thy shirts; as, one for superfluity, and another for use! But that the tennis-court-keeper knows better than I; for it is a low ebb of linen with thee when thou keepest not racket there; as thou hast not done a great while, because the

rest of thy low countries have made a shift to eat up thy holland: and God knows, whether those that bawl out the ruins
of thy linen shall inherit his kingdom: but the midwives say
the children are not in the fault; whereupon the world in-
creases, and kindreds are mightily strengthened.

Poins. How ill it follows, after you have laboured so hard, you
should talk so idly! Tell me, how many good young princes
would do so, their fathers being so sick as yours at this
time is?

Prince. Shall I tell thee one thing, Poins?

Poins. Yes, faith; and let it be an excellent good thing.

Prince. It shall serve among wits of no higher breeding than
thine.

Poins. Go to; I stand the push of your one thing that you will
tell.

Prince. Marry, I tell thee, it is not meet that I should be sad, now
my father is sick: albeit I could tell to thee, as to one it pleases
me, for fault of a better, to call my friend, I could be sad, and
sad indeed too.

Poins. Very hardly upon such a subject.

Prince. By this hand, thou thinkest me as far in the devil's book
as thou and Falstaff for obduracy and persistency: let the end
try the man. But I tell thee, my heart bleeds inwardly that my
father is so sick: and keeping such vile company as thou art
hath in reason taken from me all ostentation of sorrow.

Poins. The reason?

Prince. What wouldst thou think of me, if I should weep?

Poins. I would think thee a most princely hypocrite.

Prince. It would be every man's thought; and thou art a blessed
fellow to think as every man thinks: never a man's thought in

the world keeps the road-way better than thine: every man would think me an hypocrite indeed. And what accites your most worshipful thought to think so?

Poins. Why, because you have been so lewd, and so much engraffed to Falstaff.

Prince. And to thee.

Poins. By this light, I am well spoke on; I can hear it with mine own ears: the worst that they can say of me is that I am a second brother, and that I am a proper fellow of my hands; and those two things, I confess, I cannot help. By the mass, here comes Bardolph.

Enter Bardolph *and* Page

Prince. And the boy that I gave Falstaff: a' had him from me Christian; and look, if the fat villain have not transformed him ape.

Bardolph. God save your grace!

Prince. And yours, most noble Bardolph!

Bardolph. Come, you virtuous ass, you bashful fool, must you be blushing? wherefore blush you now? What a maidenly man-at-arms are you become! Is 't such a matter to get a pottle-pot's maidenhead?

Page. A' calls me e'en now, my lord, through a red lattice, and I could discern no part of his face from the window: at last I spied his eyes; and methought he had made two holes in the ale-wife's new petticoat and so peeped through.

Prince. Has not the boy profited?

Bardolph. Away, you whoreson upright rabbit, away!

Page. Away, you rascally Althæa's dream, away!

Prince. Instruct us, boy; what dream, boy?

Page. Marry, my lord, Althæa dreamed she was delivered of a fire-brand; and therefore I call him her dream.

Prince. A crown's worth of good interpretation: there 'tis, boy.

Poins. O, that this good blossom could ke kept from cankers! Well, there is sixpence to preserve thee.

Bardolph. An you do not make him hanged among you, the gallows shall have wrong.

Prince. And how doth thy master, Bardolph?

Bardolph. Well, my lord. He heard of your grace's coming to town: there's a letter for you.

Poins. Delivered with good respect. And how doth the martle-mas, your master?

Bardolph. In bodily health, sir.

Poins. Marry, the immortal part needs a physician; but that moves not him: though that be sick, it dies not.

Prince. I do allow this wen to be as familiar with me as my dog; and he holds his place; for look you how he writes.

Poins. [*Reads*] 'John Falstaff, knight,'——every man must know that, as oft as he has occasion to name himself: even like those that are kin to the king; for they never prick their finger but they say, 'There's some of the king's blood spilt.' 'How comes that?' says he, that takes upon him not to conceive. The answer is as ready as a borrower's cap, 'I am the king's poor cousin, sir.'

Prince. Nay, they will be kin to us, or they will fetch it from Japhet. But to the letter:

Poins. [*Reads*] 'Sir John Falstaff, knight, to the son of the king, nearest his father, Harry Prince of Wales, greeting.' Why, this is a certificate.

Prince. Peace!

Poins. [*Reads*] 'I will imitate the honourable Romans in
brevity:' he sure means brevity in breath, short-winded. 'I
commend me to thee, I commend thee, and I leave thee. Be
not too familiar with Poins; for he misuses thy favours so
much, that he swears thou art to marry his sister Nell. Repent at idle times as thou mayest; and so, farewell.

    'Thine, by yea and no, which is as much as to say, as thou
usest him, Jack Falstaff with my familiars, John with my
brothers and sisters, and Sir John with all Europe.'
My lord, I'll steep this letter in sack, and make him eat it.

Prince. That's to make him eat twenty of his words. But do you
use me thus, Ned? must I marry your sister?

Poins. God send the wench no worse fortune! But I never
said so.

Prince. Well, thus we play the fools with the time; and the spirits
of the wise sit in the clouds and mock us. Is your master here
in London?

Bardolph. Yea, my lord.

Prince. Where sups he? doth the old boar feed in the old frank?

Bardolph. At the old place, my lord, in Eastcheap.

Prince. What company?

Page. Ephesians, my lord, of the old church.

Prince. Sup any women with him?

Page. None, my lord, but old Mistress Quickly and Mistress
Doll Tearsheet.

Prince. What pagan may that be?

Page. A proper gentlewoman, sir, and a kinswoman of my
master's.

Prince. Even such kin as the parish heifers are to the town bull.
Shall we steal upon them, Ned, at supper?

Poins. I am your shadow, my lord; I'll follow you.

Prince. Sirrah, you boy, and Bardolph, no word to your master
that I am yet come to town: there's for your silence.

Bardolph. I have no tongue, sir.

Page. And for mine, sir, I will govern it.

Prince. Fare you well; go.

Exeunt Bardolph *and* Page.

This Doll Tearsheet should be some road.

Poins. I warrant you, as common as the way between Saint Alban's and London.

Prince. How might we see Falstaff bestow himself to-night in
his true colours, and not ourselves be seen?

Poins. Put on two leathern jerkins and aprons, and wait upon
him at his table as drawers.

Prince. From a god to a bull? a heavy descension! it was Jove's
case. From a prince to a prentice? a low transformation! that
shall be mine; for in every thing the purpose must weigh
with the folly. Follow me, Ned.

Exeunt.

scene 3.   [*Warkworth. Before the castle*]

Enter Northumberland, Lady Northumberland,
and Lady Percy

Northumberland. I pray thee, loving wife and gentle daughter,
Give even way unto my rough affairs:
Put not you on the visage of the times
And be like them to Percy troublesome.

Lady Northumberland. I have given over, I will speak no more:
Do what you will; your wisdom be your guide.

Northumberland. Alas, sweet wife, my honour is at pawn;
    And, but my going, nothing can redeem it.

Lady Percy. O yet, for God's sake, go not to these wars!
    The time was, father, that you broke your word,
    When you were more endear'd to it than now;
    When your own Percy, when my heart's dear Harry,
    Threw many a northward look to see his father
    Bring up his powers; but he did long in vain.
    Who then persuaded you to stay at home?
    There were two honours lost, yours and your son's.
    For yours, the God of heaven brighten it!
    For his, it stuck upon him as the sun
    In the grey vault of heaven, and by his light
    Did all the chivalry of England move
    To do brave acts: he was indeed the glass
    Wherein the noble youth did dress themselves:
    He had no legs that practised not his gait;
    And speaking thick, which nature made his blemish,
    Became the accents of the valiant;
    For those that could speak low and tardily
    Would turn their own perfection to abuse,
    To seem like him: so that in speech, in gait,
    In diet, in affections of delight,
    In military rules, humours of blood,
    He was the mark and glass, copy and book,
    That fashion'd others. And him, O wondrous him!
    O miracle of men! him did you leave,
    Second to none, unseconded by you,
    To look upon the hideous god of war
    In disadvantage; to abide a field
    Where nothing but the sound of Hotspur's name
    Did seem defensible: so you left him.

Never, O never, do his ghost the wrong
To hold your honour more precise and nice
With others than with him! let them alone:
The marshal and the archbishop are strong:
Had my sweet Harry had but half their numbers,
To-day might I, hanging on Hotspur's neck,
Have talk'd of Monmouth's grave.

Northumberland.   Beshrew your heart,
Fair daughter, you do draw my spirits from me
With new lamenting ancient oversights.
But I must go and meet with danger there,
Or it will seek me in another place
And find me worse provided.

Lady Northumberland.   O, fly to Scotland,
Till that the nobles and the armed commons
Have of their puissance made a little taste.

Lady Percy. If they get ground and vantage of the king,
Then join you with them, like a rib of steel,
To make strength stronger; but, for all our loves,
First let them try themselves. So did your son;
He was so suffer'd: so came I a widow;
And never shall have length of life enough
To rain upon remembrance with mine eyes,
That it may grow and sprout as high as heaven,
For recordation to my noble husband.

Northumberland. Come, come, go in with me. 'Tis with
my mind
As with the tide swell'd up unto his height,
That makes a still-stand, running neither way:
Fain would I go to meet the archbishop,
But many thousand reasons hold me back.
I will resolve for Scotland: there am I,

Till time and vantage crave my company.

Exeunt.

SCENE 4. [*London. The Boar's-Head Tavern
in Eastcheap*]

Enter two Drawers

First Drawer. What the devil hast thou brought there? apple-
johns? thou knowest Sir John cannot endure an apple-john.

Second Drawer. Mass, thou sayest true. The prince once set a dish
of apple-johns before him, and told him there were five
more Sir Johns; and, putting off his hat, said, 'I will now take
my leave of these six dry, round, old, withered knights.' It an-
gered him to the heart: but he hath forgot that.

First Drawer. Why, then, cover, and set them down: and see if
thou canst find out Sneak's noise; Mistress Tearsheet would
fain hear some music. Dispatch: the room where they supped
is too hot; they'll come in straight.

Second Drawer. Sirrah, here will be the prince and Master Poins
anon; and they will put on two of our jerkins and aprons; and
Sir John must not know of it: Bardolph hath brought word.

First Drawer. By the mass, here will be old utis: it will be an excellent stratagem.

Second Drawer. I'll see if I can find out Sneak.

Exit.

Enter Hostess *and* Doll Tearsheet

Hostess. I' faith, sweetheart, methinks now you are in an excellent good temperality: your pulsidge beats as extraordinarily
as heart would desire; and your colour, I warrant you, is as red
as any rose, in good truth, la! But, i' faith, you have drunk too

much canaries; and that's a marvellous searching wine, and it perfumes the blood ere one can say 'What's this?' How do you now?

Doll. Better than I was: hem!

Hostess. Why, that's well said; a good heart's worth gold. Lo, here comes Sir John.

Enter Falstaff

Falstaff. [*Singing*] 'When Arthur first in court'
—Empty the jordan.

Exit first drawer.

[*Singing*] 'And was a worthy king.'
How now, Mistress Doll!

Hostess. Sick of a calm; yea, good faith.

Falstaff. So is all her sect; an they be once in a calm, they are sick.

Doll. A pox damn you, you muddy rascal, is that all the comfort you give me?

Falstaff. You make fat rascals, Mistress Doll.

Doll. I make them! gluttony and diseases make them; I make them not.

Falstaff. If the cook help to make the gluttony, you help to make the diseases, Doll: we catch of you, Doll, we catch of you; grant that, my poor virtue, grant that.

Doll. Yea, joy, our chains and our jewels.

Falstaff. 'Your brooches, pearls, and ouches:' for to serve bravely is to come halting off, you know; to come off the breach with his pike bent bravely, and to surgery bravely; to venture upon the charged chambers bravely,—

Doll. Hang yourself, you muddy conger, hang yourself!

Hostess. By my troth, this is the old fashion; you two never meet

but you fall to some discord: you are both, i' good truth, as
rheumatic as two dry toasts; you cannot one bear with another's confirmities. What the good-year! one must bear, and
that must be you: you are the weaker vessel, as they say, the
emptier vessel.

Doll. Can a weak empty vessel bear such a huge full hogshead?
there's a whole merchant's venture of Bourdeaux stuff in
him; you have not seen a hulk better stuffed in the hold.
Come, I'll be friends with thee, Jack: thou art going to the
wars; and whether I shall ever see thee again or no, there is
nobody cares.

Re-enter First Drawer

First Drawer. Sir, Ancient Pistol's below, and would speak
with you.

Doll. Hang him, swaggering rascal! let him not come hither: it is
the foul-mouthedst rogue in England.

Hostess. If he swagger, let him not come here: no, by my faith; I
must live among my neighbours; I'll no swaggerers: I am in
good name and fame with the very best: shut the door; there
comes no swaggerers here: I have not lived all this while, to
have swaggering now: shut the door, I pray you.

Falstaff. Dost thou hear, hostess?

Hostess. Pray ye, pacify yourself, Sir John: there comes no swaggerers here.

Falstaff. Dost thou hear? it is mine ancient.

Hostess. Tilly-fally, Sir John, ne'er tell me: your ancient swaggerer
comes not in my doors. I was before Master Tisick, the de-
buty, t' other day; and, as he said to me, 'twas no longer ago
than Wednesday last, 'I' good faith, neighbour Quickly,' says
he; Master Dumbe, our minister, was by then; 'neighbour
Quickly,' says he, 'receive those that are civil; for,' said he, 'you

are in an ill name:' now a' said so, I can tell whereupon; 'for,' says he, 'you are an honest woman, and well thought on; therefore take heed what guests you receive: receive,' says he, 'no swaggering companions.' There comes none here: you would bless you to hear what he said: no, I'll no swaggerers.

Falstaff. He's no swaggerer, hostess; a tame cheater, i' faith; you may stroke him as gently as a puppy greyhound: he'll not swagger with a Barbary hen, if her feathers turn back in any show of resistance. Call him up, drawer.

Exit First Drawer.

Hostess. Cheater, call you him? I will bar no honest man my house, nor no cheater: but I do not love swaggering, by my troth; I am the worse, when one says swagger: feel, masters, how I shake; look you, I warrant you.

Doll. So you do, hostess.

Hostess. Do I? yea, in very truth, do I, an 'twere an aspen leaf: I cannot abide swaggerers.

Enter Pistol, Bardolph, *and* Page

Pistol. God save you, Sir John!

Falstaff. Welcome, Ancient Pistol. Here, Pistol, I charge you with a cup of sack: do you discharge upon mine hostess.

Pistol. I will discharge upon her, Sir John, with two bullets.

Falstaff. She is pistol-proof, sir; you shall hardly offend her.

Hostess. Come, I'll drink no proofs nor no bullets: I'll drink no more than will do me good, for no man's pleasure, I.

Pistol. Then to you, Mistress Dorothy; I will charge you.

Doll. Charge me! I scorn you, scurvy companion. What! you poor, base, rascally, cheating, lack-linen mate! Away, you mouldy rogue, away! I am meat for your master.

Pistol. I know you, Mistress Dorothy.

Doll. Away, you cut-purse rascal! you filthy bung, away! by this
wine, I'll thrust my knife in your mouldy chaps, an you play
the saucy cuttle with me. Away, you bottle-ale rascal! you
basket-hilt stale juggler, you! Since when, I pray you, sir?
God's light, with two points on your shoulder? much!

Pistol. God let me not live, but I will murder your ruff for this.

Falstaff. No more, Pistol; I would not have you go off here: discharge yourself of our company, Pistol.

Hostess. No, good Captain Pistol; not here, sweet captain.

Doll. Captain! thou abominable damned cheater, art thou not
ashamed to be called captain? An captains were of my mind,
they would truncheon you out, for taking their names upon
you before you have earned them. You a captain! you slave,
for what? for tearing a poor whore's ruff in a bawdy-house?
He a captain! hang him, rogue! he lives upon mouldy stewed
prunes and dried cakes. A captain! God's light, these villains
will make the word as odious as the word 'occupy;' which
was an excellent good word before it was ill sorted; therefore
captains had need look to 't.

Bardolph. Pray thee, go down, good ancient.

Falstaff. Hark thee hither, Mistress Doll.

Pistol. Not I: I tell thee what, Corporal Bardolph, I could tear
her: I'll be revenged of her.

Page. Pray thee, go down.

Pistol. I'll see her damned first; to Pluto's damned lake, by this
hand, to the infernal deep, with Erebus and tortures vile also.
Hold hook and line, say I. Down, down, dogs! down, faitors!
Have we not Hiren here?

Hostess. Good Captain Peesel, be quiet; 'tis very late, i' faith: I
beseek you now, aggravate your choler.

Pistol. These be good humours, indeed! Shall pack-horses,
  And hollow pamper'd jades of Asia,
  Which cannot go but thirty mile a day,
  Compare with Cæasars, and with Cannibals,
  And Troyant Greeks? nay, rather damn them with
  King Cerberus; and let the welkin roar.
  Shall we fall foul for toys?

Hostess. By my troth, captain, these are very bitter words.

Bardolph. Be gone, good ancient: this will grow to a brawl anon.

Pistol. Die men like dogs! give crowns like pins! Have we not
  Hiren here?

Hostess. O' my word, captain, there's none such here. What the
  good-year! do you think I would deny her? For God's sake,
  be quiet.

Pistol. Then feed, and be fat, my fair Calipolis. Come, give's
  some sack.
  'Si fortune me tormente, sperato me contento.'
  Fear we broadsides? no, let the fiend give fire:
  Give me some sack: and, sweetheart, lie thou there.

                              Laying down his sword.

  Come we to full points here; and are etceteras nothing?

Falstaff. Pistol, I would be quiet.

Pistol. Sweet knight, I kiss thy neaf: what! we have seen the
  seven stars.

Doll. For God's sake, thrust him down stairs: I cannot endure
  such a fustian rascal.

Pistol. Thrust him down stairs! know we not Galloway nags?

Falstaff. Quoit him down, Bardolph, like a shove-groat shilling:
  nay, an a' do nothing but speak nothing, a' shall be nothing
  here.

Bardolph. Come, get you down stairs.

Pistol. What! shall we have incision? shall we imbrue?

> *Snatching up his sword.*

Then death rock me asleep, abridge my doleful days!
Why, then, let grievous, ghastly, gaping wounds
Untwine the Sisters Three! Come, Atropos, I say!

Hostess. Here's goodly stuff toward!

Falstaff. Give me my rapier, boy.

Doll. I pray thee, Jack, I pray thee, do not draw.

Falstaff. Get you down stairs.

> *Drawing, and driving* Pistol *out.*

Hostess. Here's a goodly tumult! I'll forswear keeping house,
afore I'll be in these tirrits and frights. So; murder, I warrant
now. Alas, alas! put up your naked weapons, put up your
naked weapons.

> *Exeunt* Pistol *and* Bardolph.

Doll. I pray thee, Jack, be quiet; the rascal's gone. Ah, you
whoreson little valiant villain, you!

Hostess. Are you not hurt i' the groin? methought a' made a
shrewd thrust at your belly.

> *Re-enter* Bardolph

Falstaff. Have you turned him out o' doors?

Bardolph. Yea, sir. The rascal's drunk: you have hurt him, sir, i'
the shoulder.

Falstaff. A rascal! to brave me!

Doll. Ah, you sweet little rogue, you! Alas, poor ape, how thou
sweatest! come, let me wipe thy face; come on, you whoreson
chops: ah, rogue! i' faith, I love thee: thou art as valorous as
Hector of Troy, worth five of Agamemnon, and ten times
better than the Nine Worthies: ah, villain!

Falstaff. A rascally slave! I will toss the rogue in a blanket.

Doll. Do, an thou darest for thy heart: an thou dost, I'll canvass thee between a pair of sheets.

Enter Musicians

Page. The music is come, sir.

Falstaff. Let them play. Play, sirs. Sit on my knee, Doll. A rascal bragging slave! the rogue fled from me like quicksilver.

Doll. I' faith, and thou followedst him like a church. Thou whoreson little tidy Bartholomew boar-pig, when wilt thou leave fighting o' days and foining o' nights, and begin to patch up thine old body for heaven?

Enter, behind, Prince Henry *and* Poins, *disguised*

Falstaff. Peace, good Doll! do not speak like a death's-head; do not bid me remember mine end.

Doll. Sirrah, what humour's the prince of?

Falstaff. A good shallow young fellow: a' would have made a good pantler, a' would ha' chipped bread well.

Doll. They say Poins has a good wit.

Falstaff. He a good wit? hang him, baboon! his wit's as thick as Tewksbury mustard; there's no more conceit in him than is in a mallet.

Doll. Why does the prince love him so, then?

Falstaff. Because their legs are both of a bigness; and a' plays at quoits well; and eats conger and fennel; and drinks off candles' ends for flap-dragons; and rides the wild-mare with the boys; and jumps upon joined-stools; and swears with a good grace; and wears his boots very smooth, like unto the sign of the Leg; and breeds no bate with telling of discreet stories; and such other gambol faculties a' has, that show a weak mind and an able body, for the which the prince admits him:

for the prince himself is such another; the weight of a hair will turn the scales between their avoirdupois.

Prince. Would not this nave of a wheel have his ears cut off?

Poins. Let's beat him before his whore.

Prince. Look, whether the withered elder hath not his poll clawed like a parrot.

Poins. It is not strange that desire should so many years outlive performance?

Falstaff. Kiss me, Doll.

Prince. Saturn and Venus this year in conjunction! what says the almanac to that?

Poins. And, look, whether the fiery Trigon, his man, be not lisping to his master's old tables, his note-book, his counsel-keeper.

Falstaff. Thou dost give me flattering busses.

Doll. By my troth, I kiss thee with a most constant heart.

Falstaff. I am old, I am old.

Doll. I love thee better than I love e'er a scurvy young boy of them all.

Falstaff. What stuff wilt have a kirtle of? I shall receive money o' Thursday: shalt have a cap to-morrow. A merry song, come: it grows late; we'll to bed. Thou 'lt forget me when I am gone.

Doll. By my troth, thou 'lt set me a-weeping, an thou sayest so: prove that ever I dress myself handsome till thy return: well, hearken at the end.

Falstaff. Some sack, Francis.

Prince and Poins. Anon, anon, sir.

Coming forward.

Falstaff. Ha! a bastard son of the king's? And art not thou Poins his brother?

Prince. Why, thou globe of sinful continents, what a life dost thou lead!

Falstaff. A better than thou: I am a gentleman; thou art a drawer.

Prince. Very true, sir; and I come to draw you out by the ears.

Hostess. O, the Lord preserve thy good grace! by my troth, welcome to London. Now, the Lord bless that sweet face of thine! O Jesu, are you come from Wales?

Falstaff. Thou whoreson mad compound of majesty, by this light flesh and corrupt blood, thou art welcome.

Doll. How, you fat fool! I scorn you.

Poins. My lord, he will drive you out of your revenge and turn all to a merriment, if you take not the heat.

Prince. You whoreson candle-mine, you, how vilely did you speak of me even now before this honest, virtuous, civil gentlewoman!

Hostess. God's blessing of your good heart! and so she is, by my troth.

Falstaff. Didst thou hear me?

Prince. Yea, and you knew me, as you did when you ran away by Gadshill: you knew I was at your back, and spoke it on purpose to try my patience.

Falstaff. No, no, no; not so; I did not think thou wast within hearing.

Prince. I shall drive you then to confess the wilful abuse; and then I know how to handle you.

Falstaff. No abuse, Hal, o' mine honour; no abuse.

Prince. Not to dispraise me, and call me pantler and bread–
chipper and I know not what?

Falstaff. No abuse, Hal.

Poins. No abuse?

Falstaff. No abuse, Ned, i' the world; honest Ned, none. I dis–
praised him before the wicked, that the wicked might not fall
in love with him; in which doing, I have done the part of a
careful friend and a true subject, and thy father is to give me
thanks for it. No abuse, Hal: none, Ned, none: no, faith, boys,
none.

Prince. See now, whether pure fear and entire cowardice
doth not make thee wrong this virtuous gentlewoman
to close with us. Is she of the wicked? is thine hostess
here of the wicked? or is thy boy of the wicked? or
honest Bardolph, whose zeal burns in his nose, of the
wicked?

Poins. Answer, thou dead elm, answer.

Falstaff. The fiend hath pricked down Bardolph irrecoverable;
and his face is Lucifer's privy-kitchen, where he doth noth–
ing but roast malt-worms. For the boy, there is a good angel
about him; but the devil out-bids him too.

Prince. For the women?

Falstaff. For one of them, she is in hell already, and burns poor
souls. For the other, I owe her money; and whether she be
damned for that, I know not.

Hostess. No, I warrant you.

Falstaff. No, I think thou art not; I think thou art quit for that.
Marry, there is another indictment upon thee, for suffering
flesh to be eaten in thy house, contrary to the law; for the
which I think thou wilt howl.

Hostess. All victuallers do so: what's a joint of mutton or two in a whole Lent?

Prince. You, gentlewoman,—

Doll. What says your grace?

Falstaff. His grace says that which his flesh rebels against.

Knocking within.

Hostess. Who knocks so loud at door? Look to the door there, Francis.

Enter Peto

Prince. Peto, how now! what news?

Peto. The king your father is at Westminster;
And there are twenty weak and wearied posts
Come from the north: and, as I came along,
I met and overtook a dozen captains,
Bare-headed, sweating, knocking at the taverns,
And asking every one for Sir John Falstaff.

Prince. By heaven, Poins, I feel me much to blame,
So idly to profane the precious time;
When tempest of commotion, like the south
Borne with black vapour, doth begin to melt,
And drop upon our bare unarmed heads.
Give me my sword and cloak. Falstaff, good night.

Exeunt Prince Henry, Poins, Peto, *and* Bardolph.

Falstaff. Now comes in the sweetest morsel of the night, and we must hence, and leave it unpicked. [*Knocking within*] More knocking at the door!

Re-enter Bardolph

How now! what's the matter?

Bardolph. You must away to court, sir, presently;
A dozen captains stay at door for you.

Falstaff. [*To the* Page] Pay the musicians, sirrah. Farewell, hostess; farewell, Doll. You see, my good wenches, how men of merit are sought after: the undeserver may sleep, when the man of action is called on. Farewell, good wenches: if I be not sent away post, I will see you again ere I go.

Doll. I cannot speak; if my heart be not ready to burst,—well, sweet Jack, have a care of thyself.

Falstaff. Farewell, farewell.

Exeunt Falstaff *and* Bardolph.

Hostess. Well, fare thee well: I have known thee these twenty nine years, come peascod-time; but an honester and truer-hearted man,—well, fare thee well.

Bardolph. [*Within*] Mistress Tearsheet!

Hostess. What's the matter?

Bardolph. [*Within*] Bid Mistress Tearsheet come to my master.

Hostess. O, run, Doll, run; run, good Doll: come. She comes blubbered. Yea, will you come, Doll?

Exeunt.

act 3

scene 1. [*Westminster. The palace*]

Enter the King *in his nightgown, with a* Page

King. Go call the Earls of Surrey and of Warwick;
But, ere they come, bid them o'er-read these letters,
And well consider of them: make good speed.

Exit Page.

How many thousand of my poorest subjects
Are at this hour asleep! O sleep, O gentle sleep,
Nature's soft nurse, how have I frighted thee,
That thou no more wilt weigh my eyelids down,
And steep my senses in forgetfulness?
Why rather, sleep, liest thou in smoky cribs,.
Upon uneasy pallets stretching thee,
And hush'd with buzzing night-flies to thy slumber,
Than in the perfumed chambers of the great,
Under the canopies of costly state,
And lull'd with sound of sweetest melody?
O thou dull god, why liest thou with the vile
In loathsome beds, and leavest the kingly couch
A watch-case or a common 'larum-bell?

Wilt thou upon the high and giddy mast
Seal up the ship-boy's eyes, and rock his brains
In cradle of the rude imperious surge,
And in the visitation of the winds,
Who take the ruffian billows by the top,
Curling their monstrous heads, and hanging them
With deafening clamour in the slippery clouds,
That, with the hurly, death itself awakes?
Canst thou, O partial sleep, give thy repose
To the wet sea-boy in an hour so rude;
And in the calmest and most stillest night,
With all appliances and means to boot,
Deny it to a king? Then happy low, lie down!
Uneasy lies the head that wears a crown.

       Enter Warwick *and* Surrey

Warwick. Many good morrows to your majesty!

King. Is it good morrow, lords?

Warwick. 'Tis one o'clock, and past.

King. Why, then, good morrow to you all, my lords.
 Have you read o'er the letters that I sent you?

Warwick. We have, my liege.

King. Then you perceive the body of our kingdom
 How foul it is; what rank diseases grow,
 And with what danger, near the heart of it.

Warwick. It is but as a body yet distemper'd;
 Which to his former strength may be restored
 With good advice and little medicine:
 My Lord Northumberland will soon be cool'd.

King. O God! that one might read the book of fate,
 And see the revolution of the times
 Make mountains level, and the continent,

Weary of solid firmness, melt itself
Into the sea! and other times to see
The beachy girdle of the ocean
Too wide for Neptune's hips; how chance's mocks
And changes fill the cup of alteration
With divers liquors! O, if this were seen,
The happiest youth, viewing his progress through,
What perils past, what crosses to ensue,
Would shut the book, and sit him down and die.
'Tis not ten years gone
Since Richard and Northumberland, great friends,
Did feast together, and in two years after
Were they at wars: it is but eight years since
This Percy was the man nearest my soul;
Who like a brother toil'd in my affairs,
And laid his love and life under my foot;
Yea, for my sake, even to the eyes of Richard
Gave him defiance. But which of you was by—
You, cousin Nevil, as I may remember—

To Warwick.

When Richard, with his eye brimful of tears,
Then check'd and rated by Northumberland,
Did speak these words, now proved a prophecy?
'Northumberland, thou ladder by the which
My cousin Bolingbroke ascends my throne;'
Though then, God knows, I had no such intent,
But that necessity so bow'd the state,
That I and greatness were compell'd to kiss:
'The time shall come,' thus did he follow it,
'The time will come, that foul sin, gathering head.
Shall break into corruption:' so went on,
Foretelling this same time's condition,
And the division of our amity.

Warwick. There is a history in all men's lives,
    Figuring the nature of the times decreased;
    The which observed, a man may prophesy,
    With a near aim, of the main chance of things
    As yes not come to life, which in their seeds
    And weak beginnings lie intreasured.
    Such things become the hatch and brood of time;
    And by the necessary form of this
    King Richard might create a perfect guess
    That great Northumberland, then false to him,
    Would of that seed grow to a greater falseness;
    Which should not find a ground to root upon,
    Unless on you.

King.   Are these things then necessities?
    Then let us meet them like necessities:
    And that same word even now cries out on us:
    They say the bishop and Northumberland
    Are fifty thousand strong.

Warwick.   It cannot be, my lord;
    Rumour doth double, like the voice and echo,
    The numbers of the fear'd. Please it your grace
    To go to bed. Upon my soul, my lord,
    The powers that you already have sent forth
    Shall bring this prize in very easily.
    To comfort you the more, I have received
    A certain instance that Glendower is dead.
    Your majesty hath been this fortnight ill;
    And these unseason'd hours perforce must add
    Unto your sickness.

King.   I will take your counsel:
    And were these inward wars once out of hand,
    We would, dear lords, unto the Holy Land.

                                      Exeunt.

scene 2.   [*Gloucestershire. Before* Justice Shallow's *house*]

Enter Shallow *and* Silence, *meeting;* Mouldy,
Shadow, Wart, Feeble, Bullcalf, *a* Servant *or two*
with them

Shallow. Come on, come on, come on; give me your hand, sir,
give me your hand, sir: an early stirrer, by the rood! And how
doth my good cousin Silence?

Silence. Good morrow, good cousin Shallow.

Shallow. And how doth my cousin, your bedfellow? and your
fairest daughter and mine, my god-daughter Ellen?

Silence. Alas, a black ousel, cousin Shallow!

Shallow. By yea and nay, sir, I dare say my cousin William is become a good scholar: he is at Oxford still, is he not?

Silence. Indeed, sir, to my cost.

Shallow. A' must, then, to the inns o' court shortly: I was once of
Clement's Inn, where I think they will talk of mad Shallow yet.

Silence. You were called 'lusty Shallow' then, cousin.

Shallow. By the mass, I was called any thing; and I would have
done any thing indeed too, and roundly too. There was I, and
little John Doit of Staffordshire, and black George Barnes,
and Francis Pickbone, and Will Squele, a Cotswold man; you
had not four such swinge-bucklers in all the inns o' court
again: and I may say to you, we knew where the bona-robas
were, and had the best of them all at commandment. Then
was Jack Falstaff, now Sir John, a boy, and page to Thomas
Mowbray, Duke of Norfolk.

Silence. This Sir John, cousin, that comes hither anon about soldiers?

Shallow. The same Sir John, the very same. I see him break Sko-
gan's head at the court-gate, when a' was a crack not thus
high: and the very same day did I fight with one Sampson
Stockfish, a fruiterer, behind hind Gray's Inn. Jesu, Jesu, the
mad days that I have spent! and to see how many of my old
acquaintance are dead!

Silence. We shall all follow, cousin.

Shallow. Certain, 'tis certain; very sure, very sure: death, as the
Psalmist saith, is certain to all; all shall die. How a good yoke
of bullocks at Stamford fair?

Silence. By my troth, I was not there.

Shallow. Death is certain. Is old Double of your town living yet?

Silence. Dead, sir.

Shallow. Jesu, Jesu, dead! a' drew a good bow; and dead! a' shot a
fine shoot: John a Gaunt loved him well, and betted much
money on his head. Dead! a' would have clapped i' the clout
at twelve score; and carried you a forehand shaft a fourteen
and fourteen and a half, that it would have done a man's
heart good to see. How a score of ewes now?

Silence. Thereafter as they be: a score of good ewes may be
worth ten pounds.

Shallow. And is old Double dead?

Silence. Here come two of Sir John Falstaff's men, as I think.
      Enter Bardolph, *and one with him*

Bardolph. Good morrow, honest gentlemen: I beseech you,
which is Justice Shallow?

Shallow. I am Robert Shallow, sir; a poor esquire of this county,
and one of the king's justices of the peace: what is your good
pleasure with me?

Bardolph. My captain, sir, commends him to you; my captain, Sir

John Falstaff, a tall gentleman, by heaven, and a most gallant leader.

Shallow. He greets me well, sir. I knew him a good back-sword man. How doth the good knight? may I ask how my lady his wife doth?

Bardolph. Sir, pardon; a soldier is better accommodated than with a wife.

Shallow. It is well said, in faith, sir; and it is well said indeed too. "Better accommodated"! it is good; yea, indeed, is it: good phrases are surely, and ever were, very commendable. "Accommodated"! it comes of 'accommodo:' very good; a good phrase.

Bardolph. Pardon me, sir; I have heard the word. Phrase call you it? by this good day, I know not the phrase; but I will maintain the word with my sword to be a soldier-like word, and a word of exceeding good command, by heaven. Accommodated; that is, when a man is, as they say, accommodated; or when a man is, being, whereby a' may be thought to be accommodated; which is an excellent thing.

Shallow. It is very just.

Enter Falstaff

Look, here comes good Sir John. Give me your good hand, give me your worship's good hand: by my troth, you like well and bear your years very well: welcome, good Sir John.

Falstaff. I am glad to see you well, good Master Robert Shallow: Master Surecard, as I think?

Shallow. No, Sir John; it is my cousin Silence, in commission with me.

Falstaff. Good Master Silence, it well befits you should be of the peace.

Silence. Your good worship is welcome.

Falstaff. Fie! this is hot weather, gentlemen. Have you provided me here half a dozen sufficient men?

Shallow. Marry, have we, sir. Will you sit?

Falstaff. Let me see them, I beseech you.

Shallow. Where's the roll? where's the roll? where's the roll? Let me see, let me see, let me see. So, so, so, so, so, so, so: yea, marry, sir: Ralph Mouldy! Let them appear as I call; let them do so, let them do so. Let me see; where is Mouldy?

Mouldy. Here, an 't please you.

Shallow. What think you, Sir John? a good-limbed fellow; young, strong, and of good friends.

Falstaff. Is thy name Mouldy?

Mouldy. Yea, an 't please you.

Falstaff. 'Tis the more time thou wert used.

Shallow. Ha, ha, ha! most excellent, i' faith! things that are mouldy lack use: very singular good! in faith, well said, Sir John; very well said.

Falstaff. Prick him.

Mouldy. I was pricked well enough before, an you could have let me alone: my old dame will be undone now, for one to do her husbandry and her drudgery: you need not to have pricked me; there are other men fitter to go out than I.

Falstaff. Go to: peace, Mouldy; you shall go. Mouldy, it is time you were spent.

Mouldy. Spent!

Shallow. Peace, fellow, peace; stand aside: know you where you are? For the other, Sir John: let me see: Simon Shadow!

Falstaff. Yea, marry, let me have him to sit under: he's like to be a cold soldier.

Shallow. Where's Shadow?

Shadow. Here, sir.

Falstaff. Shadow, whose son art thou?

Shadow. My mother's son, sir.

Falstaff. Thy mother's son! like enough, and thy father's shadow: so the son of the female is the shadow of the male: it is often so, indeed; but much of the father's substance!

Shallow. Do you like him, Sir John?

Falstaff. Shadow will serve for summer; prick him, for we have a number of shadows to fill up the muster-book.

Shallow. Thomas Wart!

Falstaff. Where's he?

Wart. Here, sir.

Falstaff. Is thy name Wart?

Wart. Yea, sir.

Falstaff. Thou art a very ragged wart.

Shallow. Shall I prick him, Sir John?

Falstaff. It were superfluous; for his apparel is built upon his back, and the whole frame stands upon pins: prick him no more.

Shallow. Ha, ha, ha! you can do it, sir; you can do it: I commend you well. Francis Feeble!

Feeble. Here, sir.

Shallow. What trade art thou, Feeble?

Feeble. A woman's tailor, sir.

Shallow. Shall I prick him, sir?

Falstaff. You may: but if he had been a man's tailor, he'd ha'
pricked you. Wilt thou make as many holes in an enemy's
battle as thou hast done in a woman's petticoat?

Feeble. I will do my good will, sir: you can have no more.

Falstaff. Well said, good woman's tailor! well said, courageous
Feeble! thou wilt be as valiant as the wrathful dove or most
magnanimous mouse. Prick the woman's tailor: well, Master
Shallow; deep, Master Shallow.

Feeble. I would Wart might have gone, sir.

Falstaff. I would thou wert a man's tailor, that thou mightst
mend him and make him fit to go. I cannot put him to a private soldier, that is the leader of so many thousands: let that
suffice, most forcible Feeble.

Feeble. It shall suffice, sir.

Falstaff. I am bound to thee, reverend Feeble. Who is next?

Shallow. Peter Bullcalf o' the green!

Falstaff. Yea, marry, let's see Bullcalf.

Bullcalf. Here, sir.

Falstaff. 'Fore God, a likely fellow! Come, prick me Bullcalf till
he roar again.

Bullcalf. O Lord! good my lord captain,—

Falstaff. What, dost thou roar before thou art pricked?

Bullcalf. O Lord, sir! I am a diseased man.

Falstaff. What disease hast thou?

Bullcalf. A whoreson cold, sir, a cough, sir, which I caught with
ringing in the king's affairs upon his coronation-day, sir.

Falstaff. Come, thou shalt go to the wars in a gown; we will
have away thy cold; and I will take such order that thy friends
shall ring for thee. Is here all?

Shallow. Here is two more called than your number; you must have but four here, sir: and so, I pray you, go in with me to dinner.

Falstaff. Come, I will go drink with you, but I cannot tarry dinner. I am glad to see you, by my troth, Master Shallow.

Shallow. O, Sir John, do you remember since we lay all night in the windmill in Saint George's field?

Falstaff. No more of that, good Master Shallow, no more of that.

Shallow. Ha! 'twas a merry night. And is Jane Nightwork alive?

Falstaff. She lives, Master Shallow.

Shallow. She never could away with me.

Falstaff. Never, never; she would always say she could not abide Master Shallow.

Shallow. By the mass, I could anger her to the heart. She was then a bona-roba. Doth she hold her own well?

Falstaff. Old, old, Master Shallow.

Shallow. Nay, she must be old; she cannot choose but be old; certain she's old; and had Robin Nightwork by old Nightwork before I came to Clement's Inn.

Silence. That's fifty five year ago.

Shallow. Ha, cousin Silence, that thou hadst seen that that this knight and I have seen! Ha, Sir John, said I well?

Falstaff. We have heard the chimes at midnight, Master Shallow.

Shallow. That we have, that we have, that we have; in faith, Sir John, we have: our watch-word was 'Hem boys!' Come, let's to dinner; come, let's to dinner: Jesus, the days that we have seen! Come, come.

Exeunt Falstaff *and the* Justices.

Bullcalf. Good master corporate Bardolph, stand my friend; and
here's four Harry ten shillings in French crowns for you. In
very truth, sir, I had as lief be hanged, sir, as go: and yet, for
mine own part, sir, I do not care; but rather, because I am un-
willing, and, for mine own part, have a desire to stay with my
friends; else, sir, I did not care, for mine own part, so much.

Bardolph. Go to; stand aside.

Mouldy. And, good master corporal captain, for my old dame's
sake, stand my friend: she has nobody to do any thing about
her when I am gone; and she is old, and cannot help herself:
you shall have forty, sir.

Bardolph. Go to; stand aside.

Feeble. By my troth, I care not; a man can die but once: we owe
God a death: I'll ne'er bear a base mind: an 't be my destiny,
so; an 't be not, so: no man's too good to serve 's prince; and
let it go which way it will, he that dies this year is quit for
the next.

Bardolph. Well said; thou 'rt a good fellow.

Feeble. Faith, I'll bear no base mind.

Re-enter Falstaff *and the* Justices

Falstaff. Come, sir, which men shall I have?

Shallow. Four of which you please.

Bardolph. Sir, a word with you: I have three pound to free
Mouldy and Bullcalf.

Falstaff. Go to; well.

Shallow. Come, Sir John, which four will you have?

Falstaff. Do you choose for me.

Shallow. Marry, then, Mouldy, Bullcalf, Feeble and Shadow.

Falstaff. Mouldy and Bullcalf: for you, Mouldy, stay at home till you are past service: and for your part, Bullcalf, grow till you come unto it: I will none of you.

Shallow. Sir John, Sir John, do not yourself wrong: they are your likeliest men, and I would have you served with the best.

Falstaff. Will you tell me, Master Shallow, how to choose a man? Care I for the limb, the thewes, the stature, bulk, and big assemblance of a man! Give me the spirit, Master Shallow. Here's Wart; you see what a ragged appearance it is: a' shall charge you and discharge you with the motion of a pewterer's hammer, come off and on swifter than he that gibbets on the brewer's bucket. And this same half-faced fellow, Shadow: give me this man: he presents no mark to the enemy; the foeman may with as great aim level at the edge of a penknife. And for a retreat; how swiftly will this Feeble the woman's tailor run off! O, give me the spare men, and spare me the great ones. Put me a caliver into Wart's hand, Bardolph.

Bardolph. Hold, Wart, traverse; thas! thas! thas!

Falstaff. Come, manage me your caliver. So: very well: go to: very good, exceeding good. O, give me always a little, lean, old, chapt, bald shot. Well said, i' faith, Wart; thou 'rt a good scab: hold, there's a tester for thee.

Shallow. He is not his craft's-master; he doth not do it right. I remember at Mile-end Green, when I lay at Clement's Inn— I was then Sir Dagonet in Arthur's show—there was a little quiver fellow, and a' would manage you his piece thus; and a' would about and about, and come you in and come you in: 'rah, tah, tah,' would a' say; 'bounce' would a' say; and away again would a' go, and again would a' come: I shall ne'er see such a fellow.

Falstaff. These fellows will do well, Master Shallow. God keep you, Master Silence: I will not use many words with you. Fare you well, gentlemen both: I thank you: I must a dozen mile to-night. Bardolph, give the soldiers coats.

Shallow. Sir John, the Lord bless you! God prosper your affairs! God send us peace! At your return visit our house; let our old acquaintance be renewed: per-adventure I will with ye to the court.

Falstaff. 'Fore God, I would you would, Master Shallow.

Shallow. Go to; I have spoke at a word. God keep you.

Falstaff. Fare you well, gentle gentlemen. [*Exeunt* Justices] On, Bardolph; lead the men away. [*Exeunt* Bardolph, Recruits, & c.] As I return, I will fetch off these justices: I do see the bottom of Justice Shallow. Lord, Lord, how subject we old men are to this vice of lying! This same starved justice hath done nothing but prate to me of the wildness of his youth, and the feats he hath done about Turnbull Street; and every third word a lie, duer paid to the hearer than the Turk's tribute. I do remember him at Clement's Inn like a man made after supper of a cheese-paring: when a' was naked, he was, for all the world, like a forked radish, with a head fantastically carved upon it with a knife: a' was so forlorn, that his dimensions to any thick sight were invisible: a' was the very genius of famine; yet lecherous as a monkey, and the whores called him mandrake: a' came ever in the rearward of the fashion, and sung those tunes to the overscutched huswives that he heard the carmen whistle, and sware they were his fancies or his good-nights. And now is this Vice's dagger become a squire, and talks as familiarly of John a Gaunt as if he had been sworn brother to him; and I'll be sworn a' ne'er saw him but once in the Tilt-yard; and then he burst his head for crowding among the marshal's men. I saw it, and told John a Gaunt he beat his own name; for you might have thrust him and all his apparel into an eel-skin; the case of a treble hautboy was a mansion for him, a court: and now has he land and beefs. Well, I'll be acquainted with him, if I return; and it shall go hard but I will make him a philosopher's two stones to me: if the young dace be a bait for the old pike, I see no reason in the law of nature but I may snap at him. Let time shape, and there an end.

Exit.

act 4

scene 1. [*Yorkshire. Gaultree Forest*]

Enter the Archbishop of York, Mowbray, Hastings,
and others

Archbishop. What is this forest call'd?

Hastings. 'Tis Gaultree Forest, an 't shall please your grace.

Archbishop. Here stand, my lords; and send discoverers forth
To know the numbers of our enemies.

Hastings. We have sent forth already.

Archbishop.   'Tis well done.
My friends and brethren in these great affairs,
I must acquaint you that I have received
New-dated letters from Northumberland;
Their cold intent, tenour and substance, thus:
Here doth he wish his person, with such powers
As might hold sortance with his quality,
The which he could not levy; whereupon
He is retired, to ripe his growing fortunes,
To Scotland: and concludes in hearty prayers

That your attempts may overlive the hazard
And fearful meeting of their opposite.

Mowbray. Thus do the hopes we have in him touch ground
And dash themselves to pieces.

Enter a Messenger

Hastings.   Now, what news?

Messenger. West of this forest, scarcely off a mile,
In goodly form comes on the enemy;
And, by the ground they hide, I judge their number
Upon or near the rate of thirty thousand.

Mowbray. The just proportion that we gave them out.
Let us sway on and face them in the field.

Archbishop. What well-appointed leader fronts us here?

Enter Westmoreland

Mowbray. I think it is my Lord of Westmoreland.

Westmoreland. Health and fair greeting from our general,
The prince, Lord John and Duke of Lancaster.

Archbishop. Say on, my Lord of Westmoreland, in peace:
What doth concern your coming?

Westmoreland.   Then, my lord,
Unto your grace do I in chief address
The substance of my speech. If that rebellion
Came like itself, in base and abject routs,
Led on by bloody youth, guarded with rags,
And countenanced by boys and beggary;
I say, if damn'd commotion so appear'd,
In his true, native and most proper shape,
You, reverend father, and these noble lords
Had not been here, to dress the ugly form
Of base and bloody insurrection

With your fair honours. You, lord Archbishop,
Whose see is by a civil peace maintain'd,
Whose beard the silver hand of peace hath touch'd,
Whose learning and good letters peace hath tutor'd,
Whose white investments figure innocence,
The dove and very blessed spirit of peace,
Wherefore do you so ill translate yourself
Out of the speech of peace that bears such grace,
Into the harsh and boisterous tongue of war;
Turning your books to graves, your ink to blood,
Your pens to lances, and your tongue divine
To a loud trumpet and a point of war?

Archbishop. Wherefore do I this? so the question stands.
Briefly to this end: we are all diseased,
And with our surfeiting and wanton hours
Have brought ourselves into a burning fever,
And we must bleed for it; of which disease
Our late king, Richard, being infected, died.
But, my most noble Lord of Westmoreland,
I take not on me here as a physician,
Nor do I as an enemy to peace
Troop in the throngs of military men;
But rather show a while like fearful war,
To diet rank minds sick of happiness,
And purge the obstructions which begin to stop
Our very veins of life. Hear me more plainly.
I have in equal balance justly weigh'd
What wrongs our arms may do, what wrongs we suffer,
And find our griefs heavier than our offences.
We see which way the stream of time doth run,
And are enforced from our most quiet there
By the rough torrent of occasion;

And have the summary of all our griefs,
When time shall serve, to show in articles;
Which long ere this we offer'd to the king,
And might by no suit gain our audience:
When we are wrong'd and would unfold our griefs,
We are denied access unto his person
Even by those men that most have done us wrong.
The dangers of the days but newly gone,
Whose memory is written on the earth
With yet appearing blood, and the examples
Of every minute's instance, present now,
Hath put us in these ill-beseeming arms,
Not to break peace or any branch of it,
But to establish here a peace indeed,
Concurring both in name and quality.

Westmoreland. When ever yet was your appeal denied?
Wherein have you been galled by the king?
What peer hath been suborn'd to grate on you,
That you should seal this lawless bloody book
Of forged rebellion with a seal divine,
And consecrate commotion's bitter edge?

Archbishop. My brother general, the commonwealth,
To brother born an household cruelty,
I make my quarrel in particular.

Westmoreland. There is no need of any such redress;
Or if there were, it not belongs to you.

Mowbray. Why not to him in part, and to us all
That feel the bruises of the days before,
And suffer the condition of these times
To lay a heavy and unequal hand
Upon our honours?

Westmoreland. O, my good Lord Mowbray,
  Construe the times to their necessities,
  And you shall say indeed, it is the time,
  And not the king, that doth you injuries.
  Yet for your part, it not appears to me
  Either from the king or in the present time
  That you should have an inch of any ground
  To build a grief on: were you not restored
  To all the Duke of Norfolk's signories,
  Your noble and right well remember'd father's?

Mowbray. What thing, in honour, had my father lost,
  That need to be revived and breathed in me?
  The king that loved him, as the state stood then,
  Was force perforce compell'd to banish him:
  And then that Henry Bolingbroke and he,
  Being mounted and both roused in their seats,
  Their neighing coursers daring of the spur,
  Their armed staves in charge, their beavers down,
  Their eyes of fire sparkling through sights of steel
  And the loud trumpet blowing them together,
  Then, then, when there was nothing could have stay'd
  My father from the breast of Bolingbroke,
  O, when the king did throw his warder down,
  His own life hung upon the staff he threw;
  Then threw he down himself and all their lives
  That by indictment and by dint of sword
  Have since miscarried under Bolingbroke.

Westmoreland. You speak, Lord Mowbray, now you know
  not what.
  The Earl of Hereford was reputed then
  In England the most valiant gentleman:
  Who knows on whom fortune would then have smiled?

But if your father had been victor there,
He ne'er had borne it out of Coventry:
For all the country in a general voice
Cried hate upon him; and all their prayers and love
Were set on Hereford, whom they doted on
And bless'd and graced indeed, more than the king.
But this is mere digression from my purpose.
Here come I from our princely general
To know your griefs; to tell you from his grace
That he will give you audience; and wherein
It shall appear that your demands are just,
You shall enjoy them, every thing set off
That might so much as think you enemies.

Mowbray. But he hath forced us to compel this offer;
And it proceeds from policy, not love.

Westmoreland. Mowbray, you overween to take it so;
This offer comes from mercy, not from fear:
For, lo! within a ken our army lies,
Upon mine honour, all too confident
To give admittance to a thought of fear.
Our battle is more full of names than yours,
Our men more perfect in the use of arms,
Our armour all as strong, our cause the best;
Then reason will our hearts should be as good:
Say you not then our offer is compell'd.

Mowbray. Well, by my will we shall admit no parley.

Westmoreland. That argues but the shame of your offence:
A rotten case abides no handling.

Hastings. Hath the Prince John a full commission,
In very ample virtue of his father,
To hear and absolutely to determine
Of what conditions we shall stand upon?

Westmoreland. That is intended in the general's name:
    I muse you make so slight a question.

Archbishop. Then take, my Lord of Westmoreland, this schedule,
    For this contains our general grievances:
    Each several article herein redress'd,
    All members of our cause, both here and hence,
    That are insinewed to this action,
    Acquitted by a true substantial form,
    And present execution of our wills
    To us and to our purposes confined,
    We come within our awful banks again,
    And knit our powers to the arm of peace.

Westmoreland. This will I show the general. Please you, lords,
    In sight of both our battles we may meet;
    And either end in peace—which God so frame!—
    Or to the place of difference call the swords
    Which must decide it.

Archbishop.   My lord, we will do so.

                          Exit Westmoreland.

Mowbray. There is a thing within my bosom tells me
    That no conditions of our peace can stand.

Hastings. Fear you not that: if we can make our peace
    Upon such large terms and so absolute
    As our conditions shall consist upon,
    Our peace shall stand as firm as rocky mountains.

Mowbray. Yea, but our valuation shall be such
    That every slight and false-derived cause,
    Yea, every idle, nice and wanton reason
    Shall to the king taste of this action;
    That, were our royal faiths martyrs in love,
    We shall be winnow'd with so rough a wind

That even our corn shall seem as light as chaff
And good from bad find no partition.

Archbishop. No, no, my lord. Note this; the king is weary
Of dainty and such picking grievances:
For he hath found to end one doubt by death
Revives two greater in the heirs of life,
And therefore will he wipe his tables clean,
And keep no tell-tale to his memory
That may repeat and history his loss
To new remembrance; for full well he knows
He cannot so precisely weed this land
As his misdoubts present occasion:
His foes are so enrooted with his friends
That, plucking to unfix an enemy,
He doth unfasten so and shake a friend.
So that this land, like an offensive wife
That hath enraged him on to offer strokes,
As he is striking, holds his infant up,
And hangs resolved correction in the arm
That was uprear'd to execution.

Hastings. Besides, the king hath wasted all his rods
On late offenders, that he now doth lack
The very instruments of chastisement:
So that his power, like to a fangless lion,
May offer, but not hold.

Archbishop.   'Tis very true:
And therefore be assured, my good lord marshal,
If we do now make our atonement well,
Our peace will, like a broken limb united,
Grow stronger for the breaking.

Mowbray.   Be it so.
Here is return'd my Lord of Westmoreland.

Re-enter Westmoreland

Westmoreland. The prince is here at hand: pleaseth your lordship
　To meet his grace just distance 'tween our armies.

Mowbray. Your grace of York, in God's name, then, set forward.

Archbishop. Before, and greet his grace: my lord, we come.

Exeunt.

scene 2.   [*Another part of the forest*]

Enter, from one side, Mowbray, *attended; afterwards, the* Archbishop,
Hastings, *and others; from the other side*, Prince John of Lancaster,
and Westmoreland; Officers, *and others with them*

Lancaster. You are well encounter'd here, my cousin Mowbray:
　Good day to you, gentle lord archbishop;
　And so to you, Lord Hastings, and to all.
　My Lord of York, it better show'd with you
　When that your flock, assembled by the bell,
　Encircled you to hear with reverence
　Your exposition on the holy text,
　Than now to see you here an iron man,
　Cheering a rout of rebels with your drum,
　Turning the word to sword and life to death.
　That man that sits within a monarch's heart,
　And ripens in the sunshine of his favour,
　Would he abuse the countenance of the king,
　Alack, what mischiefs might he set abroach
　In shadow of such greatness! With you, lord bishop,
　It is even so. Who hath not heard it spoken
　How deep you were within the books of God?
　To us the speaker in his parliament;
　To us the imagined voice of God himself;

The very opener and intelligencer
Between the grace, the sanctities of heaven
And our dull workings. O, who shall believe
But you misuse the reverence of your place,
Employ the countenance and grace of heaven,
As a false favourite doth his prince's name,
In deeds dishonourable? You have ta'en up,
Under the counterfeited zeal of God,
The subjects of his substitute, my father,
And both against the peace of heaven and him
Have here up-swarm'd them.

Archbishop.   Good my Lord of Lancaster,
I am not here against your father's peace;
But, as I told my Lord of Westmoreland,
The time misorder'd doth, in common sense,
Crowd us and crush us to this monstrous form,
To hold our safety up. I sent your grace
The parcels and particulars of our grief,
The which hath been with scorn shoved from the court,
Whereon this Hydra son of war is born;
Whose dangerous eyes may well be charm'd asleep
With grant of our most just and right desires,
And true obedience, of this madness cured,
Stoop tamely to the foot of majesty.

Mowbray. If not, we ready are to try our fortunes
To the last man.

Hastings.   And though we here fall down,
We have supplies to second our attempt:
If they miscarry, theirs shall second them;
And so success of mischief shall be born,
And heir from heir shall hold this quarrel up,
Whiles England shall have generation.

Lancaster. You are too shallow, Hastings, much too shallow,
　　To sound the bottom of the after-times.

Westmoreland. Pleaseth your grace to answer them directly
　　How far forth you do like their articles.

Lancaster. I like them all, and do allow them well;
　　And swear here, by the honour of my blood,
　　My father's purposes have been mistook;
　　And some about him have too lavishly
　　Wrested his meaning and authority.
　　My lord, these griefs shall be with speed redress'd;
　　Upon my soul, they shall. If this may please you,
　　Discharge your powers unto their several counties,
　　As we will ours: and here between the armies
　　Let's drink together friendly and embrace,
　　That all their eyes may bear those tokens home
　　Of our restored love and amity.

Archbishop. I take your princely word for these redresses.

Lancaster. I give it you, and will maintain my word:
　　And thereupon I drink unto your grace.

Hastings. Go, captain, and deliver to the army
　　This news of peace: let them have pay, and part:
　　I know it will well please them. Hie thee, captain.

　　　　　　　　　　　　　　　　Exit Officer.

Archbishop. To you, my noble Lord of Westmoreland.

Westmoreland. I pledge your grace; and, if you knew what pains
　　I have bestow'd to breed this present peace,
　　You would drink freely: but my love to ye
　　Shall show itself more openly hereafter.

Archbishop. I do not doubt you.

Westmoreland. 　　　　　　　　I am glad of it.
　　Health to my lord and gentle cousin, Mowbray.

Mowbray. You wish me health in very happy season;
    For I am, on the sudden, something ill.

Archbishop. Against ill chances men are ever merry;
    But heaviness foreruns the good event.

Westmoreland. Therefore be merry, coz; since sudden sorrow
    Serves to say thus, 'some good thing comes to-morrow.'

Archbishop. Believe me, I am passing light in spirit.

Mowbray. So much the worse, if your own rule be true.

                                                    Shouts within.

Lancaster. The word of peace is render'd: hark, how they shout!

Mowbray. This had been cheerful after victory.

Archbishop. A peace is of the nature of a conquest;
    For then both parties nobly are subdued,
    And neither party loser.

Lancaster.   Go, my lord,
    And let our army be discharged too.

                                        Exit Westmoreland.

    And, good my lord, so please you, let our trains
    March by us, that we may peruse the men
    We should have coped withal.

Archbishop.   Go, good Lord Hastings,
    And, ere they be dismiss'd, let them march by.

                                            Exit Hastings.

Lancaster. I trust, lords, we shall lie to-night together.

                    Re-enter Westmoreland

    Now, cousin, wherefore stands our army still?

Westmoreland. The leaders, having charge from you to stand,
    Will not go off until they hear you speak.

Lancaster. They know their duties.

Re-enter Hastings

Hastings. My lord, our army is dispersed already:
   Like youthful steers unyoked, they take their courses
   East, west, north, south; or, like a school broke up,
   Each hurries toward his home and sporting-place.

Westmoreland. Good tidings, my Lord Hastings; for the which
   I do arrest thee, traitor, of high treason:
   And you, lord archbishop, and you, Lord Mowbray,
   Of capital treason I attach you both.

Mowbray. Is this proceeding just and honourable?

Westmoreland. Is your assembly so?

Archbishop. Will you thus break your faith?

Lancaster.   I pawn'd thee none:
   I promised you redress of these same grievances
   Whereof you did complain; which, by mine honour,
   I will perform with a most Christian care.
   But for you, rebels, look to taste the due
   Meet for rebellion and such acts as yours.
   Most shallowly did you these arms commence,
   Fondly brought here and foolishly sent hence.
   Strike up our drums, pursue the scatter'd stray:
   God, and not we, hath safely fought to-day.
   Some guard these traitors to the block of death,
   Treason's true bed and yielder up of breath.

                                        Exeunt.

scene 3.   [*Another part of the forest*]

Alarum. Excursions. Enter Falstaff *and*
Colevile, *meeting*

Falstaff. What's your name, sir? of what condition are you, and
of what place, I pray?

Colevile. I am a knight, sir; and my name is Colevile of the dale.

Falstaff. Well, then, Colevile is your name, a knight is your degree, and your place the dale: Colevile shall be still your
name, a traitor your degree, and the dungeon your place, a
place deep enough; so shall you be still Colevile of the dale.

Colevile. Are not you Sir John Falstaff?

Falstaff. As good a man as he, sir, whoe'er I am. Do ye yield, sir?
or shall I sweat for you? If I do sweat, they are the drops of
thy lovers, and they weep for thy death: therefore rouse up
fear and trembling, and do observance to my mercy.

Colevile. I think you are Sir John Falstaff, and in that thought
yield me.

Falstaff. I have a whole school of tongues in this belly of mine,
and not a tongue of them all speaks any other word but my
name. An I had but a belly of any indifferency, I were simply
the most active fellow in Europe: my womb, my womb, my
womb, undoes me. Here comes our general.

Enter Prince John of Lancaster, Westmoreland,
Blunt, *and others*

Lancaster. The heat is past; follow no further now:
Call in the powers, good cousin Westmoreland.

Exit Westmoreland.

Now, Falstaff, where have you been all this while?

When every thing is ended, then you come:
These tardy tricks of yours will, on my life,
One time or other break some gallows' back.

Falstaff. I would be sorry, my lord, but it should be thus: I never
knew yet but rebuke and check was the reward of valour. Do
you think me a swallow, an arrow, or a bullet? have I, in my
poor and old motion, the expedition of thought? I have
speeded hither with the very extremest inch of possibility; I
have foundered nine score and odd posts: and here, travel-
tainted as I am, have, in my pure and immaculate valour,
taken Sir John Colevile of the dale, a most furious knight
and valorous enemy. But what of that? he saw me, and
yielded; that I may justly say, with the hook-nosed fellow of
Rome, 'I came, saw, and overcame.'

Lancaster. It was more of his courtesy than your deserving.

Falstaff. I know not: here he is, and here I yield him: and I beseech your grace, let it be booked with the rest of this day's
deeds; or, by the Lord, I will have it in a particular ballad else,
with mine own picture on the top on 't, Colevile kissing my
foot: to the which course if I be enforced, if you do not all
show like gilt two-pences to me, and I in the clear sky of
fame o'ershine you as much as the full moon doth the cin-
ders of the element, which show like pins' heads to her, believe not the word of the noble: therefore let me have right,
and let desert mount.

Lancaster. Thine's too heavy to mount.

Falstaff. Let it shine, then.

Lancaster. Thine's too thick to shine.

Falstaff. Let it do something, my good lord, that may do me
good, and call it what you will.

Lancaster. Is thy name Colevile?

Colevile. It is, my lord.

Lancaster. A famous rebel art thou, Colevile.

Falstaff. And a famous true subject took him.

Colevile. I am, my lord, but as my betters are
That led me hither: had they been ruled by me,
You should have won them dearer than you have.

Falstaff. I know not how they sold themselves: but thou, like
a kind fellow, gavest thyself away gratis; and I
thank thee for thee.

Re-enter Westmoreland

Lancaster. Now, have you left pursuit?

Westmoreland. Retreat is made and execution stay'd.

Lancaster. Send Colevile with his confederates
To York, to present execution:
Blunt, lead him hence; and see you guard him sure.

Exeunt Blunt *and others with* Colevile.

And now dispatch we toward the court, my lords:
I hear the king my father is sore sick:
Our news shall go before us to his majesty,
Which, cousin, you shall bear to comfort him;
And we with sober speed will follow you.

Falstaff. My lord, I beseech you, give me leave to go
Through Gloucestershire: and, when you come to
court,
Stand my good lord, pray, in your good report.

Lancaster. Fare you well, Falstaff: I, in my condition,
Shall better speak of you than you deserve.

Exeunt all except Falstaff.

Falstaff. I would you had but the wit: 'twere better than your
dukedom. Good faith, this same young sober-blooded boy

doth not love me; nor a man cannot make him laugh; but that's no marvel, he drinks no wine. There's never none of these demure boys come to any proof; for thin drink doth so over-cool their blood, and making many fish-meals, that they fall into a kind of male green-sickness; and then, when they marry, they get wenches: they are generally fools and cowards; which some of us should be too, but for inflammation. A good sherris-sack hath a two-fold operation in it. It ascends me into the brain; dries me there all the foolish and dull and crudy vapours which environ it; makes it apprehensive, quick, forgetive, full of nimble, fiery and delectable shapes; which, delivered o'er to the voice, the tongue, which is the birth, becomes excellent wit. The second property of your excellent sherris is, the warming of the blood; which, before cold and settled, left the liver white and pale, which is the badge of pusillanimity and cowardice; but the sherris warms it and makes it course from the inwards to the parts extreme: it illumineth the face, which as a beacon gives warning to all the rest of this little kingdom, man, to arm; and then the vital commoners and inland petty spirits muster me all to their captain, the heart, who, great and puffed up with this retinue, doth any deed of courage; and this valour comes of sherris. So that skill in the weapon is nothing without sack, for that sets it a-work; and learning a mere hoard of gold kept by a devil, till sack commences it and sets it in act and use. Hereof comes it that Prince Harry is valiant; for the cold blood he did naturally inherit of his father, he hath, like lean sterile and bare land, manured, husbanded and tilled with excellent endeavour of drinking good and good store of fertile sherris, that he is become very hot and valiant. If I had a thousand sons, the first human principle I would teach them should be, to forswear thin potations, and to addict themselves to sack.

Enter Bardolph

How now, Bardolph?

Bardolph. The army is discharged all and gone.

Falstaff. Let them go. I'll through Gloucestershire; and there will
I visit Master Robert Shallow, esquire: I have him already
tempering between my finger and my thumb, and shortly
will I seal with him. Come away.

Exeunt.

scene 4. [*Westminster. The Jerusalem Chamber*]

Enter the King, *the* Princes Thomas of Clarence *and* Humphrey
of Gloucester, Warwick, *and others*

King. Now, lords, if God doth give successful end
To this debate that bleedeth at our doors,
We will our youth lead on to higher fields
And draw no swords but what are sanctified.
Our navy is address'd, our power collected,
Our substitutes in absence well invested,
And every thing lies level to our wish:
Only, we want a little personal strength;
And pause us, till these rebels, now afoot,
Come underneath the yoke of government.

Warwick. Both which we doubt not but your majesty
Shall soon enjoy.

King.   Humphrey, my son of Gloucester,
Where is the prince your brother?

Gloucester. I think he's gone to hunt, my lord, at Windsor.

King. And how accompanied?

Gloucester. I do not know, my lord.

King. Is not his brother, Thomas of Clarence, with him?

Gloucester. No, my good lord; he is in presence here.

Clarence. What would my lord and father?

King. Nothing but well to thee, Thomas of Clarence.
How chance thou art not with the prince thy brother?
He loves thee, and thou dost neglect him, Thomas;
Thou hast a better place in his affection
Than all thy brothers: cherish it, my boy,
And noble offices thou mayst effect
Of mediation, after I am dead,
Between his greatness and thy other brethren:
Therefore omit him not; blunt not his love,
Nor lose the good advantage of his grace
By seeming cold or careless of his will;
For he is gracious, if he be observed:
He hath a tear for pity, and a hand
Open as day for melting charity:
Yet notwithstanding, being incensed, he's flint,
As humorous as winter, and as sudden
As flaws congealed in the spring of day.
His temper, therefore, must be well observed:
Chide him for faults, and do it reverently,
When you perceive his blood inclined to mirth;
But, being moody, give him time and scope,
Till that his passions, like a whale on ground,
Confound themselves with working. Learn this, Thomas,
And thou shalt prove a shelter to thy friends,
A hoop of gold to bind thy brothers in,
That the united vessel of their blood,
Mingled with venom of suggestion—

As, force perforce, the age will pour it in—
Shall never leak, though it do work as strong
As aconitum or rash gunpowder.

Clarence. I shall observe him with all care and love.

King. Why art thou not at Windsor with him, Thomas?

Clarence. He is not there to-day; he dines in London.

King. And how accompanied? canst thou tell that?

Clarence. With Poins, and other his continual followers.

King. Most subject is the fattest soil to weeds;
And he, the noble image of my youth,
Is overspread with them: therefore my grief
Stretches itself beyond the hour of death:
The blood weeps from my heart when I do shape,
In forms imaginary, the unguided days
And rotten times that you shall look upon,
When I am sleeping with my ancestors.
For when his headstrong riot hath no curb,
When rage and hot blood are his counsellors,
When means and lavish manners meet together.
O, with what wings shall his affections fly
Towards fronting peril and opposed decay!

Warwick. My gracious lord, you look beyond him quite:
The prince but studies his companions
Like a strange tongue, wherein, to gain the language,
'Tis needful that the most immodest word
Be look'd upon and learn'd; which once attain'd,
Your highness knows, comes to no further use
But to be known and hated. So, like gross terms,
The prince will in the perfectness of time
Cast off his followers; and their memory
Shall as a pattern or a measure live,

By which his grace must mete the lives of others,
Turning past evils to advantages.

King. 'Tis seldom when the bee doth leave her comb
In the dead carrion.

Enter Westmoreland

Who's here? Westmoreland?

Westmoreland. Health to my sovereign, and new happiness
Added to that that I am to deliver!
Prince John your son doth kiss your grace's hand:
Mowbray, the Bishop Scroop, Hastings and all
Are brought to the correction of your law;
There is not now a rebel's sword unsheathed,
But Peace puts forth her olive every where.
The manner how this action hath been borne
Here at more leisure may your highness read,
With every course in his particular.

King. O Westmoreland, thou art a summer bird,
Which ever in the haunch of winter sings
The lifting up of day.

Enter Harcourt

Look, here's more news.

Harcourt. From enemies heaven keep your majesty;
And, when they stand against you, may they fall
As those that I am come to tell you of!
The Earl Northumberland and the Lord Bardolph,
With a great power of English and of Scots,
Are by the sheriff of Yorkshire overthrown:
The manner and true order of the fight,
This packet, please it you, contains at large.

King. And wherefore should these good news make me sick?
Will Fortune never come with both hands full,
But write her fair words still in foulest letters?

She either gives a stomach and no food;
Such are the poor, in health; or else a feast
And takes away the stomach; such are the rich,
That have abundance and enjoy it not.
I should rejoice now at this happy news;
And now my sight fails, and my brain is giddy:
O me! come near me; now I am much ill.

Gloucester. Comfort, your majesty!

Clarence.   O my royal father!

Westmoreland. My sovereign lord, cheer up yourself, look up.

Warwick. Be patient, princes; you do know, these fits
    Are with his highness very ordinary.
    Stand from him, give him air; he'll straight be well.

Clarence. No, no, he cannot long hold out these pangs:
    The incessant care and labour of his mind
    Hath wrought the mure, that should confine it in,
    So thin that life looks through and will break out.

Gloucester. The people fear me; for they do observe
    Unfather'd heirs and loathly births of nature:
    The seasons change their manners, as the year
    Had found some months asleep and leap'd them over.

Clarence. The river hath thrice flow'd, no ebb between;
    And the old folk, time's doting chronicles,
    Say it did so a little time before
    That our great-grandsire, Edward, sick'd and died.

Warwick. Speak lower, princes, for the king recovers.

Gloucester. This apoplexy will certain be his end.

King. I pray you, take me up, and bear me hence
    Into some other chamber: softly, pray.

                                                    Exeunt.

scene 5.   [*Another chamber*]

The King *lying on a bed:* Clarence, Gloucester,
Warwick, *and others in attendance*

King. Let there be no noise made, my gentle friends;
  Unless some dull and favourable hand
  Will whisper music to my weary spirit.

Warwick. Call for the music in the other room.

King. Set me the crown upon my pillow here.

Clarence. His eye is hollow, and he changes much.

Warwick. Less noise, less noise!
                    Enter Prince Henry

Prince.   Who saw the Duke of Clarence?

Clarence. I am here, brother, full of heaviness.

Prince. How now! rain within doors, and none abroad!
  How doth the king?

Gloucester. Exceeding ill.

Prince.   Heard he the good news yet?
  Tell it him.

Gloucester. He alter'd much upon the hearing it.

Prince. If he be sick with joy, he'll recover without physic.

Warwick. Not so much noise, my lords: sweet prince, speak low;
  The king your father is disposed to sleep.

Clarence. Let us withdraw into the other room.

Warwick. Will 't please your grace to go along with us?

Prince. No; I will sit and watch here by the king.
                    Exeunt all except the Prince.

Why doth the crown lie there upon his pillow,
Being so troublesome a bedfellow?
O polish'd perturbation! golden care!
That keep'st the ports of slumber open wide
To many a watchful night! sleep with it now!
Yet not so sound and half so deeply sweet
As he whose brow with homely biggen bound
Snores out the watch of night. O majesty!
When thou dost pinch thy bearer, thou dost sit
Like a rich armour worn in heat of day,
That scald'st with safety. By his gates of breath
There lies a downy feather which stirs not:
Did he suspire, that light and weightless down
Perforce must move. My gracious lord! my father!
This sleep is sound indeed; this is a sleep,
That from this golden rigol hath divorced
So many English kings. Thy due from me
Is tears and heavy sorrows of the blood,
Which nature, love, and filial tenderness,
Shall, O dear father, pay thee plenteously:
My due from thee is this imperial crown,
Which, as immediate from thy place and blood,
Derives itself to me. Lo, where it sits,
Which God shall guard: and put the world's whole strength
Into one giant arm, it shall not force
This lineal honour from me: this from thee
Will I to mine leave, as 'tis left to me.

Exit.

King. Warwick! Gloucester! Clarence!
      Re-enter Warwick, Gloucester, Clarence, *and the rest*

Clarence. Doth the king call?

Warwick. What would your majesty? How fares your grace?

King. Why did you leave me here alone, my lords?

Clarence. We left the prince my brother here, my liege,
  Who undertook to sit and watch by you.

King. The Prince of Wales! Where is he? let me see him:
  He is not here.

Warwick. This door is open; he is gone this way.

Gloucester. He came not through the chamber where we stay'd.

King. Where is the crown? who took it from my pillow?

Warwick. When we withdrew, my liege, we left it here.

King. The prince hath ta'en it hence: go, seek him out.
  Is he so hasty that he doth suppose
  My sleep my death?
  Find him, my Lord of Warwick; chide him hither.

                              Exit Warwick.

  This part of his conjoins with my disease,
  And helps to end me. See, sons, what things you are!
  How quickly nature falls into revolt
  When gold becomes her object!
  For this the foolish over-careful fathers
  Have broke their sleep with thoughts, their brains with care,
  Their bones with industry;
  For this they have engrossed and piled up
  The canker'd heaps of strange-achieved gold;
  For this they have been thoughtful to invest
  Their sons with arts and martial exercises:
  When, like the bee, culling from every flower
  The virtuous sweets,
  Our thighs pack'd with wax, our mouths with honey,
  We bring it to the hive; and, like the bees,
  Are murder'd for our pains. This bitter taste
  Yield his engrossments to the ending father.

Re-enter Warwick

Now, where is he that will not stay so long
Till his friend sickness hath determined me?

Warwick. My lord, I found the prince in the next room,
Washing with kindly tears his gentle cheeks,
With such a deep demeanour in great sorrow,
That tyranny, which never quaff 'd but blood,
Would, by beholding him, have wash'd his knife
With gentle eye-drops. He is coming hither.

King. But wherefore did he take away the crown?
Re-enter Prince Henry
Lo, where he comes. Come hither to me, Harry.
Depart the chamber, leave us here alone.

Exeunt Warwick *and the rest.*

Prince. I never thought to hear you speak again.

King. Thy wish was father, Harry, to that thought:
I stay too long by thee, I weary thee.
Dost thou so hunger for mine empty chair
That thou wilt needs invest thee with my honours
Before thy hour be ripe? O foolish youth!
Thou seek'st the greatness that will overwhelm thee.
Stay but a little; for my cloud of dignity
Is held from falling with so weak a wind
That it will quickly drop: my day is dim.
Thou hast stolen that which after some few hours
Were thine without offence; and at my death
Thou hast seal'd up my expectation:
Thy life did manifest thou lovedst me not,
And thou wilt have me die assured of it.
Thou hidest a thousand daggers in thy thoughts,
Which thou hast whetted on thy stony heart,

To stab at half an hour of my life.
What! canst thou not forbear me half an hour?
Then get thee gone and dig my grave thyself,
And bid the merry bells ring to thine ear
That thou art crowned, not that I am dead.
Let all the tears that should bedew my hearse
Be drops of balm to sanctify thy head:
Only compound me with forgotten dust;
Give that which gave thee life unto the worms.
Pluck down my officers, break my decrees;
For now a time is come to mock at form:
Harry the fifth is crown'd: up, vanity!
Down, royal state! all you sage counsellors, hence!
And to the English court assemble now,
From every region, apes of idleness!
Now, neighbour confines, purge you of your scum:
Have you a ruffian that will swear, drink, dance,
Revel the night, rob, murder, and commit
The oldest sins the newest kind of ways?
Be happy, he will trouble you no more;
England shall double gild his treble guilt,
England shall give him office, honour, might;
For the fifth Harry from curb'd license plucks
The muzzle of restraint, and the wild dog
Shall flesh his tooth on every innocent.
O my poor kingdom, sick with civil blows!
When that my care could not withhold thy riots,
What wilt thou do when riot is thy care?
O, thou wilt be a wilderness again,
Peopled with wolves, thy old inhabitants!

Prince. O, pardon me, my liege! but for my tears,
  The moist impediments unto my speech,

I had forestall'd this dear and deep rebuke,
Ere you with grief had spoke and I had heard
The course of it so far. There is your crown;
And He that wears the crown immortally
Long guard it yours! If I affect it more
Than as your honour and as your renown,
Let me no more from this obedience rise,
Which my most inward true and duteous spirit
Teacheth this prostrate and exterior bending.
God witness with me, when I here came in,
And found no course of breath within your majesty,
How cold it struck my heart! If I do feign,
O, let me in my present wildness die,
And never live to show the incredulous world
The noble change that I have purposed!
Coming to look on you, thinking you dead,
And dead almost, my liege, to think you were,
I spake unto this crown as having sense,
And thus upbraided it: 'The care on thee depending
Hath fed upon the body of my father;
Therefore, thou best of gold art worst of gold:
Other, less fine in carat, is more precious,
Preserving life in medicine potable;
But thou, most fine, most honour'd, most renown'd,
Hast eat thy bearer up.' Thus, my most royal liege,
Accusing it, I put it on my head,
To try with it, as with an enemy
That had before my face murder'd my father,
The quarrel of a true inheritor.
But if it did infect my blood with joy,
Or swell my thoughts to any strain of pride;
If any rebel or vain spirit of mine
Did with the least affection of a welcome

Give entertainment to the might of it,
Let God for ever keep it from my head,
And make me as the poorest vassal is,
That doth with awe and terror kneel to it!

King. O my son,
God put it in thy mind to take it hence,
That thou mightst win the more thy father's love,
Pleading so wisely in excuse of it!
Come hither, Harry, sit thou by my bed;
And hear, I think, the very latest counsel
That ever I shall breathe. God knows, my son,
By what by-paths and indirect crook'd ways
I met this crown; and I myself know well
How troublesome it sat upon my head.
To thee it shall descend with better quiet,
Better opinion, better confirmation;
For all the soil of the achievement goes
With me into the earth. It seem'd in me
But as an honour snatch'd with boisterous hand,
And I had many living to upbraid
My gain of it by their assistances;
Which daily grew to quarrel and to bloodshed,
Wounding supposed peace: all these bold fears
Thou see'st with peril I have answered;
For all my reign hath been but as a scene
Acting that argument: and now my death
Changes the mood; for what in me was purchased,
Falls upon thee in a more fairer sort;
So thou the garland wear'st successively.
Yet, though thou stand'st more sure than I could do,
Thou art not firm enough, since griefs are green;
And all my friends, which thou must make thy friends,
Have but their stings and teeth newly ta'en out;

By whose fell working I was first advanced
And by whose power I well might lodge a fear
To be again displaced: which to avoid,
I cut them off; and had a purpose now
To lead out many to the Holy Land,
Lest rest and lying still might make them look
Too near unto my state. Therefore, my Harry,
Be it thy course to busy giddy minds
With foreign quarrels, that action, hence borne out,
May waste the memory of the former days.
More would I, but my lungs are wasted so
That strength of speech is utterly denied me.
How I came by the crown, O God forgive;
And grant it may with thee in true peace live!

Prince. My gracious liege,
   You won it, wore it, kept it, gave it me;
   Then plain and right must my possession be:
   Which I with more than with a common pain
   'Gainst all the world will rightfully maintain.

               Enter Lord John of Lancaster

King. Look, look, here comes my John of Lancaster.

Lancaster. Health, peace, and happiness to my royal father!

King. Thou bring'st me happiness and peace, son John;
   But health, alack, with youthful wings is flown
   From this bare wither'd trunk: upon thy sight
   My worldly business makes a period.
   Where is my Lord of Warwick?

Prince.   My Lord of Warwick!

          Re-enter Warwick, *and others*

King. Doth any name particular belong
   Unto the lodging where I first did swoon?

Warwick. 'Tis call'd Jerusalem, my noble lord.

King. Laud be to God! even there my life must end.
　It hath been prophesied to me many years,
　I should not die but in Jerusalem;
　Which vainly I supposed the Holy Land:
　But bear me to that chamber; there I'll lie;
　In that Jerusalem shall Harry die.

Exeunt.

act 5

scene 1. [*Gloucestershire*. Shallow's *house*]

Enter Shallow, Falstaff, Bardolph, *and* Page

Shallow. By cock and pie, sir, you shall not away tonight.
What, Davy, I say!

Falstaff. You must excuse me, Master Robert Shallow.

Shallow. I will not excuse you; you shall not be excused; excuses
shall not be admitted; there is no excuse shall serve; you shall
not be excused. Why, Davy!

Enter Davy

Davy. Here, sir.

Shallow. Davy, Davy, Davy, Davy, let me see, Davy; let me see,
Davy; let me see: yea, marry, William cook, bid him come
hither. Sir John, you shall not be excused.

Davy. Marry, sir, thus; those precepts cannot be served: and,
again, sir, shall we sow the headland with wheat?

Shallow. With red wheat, Davy. But for William cook: are there
no young pigeons?

Davy. Yes, sir. Here is now the smith's note for shoeing and plough-irons.

Shallow. Let it be cast and paid. Sir John, you shall not be excused.

Davy. Now, sir, a new link to the bucket must needs be had: and, sir, do you mean to stop any of William's wages, about the sack he lost the other day at Hinckley fair?

Shallow. A' shall answer it. Some pigeons, Davy, a couple of short-legged hens, a joint of mutton, and any pretty little tiny kickshaws, tell William cook.

Davy. Doth the man of war stay all night, sir?

Shallow. Yea, Davy. I will use him well: a friend i' the court is better than a penny in purse. Use his men well, Davy; for they are arrant knaves, and will backbite.

Davy. No worse than they are backbitten, sir; for they have marvellous foul linen.

Shallow. Well conceited, Davy: about thy business, Davy.

Davy. I beseech you, sir, to countenance William Visor of Woncot against Clement Perkes o' the hill.

Shallow. There is many complaints, Davy, against that Visor: that Visor is an arrant knave, on my knowledge.

Davy. I grant your worship that he is a knave, sir; but yet, God forbid, sir, but a knave should have some countenance at his friend's request. An honest man, sir, is able to speak for himself, when a knave is not. I have served your worship truly, sir, this eight years; and if I cannot once or twice in a quarter bear out a knave against an honest man, I have but a very little credit with your worship. The knave is mine honest friend, sir; therefore, I beseech your worship, let him be countenanced.

Shallow. Go to; I say he shall have no wrong. Look about, Davy. [*Exit* Davy] Where are you, Sir John? Come, come, come, off with your boots. Give me your hand, Master Bardolph.

Bardolph. I am glad to see your worship.

Shallow. I thank thee with all my heart, kind Master Bardolph: and welcome, my tall fellow [*to the* Page]. Come, Sir John.

Falstaff. I'll follow you, good Master Robert Shallow. [*Exit* Shallow] Bardolph, look to our horses. [*Exeunt* Bardolph *and* Page] If I were sawed into quantities, I should make four dozen of such bearded hermits' staves as Master Shallow. It is a wonderful thing to see the semblable coherence of his men's spirits and his: they, by observing of him, do bear themselves like foolish justices; he, by conversing with them, is turned into a justice-like serving-man: their spirits are so married in conjunction with the participation of society that they flock together in consent, like so many wild-geese. If I had a suit to Master Shallow, I would humour his men with the imputation of being near their master: if to his men, I would curry with Master Shallow that no man could better command his servants. It is certain that either wise bearing or ignorant carriage is caught, as men take diseases, one of another: therefore let men take heed of their company. I will devise matter enough out of this Shallow to keep Prince Harry in continual laughter the wearing out of six fashions, which is four terms, or two actions, and a' shall laugh without intervallums. O, it is much that a lie with a slight oath and a jest with a sad brow will do with a fellow that never had the ache in his shoulders! O, you shall see him laugh till his face be like a wet cloak ill laid up!

Shallow. [*Within*] Sir John!

Falstaff. I come, Master Shallow; I come, Master Shallow.

Exit.

scene 2. [*Westminster. The palace.*]

Enter Warwick *and the* Lord Chief Justice, *meeting*

Warwick. How now, my lord chief justice! whither away?

Chief Justice. How doth the king?

Warwick. Exceeding well; his cares are now all ended.

Chief Justice. I hope, not dead.

Warwick.   He's walk'd the way of nature;
   And to our purposes he lives no more.

Chief Justice. I would his majesty had call'd me with him:
   The service that I truly did his life
   Hath left me open to all injuries.

Warwick. Indeed I think the young king loves you not.

Chief Justice. I know he doth not, and do arm myself
   To welcome the condition of the time,
   Which cannot look more hideously upon me
   Than I have drawn it in my fantasy.
               Enter Lancaster, Clarence, Gloucester,
                     Westmoreland, *and others*

Warwick. Here come the heavy issue of dead Harry:
   O that the living Harry had the temper
   Of him, the worst of these three gentlemen!
   How many nobles then should hold their places,
   That must strike sail to spirits of vile sort!

Chief Justice. O God, I fear all will be overturn'd!

Lancaster. Good morrow, cousin Warwick, good morrow.

Gloucester and *Clarence.* Good morrow, cousin.

Lancaster. We meet like men that had forgot to speak.

Warwick. We do remember; but our argument
   Is all too heavy to admit much talk.

Lancaster. Well, peace be with him that hath made us heavy!

Chief Justice. Peace be with us, lest we be heavier!

Gloucester. O, good my lord, you have lost a friend indeed;
   And I dare swear you borrow not that face
   Of seeming sorrow, it is sure your own.

Lancaster. Though no man be assured what grace to find,
   You stand in coldest expectation:
   I am the sorrier; would 'twere otherwise.

Clarence. Well, you must now speak Sir John Falstaff fair;
   Which swims against your stream of quality.

Chief Justice. Sweet princes, what I did, I did in honour,
   Led by the impartial conduct of my soul;
   And never shall you see that I will beg
   A ragged and forestall'd remission.
   If truth and upright innocency fail me,
   I'll to the king my master that is dead,
   And tell him who hath sent me after him.

Warwick. Here comes the Prince.

               Enter King Henry *the Fifth, attended*

Chief Justice. Good morrow, and God save your majesty!

King. This new and gorgeous garment, majesty,
   Sits not so easy on me as you think.
   Brothers, you mix your sadness with some fear:
   This is the English, not the Turkish court;
   Not Amurath an Amurath succeeds,
   But Harry Harry. Yet be sad, good brothers,
   For, by my faith, it very well becomes you:
   Sorrow so royally in you appears

That I will deeply put the fashion on,
And wear it in my heart: why then, be sad;
But entertain no more of it, good brothers,
Than a joint burden laid upon us all.
For me, by heaven, I bid you be assured,
I'll be your father and your brother too;
Let me but bear your love, I'll bear your cares:
Yet weep that Harry's dead; and so will I;
But Harry lives, that shall convert those tears
By number into hours of happiness.

Princes. We hope no other from your majesty.

King. You all look strangely on me: and you most;
You are, I think, assured I love you not.

Chief Justice. I am assured, if I be measured rightly,
Your majesty hath no just cause to hate me.

King. No! How might a prince of my great hopes forget
So great indignities you laid upon me?
What! rate, rebuke, and roughly send to prison
The immediate heir of England! Was this easy?
May this be wash'd in Lethe, and forgotten?

Chief Justice. I then did use the person of your father;
The image of his power lay then in me:
And, in the administration of his law,
Whiles I was busy for the commonwealth,
Your highness pleased to forget my place,
The majesty and power of law and justice,
The image of the king whom I presented,
And struck me in my very seat of judgement;
Whereon, as an offender to your father,
I gave bold way to my authority,
And did commit you. If the deed were ill,

Be you contented, wearing now the garland,
To have a son set your decrees at nought,
To pluck down justice from your awful bench,
To trip the course of law and blunt the sword
That guards the peace and safety of your person?
Nay, more, to spurn at your most royal image
And mock your workings in a second body?
Question your royal thoughts, make the case yours;
Be now the father and propose a son,
Hear your own dignity so much profaned,
See your most dreadful laws so loosely slighted,
Behold yourself so by a son disdain'd;
And then imagine me taking your part,
And in your power soft silencing your son:
After this cold considerance, sentence me;
And, as you are a king, speak in your state
What I have done that misbecame my place,
My person, or my liege's sovereignty.

King. You are right, justice, and you weigh this well;
Therefore still bear the balance and the sword:
And I do wish your honours may increase,
Till you do live to see a son of mine
Offend you, and obey you, as I did.
So shall I live to speak my father's words:
'Happy am I, that have a man so bold,
That dares do justice on my proper son;
And not less happy, having such a son,
That would deliver up his greatness so
Into the hands of justice.' You did commit me:
For which, I do commit into your hand
The unstained sword that you have used to bear;
With this remembrance, that you use the same

With the like bold, just, and impartial spirit
As you have done 'gainst me. There is my hand.
You shall be as a father to my youth:
My voice shall sound as you do prompt mine ear,
And I will stoop and humble my intents
To your well-practised wise directions.
And, princes all, believe me, I beseech you;
My father is gone wild into his grave,
For in his tomb lie my affections;
And with his spirit sadly I survive,
To mock the expectation of the world,
To frustrate prophecies, and to raze out
Rotten opinion, who hath writ me down
After my seeming. The tide of blood in me
Hath proudly flow'd in vanity till now:
Now doth it turn and ebb back to the sea,
Where it shall mingle with the state of floods,
And flow henceforth in formal majesty.
Now call we our high court of parliament:
And let us choose such limbs of noble counsel,
That the great body of our state may go
In equal rank with the best govern'd nation;
That war, or peace, or both at once, may be
As things acquainted and familiar to us;
In which you, father, shall have foremost hand.
Our coronation done, we will accite,
As I before remember'd, all our state:
And, God consigning to my good intents,
No prince nor peer shall have just cause to say,
God shorten Harry's happy life one day!

Exeunt.

scene 3.   [*Gloucestershire.* Shallow's *orchard*]

Enter Falstaff, Shallow, Silence, Davy,
Bardolph, *and the* Page

Shallow. Nay, you shall see my orchard, where, in an arbour, we
will eat a last year's pippin of my own graffing, with a dish of
caraways, and so forth: come, cousin Silence: and then to bed.

Falstaff. 'Fore God, you have here a goodly dwelling and a rich.

Shallow. Barren, barren, barren; beggars all, beggars all, Sir John:
marry, good air. Spread, Davy; spread, Davy: well said, Davy.

Falstaff. This Davy serves you for good uses; he is your serving-
man and your husband.

Shallow. A good varlet, a good varlet, a very good varlet, Sir
John: by the mass, I have drunk too much sack at supper: a
good varlet. Now sit down, now sit down: come, cousin.

Silence. Ah, sirrah! quoth-a, we shall
Do nothing but eat, and make good cheer,   *Singing*
And praise God for the merry year;
When flesh is cheap and females dear,
And lusty lads roam here and there
So merrily,
And ever among so merrily.

Falstaff. There's a merry heart! Good Master Silence, I'll give
you a health for that anon.

Shallow. Give Master Bardolph some wine, Davy.

Davy. Sweet sir, sit; I'll be with you anon; most sweet sir, sit.
Master page, good master page, sit. Proface! What you want in
meat, we'll have in drink: but you must bear; the heart's all.

Exit.

Shallow. Be merry, Master Bardolph; and, my little soldier there, be merry.

Silence. Be merry, be merry, my wife has all; *Singing*
    For women are shrews, both short and tall:
    'Tis merry in hall when beards wag all,
    And welcome merry Shrove-tide.
    Be merry, be merry.

Falstaff. I did not think Master Silence had been a man of this mettle.

Silence. Who, I? I have been merry twice and once ere now.

               Re-enter Davy

Davy. There's a dish of leather-coats for you.

                            To Bardolph.

Shallow. Davy!

Davy. Your worship! I'll be with you straight [*to* Bardolph]. A cup of wine, sir?

Silence. A cup of wine that's brisk and fine, *Singing*
    And drink unto the leman mine;
        And a merry heart lives long-a.

Falstaff. Well said, Master Silence.

Silence. An we shall be merry, now comes in the sweet o' the night.

Falstaff. Health and long life to you, Master Silence.

Silence. Fill the cup, and let it come; *Singing*
    I'll pledge you a mile to the bottom.

Shallow. Honest Bardolph, welcome: if thou wantest any thing, and wilt not call, beshrew thy heart. Welcome, my little tiny thief [*to the* Page], and welcome indeed too. I'll drink to Master Bardolph, and to all the cavaleros about London.

Davy. I hope to see London once ere I die.

Bardolph. An I might see you there, Davy,—

Shallow. By the mass, you'll crack a quart together, ha! will you not, Master Bardolph?

Bardolph. Yea, sir, in a pottle-pot.

Shallow. By God's liggens, I thank thee: the knave will stick by thee, I can assure thee that. A' will not out; he is true bred.

Bardolph. And I'll stick by him, sir.

Shallow. Why, there spoke a king. Lack nothing: be merry.
    [*Knocking within*] Look who's at door there, ho! who knocks?
                                   Exit Davy.

Falstaff. Why, now you have done me right.
                      To Silence, *seeing him take off a bumper.*

Silence. Do me right,   *Singing*
  And dub me knight:
  Samingo.
  Is't not so?

Falstaff. 'Tis so.

Silence. Is't so? Why then, say an old man can do somewhat.
                    Re-enter Davy

Davy. An 't please your worship, there's one Pistol come from the court with news.

Falstaff. From the court! let him come in.
                    Enter Pistol
  How now, Pistol!

Pistol. Sir John, God save you!

Falstaff. What wind blew you hither, Pistol?

Pistol. Not the ill wind which blows no man to good. Sweet knight, thou art now one of the greatest men in this realm.

Silence. By 'r lady, I think a' be, but goodman Puff of Barson.

Pistol. Puff!
    Puff in thy teeth, most recreant coward base!
    Sir John, I am thy Pistol and thy friend,
    And helter-skelter have I rode to thee,
    And tidings do I bring and lucky joys
    And golden times and happy news of price.

Falstaff. I pray thee now, deliver them like a man of this world.

Pistol. A foutre for the world and worldlings base!
    I speak of Africa and golden joys.

Falstaff. O base Assyrian knight, what is thy news?
    Let King Cophetua know the truth thereof.

Silence. And Robin Hood, Scarlet, and John.   *Singing*

Pistol. Shall dunghill curs confront the Helicons?
    And shall good news be baffled?
    Then, Pistol, lay thy head in Furies' lap.

Shallow. Honest gentleman, I know not your breeding.

Pistol. Why then, lament therefore.

Shallow. Give me pardon, sir: if, sir, you come with news from the court, I take it there's but two ways, either to utter them, or to conceal them. I am, sir, under the king, in some authority.

Pistol. Under which king, Besonian? speak, or die.

Shallow. Under King Harry.

Pistol.   Harry the fourth? or fifth?

Shallow. Harry the fourth.

Pistol.   A foutre for thine office!
    Sir John, thy tender lambkin now is king;
    Harry the fifth's the man. I speak the truth:
    When Pistol lies, do this; and fig me, like
    The bragging Spaniard.

Falstaff. What, is the old king dead?

Pistol. As nail in door: the things I speak are just.

Falstaff. Away, Bardolph! saddle my horse. Master Robert Shallow, choose what office thou wilt in the land, 'tis thine. Pistol, I will double-charge thee with dignities.

Bardolph. O joyful day!
  I would not take a knighthood for my fortune.

Pistol. What! I do bring good news.

Falstaff. Carry Master Silence to bed. Master Shallow, my Lord Shallow,—be what thou wilt; I am fortune's steward—get on thy boots: we'll ride all night. O sweet Pistol! Away, Bardolph! [*Exit* Bardolph] Come, Pistol, utter more to me; and withal devise something to do thyself good. Boot, boot, Master Shallow! I know the young king is sick for me. Let us take any man's horses; the laws of England are at my commandment. Blessed are they that have been my friends; and woe to my lord chief justice!

Pistol. Let vultures vile seize on his lungs also!
  'Where is the life that late I led?' say they:
  Why, here it is; welcome these pleasant days!

Exeunt.

scene 4. [*London. A street*]

Enter Beadles, *dragging in* Hostess Quickly *and*
Doll Tearsheet

Hostess. No, thou arrant knave; I would to God that I might die, that I might have thee hanged: thou hast drawn my shoulder out of joint.

First Beadle. The constables have delivered her over to me; and

she shall have whipping-cheer enough, I warrant her: there
hath been a man or two lately killed about her.

Doll. Nut-hook, nut-hook, you lie. Come on; I'll tell thee what,
thou damned tripe-visaged rascal, an the child I now go with
do miscarry, thou wert better thou hadst struck thy mother,
thou paper-faced villain.

Hostess. O the Lord, that Sir John were come! he would make
this a bloody day to somebody. But I pray God the fruit of
her womb miscarry!

First Beadle. If it do, you shall have a dozen of cushions again;
you have but eleven now. Come, I charge you both go with
me; for the man is dead that you and Pistol beat amongst
you.

Doll. I'll tell you what, you thin man in a censer, I will have you
as soundly swinged for this,—you blue-bottle rogue, you
filthy famished correctioner, if you be not swinged, I'll forswear half-kirtles.

First Beadle. Come, come, you she knight-errant, come.

Hostess. O God, that right should thus overcome might! Well, of
sufferance comes ease.

Doll. Come, you rogue, come; bring me to a justice.

Hostess. Ay, come, you starved blood-hound.

Doll. Goodman death, goodman bones!

Hostess. Thou atomy, thou!

Doll. Come, you thin thing; come, you rascal.

First Beadle. Very well.   *Exeunt*

scene 5. [*A public place near Westminster Abbey*]

Enter two Grooms, *strewing rushes*

First Groom. More rushes, more rushes.

Second Groom. The trumpets have sounded twice.

First Groom. 'Twill be two o'clock ere they come from the coronation: dispatch, dispatch.

Exeunt.

Enter Falstaff, Shallow, Pistol, Bardolph, *and* Page

Falstaff. Stand here by me, Master Robert Shallow; I will make the king do you grace: I will leer upon him as a' comes by; and do but mark the countenance that he will give me.

Pistol. God bless thy lungs, good knight.

Falstaff. Come here, Pistol; stand behind me. O, if I had had time to have made new liveries, I would have bestowed the thousand pound I borrowed of you. But 'tis no matter; this poor show doth better: this doth infer the zeal I had to see him.

Shallow. It doth so.

Falstaff. It shows my earnestness of affection,—

Shallow. It doth so.

Falstaff. My devotion,—

Shallow. It doth, it doth, it doth.

Falstaff. As it were, to ride day and night; and not to deliberate, not to remember, not to have patience to shift me,—

Shallow. It is best, certain.

Falstaff. But to stand stained with travel, and sweating with desire to see him; thinking of nothing else, putting all affairs else in oblivion, as if there were nothing else to be done but to see him.

Pistol. 'Tis *semper idem,* for *obsque hoc nihil est*: 'tis all in every part.

Shallow. 'Tis so, indeed.

Pistol. My knight, I will inflame thy noble liver,
And make thee rage.
Thy Doll, and Helen of thy noble thoughts,
Is in base durance and contagious prison;
Haled thither
By most mechanical and dirty hand:
Rouse up revenge from ebon den with fell Alecto's snake,
For Doll is in. Pistol speaks nought but truth.

Falstaff. I will deliver her

> *Shouts within, and the trumpets sound.*

Pistol. There roar'd the sea, and trumpet-clangor sounds.

> *Enter the* King *and his train, the* Lord Chief Justice *among them*

Falstaff. God save thy grace, King Hal! my royal Hal!

Pistol. The heavens thee guard and keep, most royal imp of fame!

Falstaff. God save thee, my sweet boy!

King. My lord chief justice, speak to that vain man.

Chief Justice. Have you your wits? know you what 'tis you speak?

Falstaff. My king! my Jove! I speak to thee, my heart!

King. I know thee not, old man: fall to thy prayers;
How ill white hairs become a fool and jester!
I have long dream'd of such a kind of man,
So surfeit-swell'd, so old, and so profane;
But, being awaked, I do despise my dream.

Make less thy body hence, and more thy grace;
Leave gormandizing; know the grave doth gape
For thee thrice wider than for other men.
Reply not to me with a fool-born jest:
Presume not that I am the thing I was;
For God doth know, so shall the world perceive,
That I have turn'd away my former self;
So will I those that kept me company.
When thou dost hear I am as I have been,
Approach me, and thou shalt be as thou wast,
The tutor and the feeder of my riots:
Till then, I banish thee, on pain of death,
As I have done the rest of my misleaders,
Not to come near our person by ten mile.
For competence of life I will allow you,
That lack of means enforce you not to evils:
And, as we hear you do reform yourselves,
We will, according to your strengths and qualities,
Give you advancement. Be it your charge, my lord,
To see perform'd the tenour of our word.
Set on.

Exeunt King, & *c.*

Falstaff. Master Shallow, I owe you a thousand pound.

Shallow. Yea, marry, Sir John; which I beseech you to let me have home with me.

Falstaff. That can hardly be, Master Shallow. Do not you grieve at this; I shall be sent for in private to him: look you, he must seem thus to the world: fear not your advancements; I will be the man yet that shall make you great.

Shallow. I cannot well perceive how, unless you should give me your doublet, and stuff me out with straw. I beseech you, good Sir John, let me have five hundred of my thousand.

Falstaff. Sir, I will be as good as my word: this that you heard
  was but a colour.

Shallow. A colour that I fear you will die in, Sir John.

Falstaff. Fear no colours: go with me to dinner: come, Lieu–
  tenant Pistol; come, Bardolph: I shall be sent for soon at
  night.

        Re-enter Prince John, *and the* Lord Chief Justice;
                Officers *with them*

Chief Justice. Go, carry Sir John Falstaff to the Fleet:
  Take all his company along with him.

Falstaff. My lord, my lord,—

Chief Justice. I cannot now speak: I will hear you soon.
  Take them away.

Pistol. Si fortuna me tormenta, spero contenta.

          Exeunt all but Prince John *and the* Chief Justice.

Lancaster. I like this fair proceeding of the king's:
  He hath intent his wonted followers
  Shall all be very well provided for;
  But all are banish'd till their conversations
  Appear more wise and modest to the world.

Chief Justice. And so they are.

Lancaster. The king hath call'd his parliament, my lord.

Chief Justice. He hath.

Lancaster. I will lay odds that, ere this year expire,
  We bear our civil swords and native fire
  As far as France: I heard a bird so sing,
  Whose music, to my thinking, pleased the king.
  Come, will you hence?

                            Exeunt.

epilogue

Spoken by a Dancer

First my fear; then my courtesy; last my speech. My fear is, your displeasure; my courtesy, my duty; and my speech, to beg your pardons. If you look for a good speech now, you undo me: for what I have to say is of mine own making; and what indeed I should say will, I doubt, prove mine own marring. But to the purpose, and so to the venture. Be it known to you, as it is very well, I was lately here in the end of a displeasing play, to pray your patience for it and to promise you a better. I meant indeed to pay you with this; which, if like an ill venture it come unluckily home, I break, and you, my gentle creditors, lose. Here I promised you I would be, and here I commit my body to your mercies: bate me some, and I will pay you some, and, as most debtors do, promise you infinitely.

If my tongue cannot entreat you to acquit me, will you command me to use my legs? and yet that were but light payment, to dance out of your debt. But a good conscience will make any possible satisfaction, and so would I. All the gentlewomen here have forgiven me: if the gentlemen will not, then the gentlemen do not agree with the gentlewomen, which was never seen before in such an assembly.

One word more, I beseech you. If you be not too much cloyed with fat meat, our humble author will continue the story, with Sir John in it, and make you merry with fair Katharine of France: where, for any thing I know, Falstaff shall die of a sweat, unless already a' be killed with your hard opinions; for Oldcastle died a martyr, and this is not the man. My tongue is weary; when my legs are too, I will bid you good night: and so kneel down before you; but, indeed, to pray for the queen.